SELLING WAR TO AMERICA

SELLING WAR TO AMERICA

FROM THE SPANISH AMERICAN WAR TO THE GLOBAL WAR ON TERROR

Eugene Secunda and Terence P. Moran

PRAEGER SECURITY INTERNATIONAL
Westport, Connecticut • London

Library of Congress Cataloging-in-Publication Data

Secunda, Eugene.
Selling war to America: from the Spanish American war to the global war on
terror / Eugene Secunda and Terence P. Moran.
     p. cm.
   Includes bibliographical references and index.
   ISBN 978-0-275-99523-2 (alk. paper)
   1. Communication in politics–United States–History.   2. Rhetoric–Political
aspects–United States–History.   3. United States–History, Military.   I. Moran,
Terence P.   II. Title.
  JA85.2.U6S43   2007
  355.02'720973–dc22   2007016229

British Library Cataloguing in Publication Data is available.

Library of Congress Catalog Card Number: 2007016229
ISBN-13: 978–0–275–99523–2
ISBN-10: 0–275–99523–2

First published in 2007

Praeger Security International, 88 Post Road West, Westport, CT 06881
An imprint of Greenwood Publishing Group, Inc.
www.praeger.com

Printed in the United States of America

The paper used in this book complies with the
Permanent Paper Standard issued by the National
Information Standards Organization (Z39.48–1984).

10 9 8 7 6 5 4 3 2 1

To our wives, Shirley and Elise,
and to our children, Ruthanne and Andrew,
Danielle and Morgan

Contents

Introduction: Selling War to America

Americans will always buy a war if it's skillfully sold to them. And to sell these wars, U.S. presidents regularly distort the truth and withhold crucial information from the public, exploiting whatever media and marketing techniques are available to them at the time. This book reveals how U.S. presidents, from William McKinley in the late nineteenth century to George W. Bush in the early twenty-first century, perpetuated a tradition of deceit or misleading dialogues with the American public whenever they sought to involve the nation in an armed conflict.

While battles are won by armies in combat, wars are won only with the support of the people. Winning the hearts and minds of its citizenry has always been the key to successfully selling war in America ever since the Revolution. We wrote this book because we believe that the U.S. public should better comprehend how U.S. presidents and their administrations exploit the media and execute marketing strategies to win support for their war policies. With this understanding, we believe the U.S. public will become a more informed and empowered electorate.

According to some historians, this duplicitous tradition of war-bent leaders was remarked on as early as 500 BC by the Greek dramatist Aeschylus, and by the Chinese General Sun Tzu in the sixth century AD.[1] At the start of the twentieth century, U.S. Senator Hiram Johnson said, "The first casualty when war comes is truth."[2]

A mixture of government persuasion, both direct and indirect, has been wedded to popular culture and the media and, with the rise of advertising agencies in the 1880s, the birth of modern marketing techniques. With the communication revolutions that produced the popular penny press in the 1840s, motion pictures in the 1890s, radio in the 1920s, television in the 1950s, cable TV in the 1970s, satellite TV in the 1980s, and the Internet in the 1990s, public media have been exploited by successive U.S. governments to facilitate the selling of wars to America.

In the early days of the American Republic, U.S. presidents had limited means of reaching voters. Before radio was introduced commercially, presidential speeches were delivered in public gathering places; pamphlets and local newspapers were then employed to spread word of the president's policies. However, speeches could only be heard by those within earshot of the speaker, and pamphlets or even newspapers could only disseminate the president's ideas in limited and frequently inaccurate ways.

With the wide public embrace of broadcast radio in the 1920s, a president could begin reaching a national audience immediately and with all his words accurately transmitted. An additional benefit was now having a way to humanize the delivery of the president's speech, dramatically increasing the impact of his words. President Franklin Delano Roosevelt more successfully exploited this medium than any other president to engage with the U.S. public. Television became the preferred mass media vehicle for presidents beginning with Harry S. Truman in 1950, at the start of the Korean War, and radio began to diminish in importance. Today, television remains a dominant communications medium in a president's array of marketing tools, but it is now just one of many communications instruments for the White House to use when a persuasive message needs to be disseminated.

In all of these presidential efforts to persuade Americans to support their decisions to go to war, lies were often told and truths withheld because the government did not trust the people to make appropriate decisions concerning their own national security interests. The Al Qaeda attacks of September 11, 2001 on the twin towers of the World Trade Center and the Pentagon provided most Americans with sufficient cause to endorse a war against terrorism directed at Osama bin Laden and his Islamic extremist allies. In his 2003 State of the Union Address, President George W. Bush successfully converted that support into public approval for the overthrow of the Taliban forces in Afghanistan and Saddam Hussein's regime in Iraq by linking them with bin Laden and other individual terrorists and terrorist states who he said were all part of one "Axis of Evil."

Selling a war in America is not very different from selling any other product, idea, or cause. The marketing techniques used in advertising, public relations, and political consulting are merely updates of Aristotle's rules for successful persuasion first inscribed some 2,500 years ago in Ancient Athens. The principles are clear: (1) understand the *context* of the sale—the time, place, events, and circumstances within which the persuasion occurs; (2) establish and maintain the *ethos* of the sources of information—their reputations for knowledge and veracity; (3) make sure that the messages have the *logos* (logic and emotional appeals) needed to convince the audience; (4) use and control all of the public media of communication available; (5) know and monitor the morale, biases, hopes, fears, and desires of the target customers, what Aristotle called the *pathos* of the audience; and (6) monitor the effects of the persuasion and adjust your campaign accordingly. In short, Americans will always buy a war if it is marketed properly.

A PEACEFUL PEOPLE

Americans believe they are a peaceful people, slow to anger but filled with righteous resolve when compelled to act. All this is part of the American Frontier Heritage, so notably articulated by Frederick Jackson Turner in his 1893 "The Significance of the Frontier in American History" address to the American Historical Society in which he stated,

> American social development has been continually beginning over again on the frontier. This perennial rebirth, this fluidity of American life, this expansion westward with its new opportunities, its continuous touch with the simplicity of primitive society, furnish the forces dominating American character.[3]

Despite revisionist criticisms of the soundness of Turner's thesis, it has remained an important insight for understanding American history as it is perceived by the public at large and celebrated in our popular culture. This is also a tradition that embraces the use of violence as necessary to overcome evil. At the core of this tradition is the mythic belief that a better and more just world can be achieved by force of arms.

One of the most insightful commentators on Turner's thesis is Richard Slotkin whose three-volume examination of the Myth of the Frontier expands Turner's premise. As Slotkin puts it in his final volume, *Gunfighter Nation: The Myth of the Frontier in Twentieth Century America,*

> The Myth of the Frontier is our oldest and most characteristic myth, expressed in a body of literature, folklore, ritual, historiography, and polemics produced over a period of three centuries. According to this myth-historiography, the conquest of the wilderness and the subjugation or displacement of the Native Americans who originally inhabited it have been the means to our achievement of a national identity, a democratic polity, an ever-expanding economy, and a phenomenally dynamic and "progressive" civilization. The original ideological task of the Myth was to explain and justify the establishment of the American colonies; but as the colonies expanded and developed, the Myth was called on to account for our rapid

economic growth, our emergence as a powerful nation-state, and our distinctively American approach to the socially and culturally disruptive processes of modernization.[4]

From their earliest history, up to the present War on Terror, Americans have found motivation and redemption in the belief that "Some men need killing" and "Some nations need defeating." During some 250 years of trials by combat, the American mythic character was formed—the frontiersman who brings law and order to the chaos of the wilderness. His image is found in real-life pioneers like Daniel Boone, Davy Crockett, John C. Fremont, and Kit Carson, and in marshals and sheriffs like Wild Bill Hickok, Wyatt Earp, Bat Masterson, and Pat Garrett. We also find his image in fictional frontier heroes like James Fenimore Cooper's Nathaniel Bumpo (alias "Hawkeye," "Deerslayer," and "Pathfinder") and lawmen like Gary Cooper's "Will Kane" in *High Noon*, and James Arness's "Matt Dillon" in television's *Gunsmoke*. More recently, this image can be found in Clint Eastwood's "Dirty Harry" movies. All of these characters, both historical and fictional, were summed up succinctly in Raymond Chandler's essay "The Simple Art of Murder" describing the hard-boiled detective hero: "Down these mean streets a good man must go who is himself not mean." Substitute "frontiers" for "streets" and you have the American frontier hero, a man of action—not reflection, of decision—not debate. It is by deeds, not by words, that progress is made and justice assured. The very names given to frontier marshals and their Colt single-action revolvers are mythic—"Peace Officers" brought law and order with "Peacemakers."

In all mythic structures, a binary polarity separates good from evil, and the resulting ethos stresses a clear division between Americans and their enemies. Quick resolutions and immediate gratifications are preferred to lengthy negotiations and delayed satisfactions. In the current "War on Terrorism," President Bush's challenge to those who seek to harm America could easily have been spoken by Wyatt Earp or "Dirty Harry": "Bring 'em on!"

Americans like to see themselves as a people of peace. When the American military engages in combat but war has not been declared by Congress, critics at home and overseas argue that America should not act without legal authority. But, as Lieutenant Colonel Gary D. Solis, U.S.M.C. (ret.) notes in the February 2002 issue of the *Marine Corps Gazette*, "The United States has employed military force more than 220 times in its history, yet has declared war only five times (The War of 1812 against the British, in 1847 against Mexico, in 1898 against Spain, and World Wars I and II)."[5]

The problem now facing President Bush is how to convince the American people to stay the course, to support a war with no formal war declaration from Congress or validation from the United Nations. Clearly, he is not the first American President to wage a war without formally seeking such a declaration, but if the lessons of the past are to be heeded, he needs more than the help of steadfast leaders, courageous warriors, technically advanced weapons, and accurate military intelligence. He will also need the loyal and continuing total support of the American people for the long struggle ahead. The question is one of morale and persuasion: How do you sell war to Americans?

THE LEGACY OF U.S. WARS

The Spanish-American War was promoted by popular journalism ("the Penny Press" and "Yellow Journalism") inciting public opinion to pressure the government into conflict with Spain. Once the U.S. Navy battleship *Maine* exploded in Havana Harbor on February 15, 1898, President William McKinley and Congress joined the press in demanding that the country mobilize for war, not only in the Caribbean, but also in the far-off Philippine Islands. In doing so President McKinley invoked both the Monroe Doctrine of the Americas for the Americans and "Manifest Destiny," which promised an American Empire in North America and across the Pacific Ocean.

World War I was won by the Allies on the battlefields of Europe and by the innovative efforts of American journalist George Creel (Chairman of the Committee on Public Information) and his propaganda organization in successfully selling U.S. involvement in that war to the American people. But war's end also brought the public's disillusionment with the Versailles Peace Treaty, resentment toward its Allies for their failure to repay war debts, rejection of the League of Nations, growing isolationism, and revulsion against the war propaganda of the American government.[6]

Building on the public outrage over the December 7 Japanese attack on Pearl Harbor, President Franklin D. Roosevelt and his Office of War Information attempted to persuade an isolationist America to overcome its reluctance to go to war again in 1941.[7] World War II saw American and Allied successes on the battlefield and on the home front. The unconditional surrenders of Nazi Germany and Imperial Japan offered clear proof that the United States and its allies won the war. The establishment of the United Nations showed that Americans thought they could win the peace to follow.

Allied victories in combat and on the home front during the Second World War built the foundation for the postwar years. The Marshall Plan and NATO (North Atlantic Treaty Organization) provided the economic and military support necessary for the recovery of Western Europe. The occupations of West Germany and Japan helped former enemies to reemerge as world-class economies and functional democracies.[8] World War II was indeed the "Good War," despite the subsequent failure of cooperation between the United States and the Soviet Union. The East–West tensions percolating beneath the surface led to a Cold War in the late 1940s that lasted fifty years.

Despite the best efforts of the U.S. government, the public never was completely convinced about the necessity of committing American forces into combat to fight global communism, and this failure profoundly affected the execution of government military strategy. The Cold War involved the United States in two hot (if undeclared) wars—Korea and Vietnam—and a number of less intense and less costly military skirmishes (Grenada and Panama City). Both major undeclared wars reflected American uncertainty and divided the country politically, emotionally, and philosophically. Americans were in conflict over both why the nation's military was fighting in Asia and the politically influenced rules which determined how the fighting was to be conducted.

The war in Korea, euphemistically termed a "Police Action" by President Harry S. Truman, was largely fought by American troops under a United Nations flag; at least that war resulted in a stalemate but kept South Korea free from Communist domination. Vietnam was another matter entirely; the American military repeatedly won the conventional battles but never succeeded in winning the hearts and minds of the Vietnamese people or even those of its own troops. The United States also failed to motivate South Vietnam's leaders to establish a form of democratic government as a viable repudiation of the communist government in the north. Most importantly, the U.S. government never succeeded in capturing the complete support of the American people in this conflict. The bloody images of Vietnam on the nightly American television news programs added fuel to a smoldering disenchantment and confusion about the way the war was being fought. Increasing draft calls, antiwar rallies, and protests further shredded the country's social fabric. Fittingly, the Vietnam Memorial in Washington, DC, is a memorial to the dead, not a celebration of victory.[9]

The abbreviated U.S. military conflicts in Lebanon, Grenada, and Panama City were concluded almost as soon as they began and never required the government to overly concern itself with public opinion. The Persian Gulf War of 1990–1991 was a relatively short technowar that made a media star of General H. Norman Schwartzkopf, but failed to help President George H. W. Bush win reelection in 1992.

The first real-time, living-room war, telecast live from Baghdad, Saudi Arabia, and Kuwait, was the first Persian Gulf War. The Bush administration never established a clear message to the public about why Americans were fighting there. At first, the government told the people that they were fighting to protect democracy in Kuwait (a palpable lie about a despotic, family-run regime); despite expert spinning by U.S. public relations agency Hill and Knowlton, this story only resonated briefly. Next, the nation was summoned to sacrifice in order to protect a cheap supply of oil, a cynical reason that few Americans embraced. A more successful message labeled Saddam Hussein the "Middle East Hitler," a label given credibility by Hussein's open admiration for the German Führer and his penchant for calling for

"The Mother of All Battles." The brevity of that war and the relatively light casualties among the all-volunteer American forces never seriously tested the resolve of American public opinion over a long struggle. In the end, the Gulf War's Operation Desert Shield and Operation Desert Storm were ultimately judged to be military and public relations success stories.[10]

Today, Americans find themselves in another long twilight struggle, this time not against International Communism and Soviet-sponsored Wars of Liberation, but against shadowy terrorist groups and possible accomplice nations providing them with safe harbors. The attacks of 9/11 roused the sleeping tiger; the task now confronting the U.S. government and its Coalition partners is to keep that tiger aroused and filled with continuing resolve to eliminate global terrorism. The quick victories over the Taliban in Afghanistan and Saddam Hussein in Iraq met with public approval, but the continuing uncertainty in both countries and the failure to capture or kill Osama bin Laden has tainted these successes. "The Global War on Terror" is becoming "The Long War."

We believe that what the U.S. public needs is information, knowledge, and understanding about the government's efforts to sell a war in order to think critically about how their elected leaders use media and messages to manipulate them. If Americans understand how wars are sold to them, they can better become the informed citizens that the Constitution requires.

Our approach to understanding how wars are sold to America combines Aristotle's ancient analysis found in his *Rhetoric* with modern marketing strategies. Our updated Aristotelian model provides six general areas of concern:[11]

1. The *context* includes time, place, people, events, and circumstances within which the persuasion is attempted; in modern usage, "The Marketing Environment."
2. The *ethos* of the Source involves the reputation of the source for knowledge about the context and truthfulness; in modern usage, "Source Credibility."
3. The *logos* of the Messages involves the clarity and appeals of these messages with regard to reason and emotion; in modern usage, "The Creative Proposition."
4. The *use and control of public media* involve the technological, economic, cultural, political, social, and institutional biases of the media used, in modern usage, "media analysis, planning, and placement."
5. The *Pathos* of the Audience involves the people's mindsets, morale, biases, hopes, fears, dreams, and desires; in modern usage, "Consumer Behavior."
6. The *Effects of the Persuasion* include both positive and negative outcomes; in modern usage, "Marketing and Consumer Research."

In our examination of American War propaganda in the 20th and 21st centuries, we are mindful of French sociologist Jacques Ellul's warning:

> With the help of propaganda one can do almost anything, but certainly not create the behavior of a free man or, to a lesser degree, a democratic man. A man who lives in a democratic society and who is subjected to propaganda is being drained of the democratic content itself—of the style of democratic life, understanding of others, respect for minorities, re-examination of his own opinions, absence of dogmatism.[12]

Any study of war cannot ignore the work of the great Prussian military theorist Carl von Clausewitz. In his influential work, *On War*, he provided a number of key points about armed conflict. War, itself, he defined as " . . . an act of force to compel our enemy to do our will."[13] Rejecting calls for restraint in war, Clausewitz predicted the disastrous results of the first President Bush's reluctance to annihilate Saddam Hussein's Republican Guards in the Gulf War: "War is such a dangerous business that the mistakes which come from kindness are the very worst."[14] He further cautioned us with three guiding principles:

> War is never an isolated act.
> War does not consist of a single blow.
> In war the result is never final.[15]

Therefore, "the political object now comes to the fore again."[16]

In keeping both the combat and political objects prominently in mind, we need to remember one of Clausewitz's most famous sayings: "Everything in war is very simple, but the simplest thing is difficult."[17] That difficulty comes from what he calls "friction" and the "fog" of war. In stressing moral elements over purely physical efforts, Clausewitz identified three main principles sustaining the morale of any army at war: "The skill of the commanders, the experience and courage of the troops, and their patriotic spirit."[18] In this age of mass media and government based upon the consent of the people, we would suggest a fourth principle: the willing and patriotic support of a nation's citizenry.

Our task, then, is to provide some reasons for success and failure in selling a war to the American people that won't be a formula for totalitarian brainwashing and mind control. The fiasco with the Pentagon's proposed Office of Strategic Influence (in which the U.S. government was forced to acknowledge that its military was planning to follow a policy of disinformation) is testament to the failure of the Big Lie. This approach works reasonably well in a totalitarian state that can completely control the media, but is extremely difficult to achieve in a free society. To deceive one's enemies in wartime is both necessary and strategic; to deceive one's own citizens is both evil and stupid.[19]

The government must trust both its own conviction in the justice of the cause and respect the intelligence of the public to successfully sell a war to the American people. No nation can protect a democratic society by employing the propaganda techniques of totalitarian systems which depend on total control of content and the channels of communication. In a democracy, honest persuasion is not only permissible but required; it provides the stimulus for the Great Debate that is democracy.

If the government is unsure of its cause, unable to explain it truthfully and logically, unwilling to trust its fellow citizens, then no amount of spinning, public relations gimmicks, pressure on the media, advertising ploys, or marketing strategies is going to succeed. The hearts and minds of the American people can be won with rational argument, respect for the truth, and open debate. If the cause is just and the arguments credible, the government can convince its citizens of the need for action. To the well-known military dictum of not starting a war you cannot win, we offer an addendum: Don't start a war you cannot sell to the American people and assure that they are comfortable with having made that decision in the long term.

The relative skillfulness of the U.S. government's propaganda efforts has largely determined the American public's willingness to support the wars that the United States has waged. The job of informing and persuading America to endorse its war efforts has become increasingly more challenging as media technologies, like instant global coverage of television news and the Internet, have begun to reach into every American home. We analyze each of these wars within the context of the techniques that the government used to generate public support. We also examine the results of these selling efforts before, during, and after each conflict.

Our examination begins with the propaganda campaign undertaken by government and nongovernment forces to generate enthusiasm for the United States to wage a war against Spain in 1898. It ends with a review of the methods the U.S. government is using now to engender support for the Global War against Terror. From these historical analyses, noting both government selling blunders and triumphs of the past century, we try to pinpoint the pitfalls and offer keys for successfully persuading the American public to support fighting those wars in the future that the U.S. government decides are necessary to fight.

For each military engagement, we identify the stories told, the messages sent, and the information disseminated that mobilized enthusiastic support, and those communications elements that failed to do so.

We focus on some key battles in each war because the delivery of the product must fulfill the promise of the promotion. As Barry Goldwater said in his 1964 acceptance speech as the Republican candidate for President, "In war there is no substitute for victory." That principle seems to find a responsive chord in the American public and, while it did not help elect Goldwater in 1964, it certainly helped Richard Nixon in 1968 with his campaign attacks on the Democrats for failing to achieve victory in Vietnam. We also show how the U.S. government attempted to manipulate the many channels of communication, such as the mass media, the entertainment industry, and educational institutions, to assure a positive public perception of the wars it has waged. We identify and analyze the forms of media available at the time of each conflict, including the symbols, slogans, posters, songs, motion pictures, live theater, and other vehicles like the Internet that were used as campaign components. In addition, we examine those aspects of popular culture that occurred outside government influence that enhanced or frustrated the selling efforts.

In the final segment of the book, a chapter is devoted to analyzing and distilling the lessons gleaned from the persuasive communications aspects of American wars fought since 1898, noting the successes and failures of government propaganda campaigns. We conclude by showing how these principles might be applied to the conduct of future persuasive programs that can assure U.S. civilian support of armed conflicts based on honest presentation of the facts and realistically set objectives.

Our objective is not politically motivated: we neither extol nor condemn America's wars or the efforts to sell these wars to America; rather we attempt to identify what worked and what failed in these efforts to persuade. We do not share the triumphant traditions of those, like David Frum and Richard Perle in *An End to Evil: How to Win the War on Terror*, who think that the United States of America can do no wrong and was justified in all of its wars and undeclared conflicts. Equally, we do not share the negative views of those, like Noam Chomsky in *Hegemony or Survival: America's Quest for Global Dominance*, who see the United States as "the Great Satan of Capitalism, Consumerism, and Global Imperialism." To us, such extreme positions do little to advance the type of informed debate that is central to American democracy.

Our hope is that this book will provide information and insight needed by citizens concerned with how decisions are reached about the great questions of war and peace in the modern world. This hope is shaped by our view that war, rather than being an aberration, has long been a central and recurring element in the lives of most people and civilizations from the ancient world (Sumer, Egypt, China, India, Persia, Greece, and Rome) to today's nation states. Our task is to help people to become more careful customers when buying a war. In place of the old Roman warning—"Let the buyer beware"—we offer a new maxim—"Let the buyer be aware."

1

The Splendid Little War—
The Spanish-American War

MANIFEST DESTINY

The Frontier as Ideal and Ideology

It is every marketer's nightmare to have customers demanding a product that
the marketer is unprepared to sell them. That's the dilemma that U.S. President William McKinley initially faced in 1898 during the months leading
up to America's War with Spain.

To understand what led to the President's predicament, and how the
Spanish-American War was marketed successfully to the American public,
we need to appreciate the national *context* in which the war was sold, what
marketers today describe as "The Marketing Environment." What follows
is a description of what the American public of the 1890s believed was true
about their country and its place in history, leading to a general resolve
that a war must be fought with Spain if the United States was to fulfill its
"Manifest Destiny."

On July 12, 1893, Frederick Jackson Turner, a thirty-two-year-old in-
structor in history from a small college, presented a paper at the American
Historical Society on "The Significance of the Frontier in American History,"
linking the American character and political development to the frontier as
both ideology and reality. Citing data from the U.S. Census of 1890, Turner
specifically noted the closing of the frontier, with more Americans now living
in urban rather than in rural areas, and the United States now secure from

the Rio Grande River to the Forty-Ninth Parallel and from sea to shining sea.[1] John L. O'Sullivan's 1845 editorial in *The United States Magazine and Democratic Review* calling for the "fulfillment of our manifest destiny to rule the North American continent" had become reality.

From the original thirteen English colonies huddled on the shores of the Atlantic Ocean and the Revolution that transformed them into the thirteen states of the United States of America in 1787, the new nation grew rapidly in size and power through purchase, exploration, and conflict. The Louisiana Purchase of 1803 doubled the country's size by adding 828,000 square miles at a cost of only $15 million (paid to Napoleon Bonaparte to finance France's European wars) and provided land originally promised to Native Americans exiled from the new America. The Lewis and Clarke Expedition (1804–1806) claimed all the lands from the Missouri River to the Pacific Ocean for America. While the War of 1812 with Great Britain failed to achieve the U.S. goal of expanding into either Canada or Florida, and divided the country over "Mr. Madison's War," the American people were able to comfort themselves with the naval victories on the Great Lakes, the defense of Fort McHenry (during which Francis Scott Key wrote "The Star-Spangled Banner") and General Andrew Jackson's victory in the Battle of New Orleans (December 23, 1814–January 8, 1815). Although the December 24, 1814, Treaty of Ghent ended the war as a stalemate, the American people became convinced that the consummation of both that treaty and Jackson's military victory were proof that the United States had, in fact, won the war against the British. In war and politics, as in all modern marketing communications, image can triumph over reality.[2]

In 1821, Spain ceded Florida to the United States, adding territory and increasing American confidence. The U.S. war against Mexico (1846–1848) added Arizona, California, New Mexico, Nevada, and Texas to the growing Union. As each new territory was acquired, Native Americans were driven away from an ever-expanding American nation, destroying their tribal heritages and offering only relocation, dispersal, remote reservations, and annihilation.[3]

The Civil War (1861–1865) pitting North against South stalled, but did not halt, American expansion which surged again after the Federal triumph. The United States emerged from the war reunited in law, if not yet in sentiment, but stronger militarily, industrially, technically, and economically.[4] In 1867, America paid Russia $7.2 million for Alaska's 570,833 square miles and claimed Midway Island in the Pacific by discovery. In 1893, Hawaii became an American possession by force-of-arms when an American-settlers-led revolt was quickly supported by the U.S. Navy.[5] In less than a century of expansion, the United States held title to most of North America and was now looking beyond its West Coast to the vast reaches of the Pacific Ocean.

America as a Sea Power

By 1890, Americans had come to regard the Caribbean as their sea and now regarded their country as both an Atlantic and a Pacific power. Spurred by the brilliant lectures of Navy Captain Alfred Thayer Mahan at the Newport War College, collected and published in 1890 as *The Influence of Sea Power upon History 1660–1783*, Americans began defining their country as a major sea power. The U.S. Navy's mission was transformed from protecting America's shores to projecting American ideas, ideals, interests, people, and power around the globe.[6] Mahan's Sea Power Thesis would be integrated with Turner's Frontier Thesis. America's anticolonial idealism now confronted America's imperial ambitions.

The Monroe Doctrine of 1823 had declared, in essence, that "the Americas were for the Americans" and warned Europe against further European colonial expansion in the Western Hemisphere. While the doctrine had few teeth, by 1890, Mexico and much of Latin and South America were largely free of Portuguese and Spanish domination through the efforts of such revolutionary leaders as Antonio Lopez de Santa Ana, Simon Bolivar, Bernardo O'Higgins, and José de San Martin. In the late 1890s, American popular opinion favored the removal of the last vestiges of Spanish colonialism in the Caribbean, with Cuba and Puerto Rico as the focal points of this sentiment. Combining the Monroe Doctrine with Manifest Destiny and the Frontier Thesis with the Sea Power Thesis, successive U.S. administrations had forged a powerful weapon that needed only the proper fuse to ignite a full-scale war between Spain and the United States of America, beginning the country's expansionist thrust overseas.

The Role of the Press

At first, the primary source promoting the war was not the government but the popular daily newspapers. It was this media vehicle, driven by its individual publishers' marketing needs that would supply both the fuse and the spark. In the age of the penny press, requiring mass circulation to attract advertisers to subsidize publication costs, these newspapers needed a steady stream of timely and sensational headlines and copy to attract and hold the mass readership necessary for the enterprise to flourish. Publishers like Joseph Pulitzer and William Randolph Hearst battled each other for readers, advertisers, and influence. Choosing to interpret American public concern for the plight of the Cuban people as a product of American idealism, mixed with a desire for economic and territorial expansion, American newspapers quickly satisfied their readers' appetites with lurid stories of Spanish brutality, cruelty, and injustice. As Joseph E. Wilson noted in his 1934 study, between 1895 and 1898 (the three years from the Cuban rebellion to America's entry into the war with Spain), there were fewer than twenty days without a story about Cuba in New York City newspapers.[7] These influential newspapers were the public's major sources of news and information of the day. Their stories and opinions were trusted by the people and had a powerful influence on shaping politicians' policies.

Joseph Pulitzer's *World* and William Randolph Hearst's *New York Journal* competed not only for circulation and advertising revenues, but also for the role of head cheerleader for American political and military intervention in the Cuban crisis, which was largely media-generated. They fought over who best could report the Cuban Revolution, sending their top reporters and artists to cover the fighting. Foremost among Hearst's journalists were Richard Harding Davis, who supplied the copy, and the great artist of the American Frontier, Frederick Remington, who supplied the drawings.

In 1897, the development of the half-tone process allowed newspapers and magazines to print photographs directly, thus lending increased credibility to the images; photojournalism was born. It was during this time that Remington is supposed to have sent a telegram to Hearst complaining of the lack of conflict in Cuba: "Everything here is quiet. There is no trouble here. There will be no war. I wish to return." To this cable, Hearst is reported to have replied: "Please remain. You furnish the pictures; and I'll furnish the war."[8] Although there is no documentation that either cable was ever sent, historians and critics of the press like to use them as evidence of media manipulation, rather like the fictional editor in John Ford's film, *The Man Who Shot Liberty Valence*, who says of fact and fiction, "When the legend becomes fact, print the legend." Whatever the truth about these telegrams, there is little question that the American press openly advocated war with Spain by portraying Cuba as a land yearning to be free while suffering atrocities at the hands of their Spanish oppressors. They sought every opportunity to fan the flames of war and excite their readers' emotions. For example, on February 9, 1898, Hearst's *Journal* published an intercepted letter from the Spanish Ambassador to the United States which described U.S. President William McKinley as "weak and catering to the rabble, and besides, a low politician."[9]

The Sinking of the *Maine*

Despite such warmongering in the popular press, President William McKinley's administration concluded that America lacked sufficient justification to intervene in Cuba. Those grounds were provided when the U.S. Navy's battleship *Maine* suddenly exploded and sank in Havana Harbor, with great loss of U.S. lives. This incident would mirror an earlier moment in American history—the attack on the Alamo in 1836—as well as every subsequent action in the decades that followed that would be exploited to justify American military action—the sinking of the *Lusitania* in May 1915, the Japanese attack on Pearl Harbor on December 7, 1941, the North Korean invasion of South Korea in June 1950, the supposed Gulf of Tonkin attacks in 1964, the Iraqi invasion of Kuwait in 1990, and most recently the Al Qaeda attacks on the Pentagon and the World Trade Center towers on September 11, 2001. Each of these acts would be used to sell a war to the American people with a cry of "Remember...!" In 1898, it was the people, stirred to fury by the popular press that sold the war to a reluctant American government. It was the beginning of an American tradition—the tail wagging the dog.

The explosion that destroyed the American battleship *U.S.S. Maine* in Havana Harbor on February 15, 1898, killing 266 of the 354 sailors and Marines on board, may have been an accident or a deliberate act of war. Although the exact cause is still debated, the American popular press then had little doubt as to the cause and the culprit. The front-page headline of Hearst's *New York Journal* of February 17, 1898, declared: "Destruction of the War Ship *Maine* Was the Work of an Enemy" and offered "$50,000 Reward! For the Detection and Perpetrator of the *Maine* Outrage!" A second page-one headline reported, "Naval Officers Think the *Maine* Was Destroyed by a Spanish Mine." That same day, Pulitzer's *World* was no less certain of who they thought was responsible for this disaster, posing a question on its front page: "*Maine* Explosion Caused by Bomb or Torpedo?" In either case, an accident was not considered, as a second headline stated: "Capt. Zalinski, the Dynamite Expert, and Other Experts Report to *The World* that the Wreck Was Not Accidental." Although the European edition of *The New York Herald* of February 17, 1898, was more cautious in its reporting, noting that the blast could have been accidental or deliberate, it also reported the effects of the incident on American public opinion, stating that American public opinion had already prejudged the affair and suggesting that it would take direct evidence absolving Spanish involvement in the catastrophe to alter public suspicions. In short, Spain was held to be guilty until proven innocent in the court of American public opinion.

The Creative Proposition

While it is possible to debate the *logos* (logic) of the calls for war, there is no question that the sinking of the Maine struck a responsive chord with the American people. The event itself justified the war for most Americans, causing them to immediately embrace what in modern marketing terminology would be defined as "The Creative Proposition"—that the war was forced upon the United States by Spain. It could be argued that the alleged attacks by North Vietnamese torpedo boats on American destroyers off the coast of North Vietnam sixty-six years later similarly provided President Johnson's Administration with justification for deeper American involvement in an escalation of the Vietnam War.

Following the sinking of the *Maine*, the popular press increased their demands for American military action against the Spanish. Magazines joined newspapers in promoting the war and the fledgling medium of motion pictures quickly provided "newsreel" scenes with titles like *Wreck of the Battleship "Maine"* and *Burial of the "Maine" Victims*, the latter with scenes of the funeral procession and interment in Arlington Cemetery of the ship's crew.[10] Among the popular music of the day that exploited the disaster were such songs as "Before the *Maine* Went Down" and "We Remember the *Maine*."

The Call to Arms

President McKinley initially struggled to avoid war with Spain, hoping for a diplomatic settlement to the crisis, while what would later be termed "a media frenzy" ensued. For his efforts to avoid war, McKinley was criticized by superpatriots like Under Secretary of the Navy Theodore Roosevelt who compared the president's backbone to "a chocolate éclair." In the end, McKinley surrendered to the battle cries of a press and public so hungry for war that they needed no government efforts to sell it to them. The government was like a manufacturer who had to be prodded into providing the customers with what they not only wanted, but demanded. In such a seller's market, it would have taken a more courageous and principled politician than McKinley to refuse such a call.

When President McKinley's request to Congress for aid for Cuba was approved overwhelmingly, Spain declared war on the United States on April 23, 1898. America declared war on Spain two days later. *The New York Herald's* European edition of April 26, 1898, trumpeted on its front page: "War Declared by Congress on Spain." A second headline reported: "Fleet to Attack the Philippines," signaling that the war would be fought not only to protect Cuba and the Caribbean from Spanish colonialism, but also to extend America's reach across the Pacific to the edges of Asia, an extension that would have dangerous consequences in 1941. It was the first successful realization of the country's sense of *Manifest Destiny* on an international stage. In modern marketing terms, America was now undertaking a program of *market expansion*.

REMEMBER THE *MAINE*!

Media Analysis, Planning, and Placement

Once the war was declared, the McKinley administration quickly exploited the media in order to better sell the war to an all-too-willing public. Unlike the wars that followed, the Spanish-American War did not need intensive government manipulation of public media to disseminate its message. Little attention was paid by the McKinley administration to "Media Analysis, Planning, and Placement," fundamental requisites of any modern marketing communications campaign, for a very simple reason: the popular press was, if anything, more eager for the war than was the administration. If anything, the McKinley administration frequently found itself struggling to catch up with public opinion fanned to white-hot anger by the popular penny press.

It took relatively little time for the American military to defeat the Spanish forces, but a bloody campaign against Filipino insurgents who fought their American "liberators" took much longer. The war itself would play out in three acts—first, a decisive naval battle in the Philippines, then naval and land engagements in the Caribbean, and finally the Filipino Insurrection against the Americans after the Spanish military had surrendered. The American media would cover the first two acts well but act three would not command much public attention. The actual war with Spain would be short, lasting less than four months from the American declaration of war on April 26 to the Spanish surrender on August 7, 1898.

On paper, Spain appeared to be a potent imperial power: an army with 150,000 troops in Cuba, 8,000 in Puerto Rico, 20,000 in the Philippines, and reserves of 150,000 in Spain. But its navy was no Spanish Armada, lacking modern ships and armaments and manned by ill-trained crews. Although the United States lacked a sufficient army for the conflict, the U. S. Navy was more than equipped to win the war at sea. As early as 1896, the Naval War College had prepared a document, "War with Spain," that "assumed that the war would be fought to achieve independence for Cuba, that the U.S. did not contemplate major territorial acquisitions, and that command of the sea would determine the outcome."[11] This Mahan-inspired document would provide the blueprint for the naval war but the second assumption would be ignored in both the Caribbean and the Pacific.

Unlike the Navy, the U.S. Army was not prepared to fight a war with anybody after the final defeat of the Native Americans at Wounded Knee in 1890. With a small regular army supplemented, in theory, by individual state guard units, the Army was incapable of mustering sufficient troops for any real conflict. In April 1898, the U.S. Congress authorized a regular army of 65,700 soldiers and volunteer forces of 3,000 cavalry, 3,500 engineers, and 10,000 infantry in response to the impending conflict. One of the volunteer cavalry units would achieve fame for itself and its lieutenant colonel, Theodore Roosevelt of the Rough Riders.[12]

Naval Victory in the Philippines

Although the sinking of the *Maine* in Cuba was supposedly the cause of the war, the "splendid little war," as Secretary of State John Hay called it, actually began on May 1, 1898, when Commodore (later Admiral) George Dewey destroyed the Spanish Pacific Fleet in the battle of Manila Bay. Manila was ripe for the taking, but Dewey's fleet lacked sufficient ground troops to seize the city or the rest of the Philippine Islands.[13] Overnight, Dewey became a national hero for his brilliant victory and his order to Captain Charles V. Gridley that was a model of American efficiency and grace under pressure: "You may fire when ready, Gridley." Dewey was celebrated with songs like "Brave Dewey and His Men" and newsreels like *Admiral Dewey Receiving Washington and New York Committees*, *Admiral Dewey Leading Land Parade*, and *The Dewey Attack*. *The Battle of Manila Bay*, a popular reenactment in miniature of the naval battle in the Pacific, was actually filmed in a large tub on the roof of a building on Nassau Street in Manhattan where Vitagraph, an early motion picture studio, then had its offices.[14] The promotion cycle had begun: success in war led to favorable media coverage for both Commodore Dewey and the McKinley administration, which then led to more favorable media coverage.

The U.S. invasion troops finally arrived in the Philippines only after the August 12, 1898, peace protocol officially ended the war. A sham battle was prearranged in which the Americans would pretend to attack and the Spanish, after a token resistance, would surrender with honor. This staged incident increased Filipino suspicion of their American "liberators," eventually erupting into a full-scale war against the American forces.[15]

War in America: The Caribbean Campaign

Matching Dewey's success in the Philippines, the U.S. Navy in the Caribbean blockaded Cuba in April 1898 while the Marines seized Guantanomo Bay for use as a fueling station. On July 3, the Spanish fleet emerged from Santiago Bay and engaged Rear Admiral William T. Sampson's fleet. It was another disaster for the Spanish Navy, with the entire fleet either sunk or captured.[16] Again, success in battle was heralded in the media of the day. On land, the Army and Marine Corps disembarked 17,000 troops in Cuba on June 22–23, 1898, to begin the land campaign. Major General William R. Shafter's forces fought weather, insects, diseases, and the terrain before confronting the Spanish forces on July 1 with coordinated attacks on El Caney and San Juan Heights. Despite the fierce defense by the Spanish, the Americans prevailed, but at a high cost in casualties. Teddy Roosevelt and his Rough Riders won enduring fame for "the charge up San Juan Hill" and Roosevelt would parlay his war hero image into elections as governor of the state of New York and later as vice president in 1901. By July 17 the Spanish forces in Cuba were defeated, as much by their military incompetence and the Cuban rebels as by American might. On July 25, General Nelson A. Miles (of Indian–fighting fame), led the American invasion of Puerto Rico and largely defeated the Spanish forces by the August 12 peace protocol.[17]

The McKinley administration benefited from the quick victories in the Caribbean that provided Americans with new heroes and heroics. In addition to the newspaper and magazine stories and illustrations, the newsreels provided such crowd-pleasing titles as *The Battle of Santiago Bay*, a studio-created fiction that passed as reality, and *Fighting with Our Boys in Cuba* which depicted a reenactment of the Rough Riders Charge up San Juan Hill.[18] Popular songs included "The Charge of the Roosevelt Rough Riders" (conveniently ignoring Roosevelt's superior, Colonel Leonard Wood), "Just Before the Battle, Mother," "Bugle Calls by T. Roosevelt's Bugler at San Juan Hill," John Philip Sousa's "El Capitan" and "Stars and Stripes Forever," and "There'll Be a Hot Time in the Old Town Tonight," not inspired by the war itself but extremely popular with both the military and the civilians at home.

Across the Pacific

The peace protocol of August 12 and the surrender of Manila on August 13 signaled America's triumph in the war with Spain, but the Filipinos grew increasingly distrustful of the Americans, seeing them less as liberators than as a new army of occupation. Soon, fighting broke out between Filipino and American forces, lasting from February 1899 to July 1901. American casualties during this "pacification" of its former allies totaled 4,234 dead and 2,818 wounded, far exceeding the 379 Americans combat deaths in the war with Spain (an additional 5,083 deaths were from noncombat causes, mainly sickness and accidents). On the Filipino side, at least 16,000 combatants were killed or wounded, along with some 200,000 civilians caught in the fog and friction of war.[19] This would not be the last time in American history that winning the battles would be easier and less costly than winning the hearts and minds of the people the country's military claimed to be liberating.

America promised the Filipino people freedom and self-rule; what America delivered was annexation of the Philippines and American military and civilian control that would last until after World War II. As President McKinley explained his decision to sanction the occupation of the Philippines to a group of Methodist Ministers, God called upon America "... to educate the Filipinos and uplift them and civilize them and Christianize them and by God's grace do the best we could by them, as our fellowmen for whom Christ died."[20] No clearer statement of America's Manifest Destiny to civilize the world could be stated, although the president seemed to think that the Roman Catholic majority in the Philippines were not Christian enough for America.

The Treaty of Paris on December 10, 1898, ended the Spanish-American War and allowed the United States to annex the Philippine Islands, Puerto Rico, and Guam, and to establish a protectorate in Cuba. In fact, if not in name, the United States had become a genuine world power, complete with colonies and territories to be policed by its Army, Marine Corps, and Navy. Thus by far, the promises to the American people and the world had been performed, establishing the credibility of the government and demonstrating the reality of the creative proposition that promised guides and decisive victories to avenge the *Maine*.

It is significant that the 1896 presidential election that pitted the Republican William McKinley against the Democrat William Jennings Bryant did not focus on freeing Cuba, but on domestic economic issues—free silver versus the gold standard and free trade versus protectionism. In 1900, McKinley ran for reelection with the claim that "The American flag has not been planted on foreign soil to acquire more territory but for humanity's sake." This catchphrase appeared under campaign pictures of McKinley and his running mate Theodore Roosevelt accompanied by the slogan, "The Administration's Promises Have Been Kept." Another campaign theme exploited Roosevelt's Rough Rider image, complete with uniform, sword, and campaign hat. Additional campaign messages were: "Prosperity at Home, Prestige Abroad," "Commerce and Industries," "Commerce and Civilization," and "Patriotism, Protection and Prosperity." Clearly, success in battle provided increased credibility for the McKinley administration and support for the creative proposition used to sell the war.[21]

WINNING HEARTS AND MINDS IN THE PHILIPPINES

An Unfinished Peace

Sixty years before President Lyndon B. Johnson established the American goal of "winning the hearts and minds" of the Vietnamese people, President William McKinley called upon the U.S. Army to prove to the Filipino people "...that the mission of the United States is one of benevolent assimilation, substituting the mild sway of justice and right for arbitrary rule."[22] In attempting to quell the Filipino Insurrection, Americans set out to reform the education, health, and transportation systems of the Philippines. Despite success in these crucial services, the Americans were thwarted by small but dedicated bands of guerrillas who hid safely among the civilian population until the time was ripe for ambush, sniping, sabotage, and disruption of daily life.[23] The reports from that time suggest uncomfortable parallels with both Vietnam and the current pacification programs in Iraq. The *pathos* of the audience, so supportive of the war thus far, would be tested by events in the Philippines that raised doubts about America's role in liberating the Filipino people themselves.

As in Vietnam and Iraq, the Americans were able to win the battles but found victory elusive and peace difficult. In December 1900, General Arthur MacArthur (father of World War II and the Korean War's General of the

Army Douglas MacArthur) established rules of engagement that exempted partisans and guerrillas from the accepted rules of war and allowed military commanders to use force against civilians in cases of "military necessity" and "retaliation."[24] As would later be true in Vietnam and Iraq, such orders all but invited abuses, if not outright war crimes, by the U.S. soldiers and Marines responsible for carrying out these orders.

American Atrocities

With increasing numbers of American military and Filipino civilian casualties, Filipino insurgents clearly hoped that the continuing conflict would sap the will of the U.S. military in the Philippines. The insurgents also hoped to undermine American public support for the Philippine occupation by exploiting the U.S. public's concern about charges of American imperialism in the Pacific. The insurgents also attempted to gain support from countries becoming wary of America's growing power. Stories of atrocities by American forces helped fuel these hopes. The soldiers and Marines responsible for pacifying the Philippines never achieved the glory afforded to the dramatic victories of Admiral Dewey for Manila Bay, Admiral Sampson for Santiago Bay, and Teddy Roosevelt and his Rough Riders for the charge up San Juan Hill. Instead, they faced the grueling task of finding and defeating an elusive enemy totally embedded in the civilian population, an operation not conducive to the marketing of quick victories and smiling heroes.

Among the many atrocity charges was the Samar Expedition. In October 1901, Marine Major Littleton Waller was ordered by Army Brigadier General Jacob H. Smith to pacify the island of Samar in the Philippine Islands chain. Although largely successful overall, Waller led a disastrous march across the interior of the island that resulted in the deaths of eleven of the fifty-four Marines on the mission; all of the survivors were hospitalized when they reached safety. After some of the thirty-five Filipino scouts and bearers accompanying the unit attacked a Marine lieutenant, Waller ordered eleven shot as mutineers.

The outrage in the American press and among the American public was clearly bad news for the administration, now headed by President Theodore Roosevelt following the assassination of President McKinley on September 14, 1901. Embracing American expansionism and seeking to justify its aggressive foreign policies, the Roosevelt administration pressed for the court martial of Waller, who was charged with murder on February 29, 1902. The U.S. Senate was already holding hearings on war atrocities at the time and the new president gave into public opinion and ordered Waller to stand trial on March 17, 1902, in Manila. Waller readily admitted ordering the executions, justifying his actions under General Order 100 which authorized force in cases of "military necessity." After General Smith denied issuing such orders and called Waller "a rogue officer," Waller retestified that Smith had actually ordered him to take no prisoners. The front page of Hearst's *New York Evening Journal* of April 8, 1902 was a public relations disaster for the Roosevelt administration: "Kill All; Major Waller Ordered to Massacre the Filipinos!"

Waller was acquitted on a technicality and continued his career while his commander, Smith, was later convicted of "conduct to the prejudice of good order and military disciple" and forced to retire.[25] As happened later in Vietnam and Iraq, the administration and the military command tried shifting the blame to the troops in the field, arguing that lapses by individuals did not represent the higher command or all Americans. In spinning the stories of the Samar executions, the May Lai Massacre, and the Abu Ghraib prison abuses, the official line was that the leaders were blameless for the actions of a few misbehaving individuals who had acted beyond their authority. And the individuals involved, from Major Waller in the Philippines, to Lieutenant William Calley in Vietnam, to the guards at Abu Ghraib prison in Iraq, all justified their actions with the Nazi Adolf Eichmann's defense against war crimes and crimes against humanity: "I was just following orders."

Anti-Imperialism Meets American Patriotism

The media and the public continued to back U.S. actions in the Pacific, despite the revelations of the Waller case and the best efforts of the Anti-Imperialist League, with 500,000 members in the United States, including such notables as Carl Schurz, Jane Addams, Andrew Carnegie, William James, Samuel Gompers, and Mark Twain. The public was also not swayed by a heated debate in the U.S. Senate where Senator George H. Hoar argued against U.S. expansionist policies, describing search and destroy missions, water tortures and internment camps for Filipinos. In opposition was Senator Henry Cabot Lodge who defended America's Manifest Destiny policies. The *pathos* of the audience, involving U.S. public opinion, remained resolutely sympathetic to the Roosevelt administration, supporting continuation of U.S. military occupation of the Philippines. Faced with a choice between limiting and expanding the American Frontier in the Pacific, the majority of Americans chose expansion.[26]

President Roosevelt and his administration were successful in selling this war for pacification and American rule to the public. In the Philippines, new policies that dealt harshly with insurgents blunted the guerrillas' efforts. The capture of Emilio Arguinaldo, the most prominent insurgent leader, contributed to the end of the dream of an independent Philippines. Pacification succeeded with the use of the twin weapons first used by the U.S. Army in controlling Native Americans: ruthless military power combined with civilian infrastructures to make the Filipinos dependent upon Americans for law, order, and subsistence. It is not insignificant that twenty-six of the thirty generals who served in the Philippines had earlier served on the Frontier in America's conquest of the Indians.[27]

In the end, military success over the insurgents and civilian efforts to improve the lives of the average Filipino quieted the public uproar over the atrocity charges. In selling war, as in marketing any consumer product, nothing succeeds like success. In the beginning, the war was easily sold to the American people as a noble struggle to free the people of Cuba, Puerto Rico, and the Philippines from oppressive Spanish rule. Later, the quick war and the longer struggle to subdue the Filipinos were sold to the U.S. public as a realization of America's Manifest Destiny. Both efforts were successful.

The Platt Amendment of 1901 gave America total control over Cuba for many decades, and even after Fidel Castro overthrew the Batista regime sympathetic to the United States in 1959, the United States retained control of a naval station at Cuba's Guantanomo Bay. Puerto Rico became a U.S. Commonwealth in 1967 and remains so to this day.

Selling a Wanted War

While John Hay's "splendid little war" was not without setbacks and difficulties, the McKinley administration, after being pushed into the war by a public mobilized by a jingoistic American press, was able to keep selling the war to the American people. Further, the Roosevelt administration was able to sell the pacification of the Philippines that followed the peace treaty with Spain, overcoming changes of imperialism and betrayal of American commitment to freedom and democracy. The government won the battles on both the front lines and the home front, performing the promise to make America a great sea power and expand its frontier across the Pacific Ocean. Once more, America was empowered by its use of military power, with the U.S. public accepting the war and the subsequent occupation of the Philippines and Puerto Rico as necessary sacrifices for the greater good of the Cuban, Puerto Rican, and Filipino peoples.

To a large extent, this was an easy marketing program since the public demanded the war even before the government was ready to sell it. The customers who demanded the product were largely satisfied with its delivery. From this first American war of the twentieth century, some lessons seem crystal clear.

First, the *context* must be examined; if the marketing environment is fertile for exploitation because of history and prior media efforts, the public will support the administration, especially if there has been what the public perceives as an unprovoked and cowardly attack on the country or its military forces. ("Remember the *Maine*" would remain a rallying cry throughout the war.)

Second, the administration has *ethos* simply by having been popularly elected. Its credibility will be strengthened or diminished by a number of factors, primarily the success or failure of the U.S. military against the enemy and the ability to control the negative effects of bad news. In the Philippine Insurrection, the Roosevelt administration was able to explain away the atrocity charges as not representative of official policy.

Third, the *logos* of the messages, or selling proposition, will appeal to both logic and emotion if they are connected to some core American values like "freedom, democracy, peace," and America as the "Guiding Light of the World."

Fourth, the administration, either through happenstance or planning, needs to *use and control the public media* in order to influence how the news media will cover the war. While the American media were initially more war-minded than the first McKinley administration, President Roosevelt later needed to work hard at damage control during the Waller trial. In general, however, despite frequent criticisms by the news media, American journalism traditionally supports America's wars, at least at the onset.

Fifth, understanding the *pathos* of the people, in modern marketing parlance, its "psychographics," is paramount if the administration is going to shape "consumer behavior" to its own ends. In the Spanish-American War, the people's biases, morals, hopes, fears, dreams, and desires were shaped more by the press than by the presidency; that is not always the case and contemporary U.S. presidents can ill-afford to allow the news media to shape their decisions.

Finally, since the *effects* of all persuasion include both positive and negative outcomes, administrations are successful in selling a war when they trumpet their successes (the victories at Manila Bay and Santiago Bay and the charge up San Juan Hill) while downplaying their failures (the Samar executions and the torture charges during the occupation of the Philippines). No modern marketing and consumer research methods existed during the Spanish-American War as we understand them today, but it may have been a sign of public approval that while the McKinley–Roosevelt ticket of 1900 received 51.7 percent of the vote, in 1904, the Roosevelt–Fairbanks ticket received 56.4 percent. The difference may have resulted from Roosevelt's more direct use of the war to market himself, as well as from the effects of McKinley's assassination in 1901.

In the Spanish-American War and during the Philippine Insurrection, the McKinley and Roosevelt administrations were successful in maintaining their *ethos* (credibility), in selling the *logos* (logic and appeals) of the messages, and in exploiting public media to reach the people, achieving positive responses (*pathos*) in the American people. The Spanish-American War was a relatively easy war to sell to a U.S. public clamoring for American intervention. Selling the annexation of Puerto Rico and U.S. control of the Philippines was a bit harder, but appeals to patriotism undermined the naysayers and assuaged the concerns of the American people. What began as "Mr. Hearst's War" ended up as "America's War," the war America wanted, perhaps needed, to continue its frontier heritage by wedding it to sea power, bringing enlightenment, peace, justice, and freedom to the less fortunate peoples of the world. The American Colossus no longer enlightened the world by example alone but with deeds as well. Destiny was now manifest.

2

The Great War—World War I

AVOIDING FOREIGN ENTANGLEMENTS

Nineteen years after the Spanish-American War ended, a combination of marketing communications techniques and outright propaganda employed by foreign and U.S. government officials and abetted by the public media gradually entangled America in a global war being fought three thousand miles from the nation's nearest shores. America's national security was never at stake. A naïve public, initially opposing America's involvement in the brutal conflict between the Allied forces and the Central Powers in Europe and the Middle East, was slowly persuaded to abandon its isolationist views and enthusiastically embrace the country's entry into the war on the side of the Allied forces.

World War I was sparked on June 22, 1914, by the assassination of the Austrian Archduke Franz Ferdinand and his wife in Sarajevo by Serbian terrorists. The principal opposing sides ultimately pitted France, Great Britain, Russia, and, later, Italy against Austria-Hungary, Bulgaria, Germany, and, later, the Ottoman Empire. Both sides had old scores to settle and colonial empires to protect or expand. The guns of August 1914 ushered in four years of battle, blockade, sacrifice, and enormous slaughter. After rapid German advances on the Western Front degenerated into static trench warfare from the Alps to the North Sea, Germany and Russia mauled each other in fierce fighting on the Eastern Front.[1]

The View from America

In the early years of the war, the United States remained decidedly neutral. As President Woodrow Wilson said in his message to the U.S. Senate on August 19, 1914, "The United States must be neutral in fact as well as in name." In an address to foreign-born citizens on May 10, 1915, the president was even blunter: "There is such a thing as a man being too proud to fight." Geography, history, policy, transportation, and communication had combined to make neutrality a logical and safe international policy for America.

Two vast oceans separated the United States from Europe and Asia. The American Revolution and the War of 1812 were fought to free the country and the people from British rule and domination. After the war of 1812, the border with Canada became fixed and permanent. The Mexican War of 1848 ended with Mexico recognizing the Rio Grande as the American–Mexican boundary, ceding Arizona, California, New Mexico, Nevada, and Texas to the United States. The Spanish-American War of 1898 not only enforced the Monroe Doctrine that the Americas were for Americans but reenforced George Washington's Farewell Address warning "to steer clear of permanent alliances, with any portion of the foreign world."

Until the twentieth century, transportation had also favored American isolationism and self-reliance. Railroads now linked the country but the sailing ships made transatlantic crossings lengthy, difficult, and expensive. Steamships reduced these problems but did not eliminate them entirely. For most of the millions of European immigrants streaming into the United States at the end of the nineteenth and beginning of the twentieth centuries, it still was a one-way voyage from the Old Country to the New World.

The United States was also isolated from distant countries because of the limitations of communication. Until the technological miracle of Samuel F. B. Morse's electric telegraph in 1844, communication could move only in the time and space provided by means of physical transportation. Now, communication was free to travel with the speed of light but was still restricted to the wires that carried the current. When the Atlantic Cable was laid in 1858, electricity carried messages across the ocean to Europe. After 1897, Gugliemo Marconi's wireless telegraph extended the reach of Morse's telegraph by freeing it from wires, increasing the flow of information between Europe and the United States.

In 1914, motion pictures were just emerging from their infancy; in America, D. W. Griffith's monumental *The Birth of a Nation* would overwhelm audiences in 1915, establishing the motion picture as a powerful form of communication that, in words attributed to President Wilson, himself a noted historian, was "History writ with lightning."

Despite these advances in electronic communication technology, printed newspapers, magazines, books, and pamphlets continued to provide most

Americans with most of their local, regional, national, and international news and opinion.

Propaganda Aimed at America

In time of war, each nation strives to inspire its citizens, influence neutral nations, reinforce allies, and demoralize the enemy. In the Great War, both Germany and Great Britain attempted to use propaganda to promote their positions to the American people and its government. Germany's goal was not so much to gain America as an ally as to ensure her neutrality. Toward this goal, Germany appealed to the millions of Americans of German descent who still identified with their German ancestry and culture. Their *creative platform* stressing the need to protect German honor and the rightness of their cause ("*Gott mit uns*—God is with us") had some influence on German Americans but little on the rest of the population. Also sympathetic to the German side, however, were many Irish-Americans who harbored hatred for the British after centuries of brutal occupation and oppression in Ireland, especially the Great Famine of 1845–1852 that caused over a million deaths and the exile of another million-and-a half, mostly to the United States. The Irish Rebellion of Easter Monday 1916, erupting in the second year of the Great War, added to anti-British feelings among Irish-Americans, reinforcing, at the least, a desire for America to stay neutral.

The British began their marketing campaign aimed at the American people with some distinct disadvantages. In addition to the hostility to be expected from the German and Irish communities, there was an unfortunate history between the two nations. Americans had fought two wars against the British, the first to win its independence, the second to establish its freedom of the seas as well as to expand its northern frontier into Canada. During the American Civil War, Britain had openly sided with the Confederate States of America, choosing to overlook the Southern practice of slavery in order to serve the financial interests of British textile manufacturers who needed the South's cotton for their mills. On this still sore point, Nativist Americans shared hostility toward the British with their usual antagonists, Catholic German-Americans and Irish-Americans. Against these handicaps, however, Great Britain had one clear advantage over Germany: a common English language that not only made communication between the two countries easy but also encouraged a shared culture in terms of political theory, laws, literature, and even history. The establishment of the Rhodes Scholarships in 1902 enabled young men from the British Empire and the United States to study at England's celebrated Oxford University, with the specific intention "to further harmony and compatibility between English-speaking peoples."

Early in the war, the British established a number of committees to support their propaganda efforts. Of particular relevance for the United States was the work of the Neutral Countries Subcommittee of the Central

Committee for National Patriotic Associations, established in 1914. Its goal was to gain support for the Allied cause in neutral countries. The United States was the key nation on their agenda for the simple reason that Britain was using the Royal Navy to blockade all shipping in and out of largely landlocked Germany. At the same time, Britain was relying upon the United States for its own imports despite the threat of attacks on shipping by German *Unterzeeboaten* (U-boats).

Central to these propaganda efforts targeted at Americans was the promotion of a key slogan provided by the noted English author H. G. Wells: "The War That Will End War." With one brilliant slogan, the British could now present themselves as peacemakers forced to fight against war itself. Other messages that resonated well with Americans publicized the German invasion of neutral Belgium, anthropomorphized in lurid color posters as a damsel in distress in the clutches of a barbaric German soldier bent on pillage, rape, and murder. This image was reinforced with slogans: "Defend Brave Little Belgium" and "Stop the Dreaded Hun." (Ironically, it was the German Kaiser, Wilhelm II, who provided the Allies with the label "Hun" when he urged his troops to attack like the Huns of old.)[2]

"He Kept Us Out of War"

As the years of combat passed, President Woodrow Wilson and the people stayed neutral. In 1916, Wilson ran for reelection on the slogan: "He Kept Us Out of War." Despite the urgings of Spanish-American War hero and former President Theodore Roosevelt and other interventionists, public opinion strongly supported President Wilson's policy of neutrality. This war across the ocean seemed alien to most Americans, one more disease plaguing the Old World. Americans, whether descendents of the original colonists or of the more recently arrived "huddled masses yearning to breathe free," turned their faces away from the past toward the bright American future of peace, prosperity, and progress. One popular song of 1915 summed up American public opinion in its title: "I Didn't Raise My Boy to Be a Soldier."

Still, the Allied propaganda aimed at winning America as an ally had some success. New reports stressing German atrocities against Belgium, the execution of British nurse Edith Cavill for aiding Allied soldiers, the reported bayoneting of innocent women and children, the alleged corpse factory in which bodies were turned into soap (a fabrication that would become terrifyingly real in World War II) all contributed to a gradual polarization of the U.S. public. In this effort, the British were helped by those Americans with interventionist sympathies, predominantly East Coast Republicans who identified with the Allies.

The Germans made the British propaganda effort easier by committing two major blunders that antagonized American public opinion. The first was

Germany's decision to conduct unrestricted submarine warfare, epitomized by the sinking of the British Cunard liner *Lusitania* off the coast of Ireland on May 7, 1915, killing 128 Americans. The front page of *The New York Herald* European edition of May 8, 1915, tells the story: "The Lusitania Sunk Off the Irish Coast By German Pirates." This threat to American freedom to sail the seas not only helped to turn American public opinion against Germany but also resulted in increased U.S. military spending for self-defense.

The second blunder was even more destructive to Germany's cause. Alfred Zimmermann, the German Undersecretary of State in Berlin, sent a telegram to the German Ambassador in Mexico instructing him to tell the Mexican government that if the United States declared war on Germany and Mexico attacked the United States, Germany, anticipating victory, would help Mexico reclaim Arizona, New Mexico, and Texas. The "Zimmermann Telegram" was intercepted, decoded, and made public by the British who controlled the Atlantic Cable.[3] Pancho Villa's raid across the border on Columbus, New Mexico, on March 9, 1916, made the telegram's proposal seem all too real. *The New York Herald* front page on March 10 carried this headline: "Gen. Villa Raids American Town, Killing Many." Public pressure for America to join the Allied side was steadily increasing. While President Wilson remained silent on what he would do, former President Teddy Roosevelt was quite outspoken, as reported on the same front page: "I am disgusted with its [America's] unmanly failure to do its duty in an international crisis, and its abandonment of national honor."

Considerations involving American overseas trade, identification with "democracy" over "imperialism" (despite the undemocratic nature of the British, French, and Russian Empires), and effective Allied propaganda gradually shifted both U.S. public opinion and the Wilson administration toward supporting the Allied cause directly. Although German General Erich Ludendorff dismissed America's potential entry into the war saying, "What can she do? She cannot come over here.... I do not give a damn about America"—the Yanks were coming and they would make a difference.

More Precious Than Peace

On April 2, 1917, bowing to public pressure and his own sympathies for the Allied cause, President Woodrow Wilson stood before a Joint Session of Congress and asked for a declaration of war against Germany. It was only the fourth time in the country's history that an American president had requested such a declaration. In asking for war to make the "world safe for democracy," Wilson struck a responsive chord in Americans and the way they view themselves: the reluctant warriors who fight only when no other option is open, the noble knights who fight not for gain or glory but for peace, democracy, and right.

It is a fearful thing to lead this great peaceful people into war, into the most terrible and disastrous of all wars, civilization itself seeming to be in the balance. But the right is more precious than peace, and we shall fight for the things we have always carried nearest our hearts—for democracy, for the rights of those who submit to authority to have a voice in their own governments, for the rights and liberties of small nations, for a universal domination of right by such a concert of free peoples as shall bring peace and safety to all nations and make the world itself at last free.

Four days later, on April 6, Congress voted for a declaration of war against Germany. The overture was over. Now the full American orchestra of public communication would be used to swell the chords and choruses of a mighty nation, summoning the American people to a war to save the Old World from itself and to make the world safe for democracy by bringing American values and dreams to all the peoples of the earth. The British started their marketing campaign to recruit America as an ally in the war. Now, the American administration would have to continue to persuade the American people to support this war. The promises were easy to make and easy to sell; performing the promises would be much more difficult. America's decision to enter this European War was an altruistic effort to bring nobility and selflessness to what was essentially an ignoble and selfish cause. This high-minded mission was doomed to failure.

WINNING THE WAR OVER HERE AND OVER THERE

Preparing for War

In 375 C.E., Flavius Vegetius Renatus provided a maxim for all those who advocate a strong military: "*Qui desidenat pacem, praoparet bellum*—Let him who desires peace, prepare for war." In April 1917, President Wilson and America desired peace but were totally unprepared for the war that Congress had just declared. Despite the President's strong words, U.S. military forces were extremely weak.

The U.S. Navy, spurred by the writings of Admiral Alfred Thayer Mahan on the influence of sea power, was mighty enough, second only to the British Navy in ships and total tonnage; however, the U.S. Army, which would bear the brunt of battle in the trenches on the Western Front, was woefully unprepared. In 1916, the Army's 107,642 troops ranked seventeenth in the world. It was seriously deficient in both modern arms and large-scale strategy and tactics. The National Guard had 132,000 soldiers, but they were part-time and ill-prepared for modern warfare. The Marine Corps had 10,397 well-trained professionals, but they were spread thin policing American areas of interest around the globe.

But America rose to the challenge. By 1917, the American Expeditionary Forces (AEF) numbered over 2 million men, augmented by over a half million sailors in the Navy and a Marine Corps of over 75,000 Leathernecks. Despite this dramatic increase in troop strength, the Americans were deficient in both training and in such weapons as rifles, machine guns, tanks, artillery, and the newly significant airplane. Fortunately, the French were able to provide the needed arms and other equipment.

Although the Marine Corps easily achieved its recruiting goals with 60,189 new men out of 239,274 volunteers who tried to enlist, the Army, with over 700,000 volunteers, needed a draft to secure an additional half million to fill its ranks. The Selective Service list of May 1917 provided the means to conscript these additional men.[4]

In order to encourage volunteers and to gain public support for the Draft, the U.S. government had to market the war as a realization of the American dream, not as an unnecessary sacrifice for foreign entanglement. All Americans, native-born and immigrant alike, were invited to join the "Crusade for Democracy," whether in combat on the Western Front or in support on the home front.

Committee on Public Information

President Wilson, previously the protector of America's neutrality but now the drumbeater for war, ordered that a Committee on Public Information (CPI) be formed. It was comparable to the British propaganda committees that were so effective in previously mobilizing American support for their side. Wilson asked George Creel, a self-styled "crusading journalist for the weak against the strong," to head the committee which was established as the central coordinator for all government effort to sell the war to America. As Newton D. Baker, the Secretary of War, recalled in a postwar dinner speech in Washington on November 29, 1918, "... [this]war wasn't won by sword alone. It was won by the pen as well as the sword." In this speech, Secretary Baker also articulated what would become a common theme for America's image in the twentieth century: "... it was of the greatest importance that America in this war should be represented not merely as a strong man fully armed, but as a strong man fully armed and believing in the cause for which he was fighting."[5] Hearts and minds were now as important as guns and ammunition.

George Creel accepted Wilson's offer with the enthusiasm of any super salesman. Indeed, the very title of Creel's postwar book about his efforts contains what the novelist Sinclair Lewis would later describe as "boosterism": *How We Advertised America: The First Telling of the Amazing Story of the Committee on Public Information that Carried the Gospel of America to Every Corner of the Globe.*

The book itself is a testament to Creel's faith in America and in American advertising. Rejecting the term *propaganda* because of its association with

German lies and deceits in the public's mind, Creel stressed *education* and *information* as the keys to selling this war to America. His basic strategy has guided American war marketing policy since its entry into World War I up to today's War on Terrorism:

> The *war-will*, the will to win, of a democracy depends upon the degree to which each one of all the people of that democracy can concentrate and consecrate body and soul and spirit in the supreme effort of service and sacrifice.[6]

What Creel and the Committee on Public Information achieved in the nineteen months of America's participation in the war is impressive. The organization was largely staffed by volunteers. Journalists and editors readily imposed voluntary censorship upon themselves to "safeguard military information useful to the enemy."[7]

Seventy-five thousand volunteers were recruited by the Committee to serve as "Four-Minute Men," delivering 755,190 speeches in 5,200 American communities to 14,454,514 listeners. Each "Four-Minute Man" was prepared to deliver a seemingly impromptu pro-war speech on a series of topics—Universal Service, The Red Cross, Liberty Loans, Food Conservation, Why We Are Fighting, The Enemy, German Propaganda, The Navy, The Army, A Tribute to Our Allies, The Meaning of America—to audiences in movie theaters, fraternal lodges, labor unions, garages, lumber camps, churches, colleges, and even Indian reservations. A Woman's Division was founded to speak to women's groups on the general theme of "What women were doing to help win the war" and Junior Four-Minute-Men teams composed of both boys and girls who spoke in elementary and high schools.[8] Special "war expositions," containing graphic representations of the war, toured twenty-one cities and reached a total audience of over 10 million visitors.

A daily news service was established to provide information to news organizations via wire, radio, and the mail. The division of news held to a sound principle of successful advertising: disseminate both good and bad news. It also tried to negotiate between the military and the press, which, then as now, were mutually suspicious of each other.

President Wilson's speeches were printed and distributed in pamphlet form. Among other pamphlets that were distributed was one by a university professor with a title that would be recycled in a seminal World War II Army propaganda film: *How War Came to America*; 6,250,000 copies of this particular pamphlet were distributed free of charge.

The Committee on Public Information (CPI) had three main goals for these publications, goals that were in harmony with the Committee's central mission:

1. To make America's own purposes and ideals clear both to ourselves and to the world, whether ally or enemy.

2. A thorough presentation of the aims, methods, and ideals of the dynastic and feudal government of Germany.
3. Giving information which would help in a constructive way in the daily tasks of a nation at war.[9]

While employing the accepted media of speech and print, Creel and the Committee were quick to exploit new forms of communication. The Army Signal Corps provided raw film footage that was then edited into seven-reel features with such titles as *Pershing's Crusaders, America's Answer, and Under Four Flags*. In addition to these feature films, the Committee distributed weekly newsreels, supplemented by one-reel war films. Significantly, and in direct contrast with what would be the norm in World War II, the Committee did not seek close cooperation with commercial filmmakers.

In contrast to this hand-off policy for American films distributed within the United States, the War Trade Board controlled licenses for exporting films and the Committee on Public Information had to endorse a film before it could be sent to overseas audiences. The Committee's rules were short, simple, and restrictive[10]:

1. That every shipment for entertainment film from the United States should contain at least 20 percent "educational material."
2. That not a single foot of American entertainment film would be sold to any exhibitor who refused to show the Committee's war films.
3. That no American picture of any kind would be sold to houses where any sort of German film was being used.

In this effort at control, the Committee had one clear advantage: the war had brought commercial film production in both allied and enemy nations to a near standstill. In contrast, American commercial film production had soared with neutrality. The studio system that would establish Hollywood as the film capital of the world emerged and has remained dominant ever since that time. As Creel himself noted, "What war-weary foreigners liked and demanded was American comedy and dramatic film."[11]

This proved to be very disadvantageous for the German film industry. While film exhibitors in many neutral countries were either owned or controlled by German companies, the hardball policies of Creel's Committee paid off. Neutral countries like Sweden, Norway, Switzerland, and Holland began opting for U.S.-produced films over German productions (of which there were few new titles). Success was also achieved in Latin and South America with Mexico, Argentina, Peru, and Chile falling in line. Across the Pacific, China joined the American film bandwagon. In the end, Creel achieved his goal of "Not only putting [American] movies into foreign countries but keeping those with negative images of America out."[12]

These events led to America's domination of commercial film distribution across the globe, the beginning of what some critics later termed "American cultural imperialism." To the charge that America dominates global culture through capitalism and tough negotiations, defenders of American culture from George Creel to Jack Valente, recent head of today's Motion Picture Association, suggest that the obvious excellence of American films is attested to by their wide acceptance with audiences all over the globe.[13]

Supporting the War

The burgeoning Hollywood film industry also served the nation by providing easily recognizable celebrity faces for the four Liberty Loan Drives, the Victory Loan Drive, and the War Saving Stamps Drive that raised the money needed to finance the war effort. Although the Hollywood star system was still in its infancy, names and faces like Charlie Chaplin, Mary Pickford, Douglas Fairbanks, Buster Keaton, Norman Talmadge, Theda Bara, Dorothy and Lillian Gish, and Lon Chaney brought out massive crowds which not only cheered the stars but bought the Liberty Bonds: $3 billion for the first loan, $4 billion for the second, $7 billion combined for the third and fourth loans and $1 billion for the postwar Victory Loan, a total of $22 billion in $100 bonds in all. The War Saving Stamps Drive asked people, especially children, to buy twenty-five-cent stamps to support the war effort.

While not required to make films supporting the war effort, Hollywood did provide a number of films with clear pro-American, pro-Allies slants: in 1917, *Escaping the Hun, The Lone Eagle*, and *Over There*; in 1918, *Claws of the Hun, The Beast of Berlin, Over the Top, The Prussian Air*, D. W. Griffith's *Hearts of the World, The Hun Within*, and three films with the Kaiser as movie villain *The Kaiser's Finish, The Kaiser's Shadow*, and *The Kaiser*.[14]

The advertising industry, barely thirty-five years old in 1917, was enlisted in the fight to market the war to America. It quickly responded with over 800 publishers of weekly and monthly periodicals pledging space worth $160,000 per month to support the war. In addition, the Advertising Division of the Committee on Public Information secured another $340,981 in advertising space for government propaganda use. Media advertising thus joined government in a partnership that continues today, shaping American public opinion, its elections, and its wars. In Creel's words, "The Committee mobilized the advertising forces of the country—press, periodical, car and outdoors—for the patriotic campaign." In helping the country, the advertising world also helped itself, bringing good publicity to a new profession longing for respectability.[15]

In the world of graphic communication, many leading artists and illustrators enlisted eagerly in the struggle, including Howard Chandler Christy, James Montgomery Flagg, Charles Dana Gibson, and a dozen other lesser known illustrators. Perhaps the earliest pro-war poster was one created in 1915 by James Montgomery Flagg for the Boston Committee on Public Safety and distributed quickly when war was declared in April 1917. It personifies America as Columbia, wearing her red, white, and blue costume, asleep in a chair. At the top, the headline cries out: "Wake Up, America!" At the bottom the message is clear: "Civilization Calls Every Man, Woman, and Child!"

Posters encouraged enlistment in the Army, Navy, and Marines, including specific units like the Tank Corps, the Coast Artillery, and the Air Service. Of all the recruitment posters, perhaps the best known and possibly most effective was James Montgomery Flagg's striking portrait of Uncle Sam, in full Fourth of July costume of red, white, and blue with a top hat, looking you straight in the eye and pointing his right index finger directly at you, with the command, "I Want You." For the Army, the words "For U.S. Army" were added. For the Navy, the words were "I want You in the Navy and I Want You Now." For the Marines, an unnamed illustrator substituted a Marine sergeant for Uncle Sam and used these words: "The U.S. Marines Want You." The Uncle Sam poster was also used in World War II and continues to be used, sometimes in ironic form, today. Flagg also created a special Marine Corps recruiting poster of a Marine, in combat gear and campaign hat, holding a pistol, staring at the viewer. The American flag provides the background for the image. The words at the bottom are "First in the Fight—Always Faithful—Be a U.S. Marine."

Other posters advanced themes central to the Committee's mission: Conservation of food ("Food Will Win the War") and coal ("Save Your Coal to Fire the Kaiser"); Liberty Loans ("Let's End It Quick with Liberty Bonds," "Halt the Hun! Buy U.S. Government Bonds," "Fight or Buy Bonds," "Beat Back the Hun with Liberty Bonds"); War Saving Stamps ("Boys and Girls! You can help Uncle Sam Win the War," "Share in the Victory—Save for Your Country, Save for Yourself"); tributes to our Allies ("America's Tribute to Britain," "All for One and One for All! Vive La France!"); United War Work Campaign (Salvation Army, YMCA, YWCA, National Catholic War Council Charities, The Jewish Welfare Board); the Red Cross ("The Spirit of America"); relief ("They Shall Not Perish," "Save Serbia, "Give or We Perish—Armenia, Greece, Syria, Persia," "Help the Belgium Babies," "Free Milk for France," "For the Fatherless Children of France"); shipping ("Together We Win," "Another Ship—Another Victory," "On the Job for Victory"); and special causes ("Don't Talk, Spies Are Listening," "Books Wanted for Our Men in Camp," "Over There," and "Team Work Will Win the War!").

Singing of Arms and Men

Other aspects of popular culture were also enlisted in marketing the war, from dime novels and pulp fiction to popular music. Among the songs about the war were these: "When the *Lusitania* Went Down," "Wake Up, America!" "Good-bye Broadway, Hello France," "America, Here's My Boy," "Hinkey Dinky Parlay Voo?" "It's Time for Every Boy To Be a Soldier," "We'll Carry the Star Spangled Banner thru the Trenches," "Over the Top," "The Rose of No Man's Land," "When the Kaiser Does the Goosestep," "It's a Long Way to Berlin, but We'll Get There," "Tell That to the Marines," "The Battle Song of Liberty."[16]

Of all of the war songs, none was more popular or more central to the war effort than George M. Cohan's "Over There." By World War I, Cohan was already an American show business legend, a performer since childhood in his family act, The Four Cohans. He also wrote songs and plays, danced, and produced both musicals and dramas for the stage. Among his songs were some of America's favorites: "Mary is a Grand Old Name," "Give My Regards to Broadway," "Grand Old Flag," and "Yankee Doodle Dandy." Now, Cohan invited Johnnie to get his gun and take it and himself "Over There." The chorus is a call to arms for Americans, a reassurance for the Allies and a threat to Germany:

> Over there, over there
>> Send the word, send the word over there
>> That the Yanks are coming, the Yanks are coming,
> The drums rum-tumming everywhere
>> So prepare, say a prayer
>> Send the word, send the word to beware
>> We'll be over, we're coming over,
>> And we won't come back till it's over over there!

Performed and recorded by many singers, "Over There" was the most popular song of the war, becoming a second National Anthem, celebrating American optimism, confidence, and determination.[17]

We note in these words not only American idealism but naivety as well. It was naïve to believe that force of arms alone will result in a peace worth having, forgetting that a bad peace would lead to a new war. In *On War*, Clausewitz had warned against this very naivety of seeing war as combat alone: "War cannot be divorced from political life; and whenever this occurs in our thinking about war, the many links that connects the two elements are destroyed and we are left with something pointless and devoid of sense."

The Yanks Are Coming

Meanwhile, accompanying these advertising and political maneuvers, American military forces were being recruited and drafted, trained, shipped overseas, retrained and equipped, and sent into battle. The president's speeches and Cohan's "Over There" had promised that "the Yanks are coming" but it took time to deliver that promise. Under U.S. Army General

John J. "Black Jack" Pershing, the American Expeditionary Forces would eventually ship over a million men in France.

Before the American forces could be deployed in battle, the Germans hoped to end the war with Russia and overwhelm the British and French Forces on the Western Front. After crushing defeats by the Austrian–German armies, Russia was overtaken by internal revolt, resulting in the abdication of Czar Nicholas II on March 2, 1917. A provisional government attempted to continue the war, but the Communist Revolution of October 1917 and German military victories in the Ukraine in February 1918 would conclude in a Bolshevik surrender to Germany.[18]

Freed from fighting on the Eastern Front, German armies moved West for one final desperate gamble to smash the Allied Armies before the American forces could be thrown into the struggle. German offenses on March 21, April 9, and May 27, 1918, initially achieved some success in pushing back the Allies. Against the third attack, the American First Division entered the battle, followed by the Second and Third Divisions at Chateau Thierry and Belleau Wood on June 1 and 6. The Yanks were finally "Over There" and on the killing ground.[19]

Although green to combat, the Americans proved to be tough, courageous, even foolhardy, troops who overcame high casualty rates to confront and, eventually, force the German veterans to retreat. Once in combat, the American Expeditionary Forces soon provided heroes and heroic deeds to be celebrated in the American campaign to sell the war at home.

The Allied Aisne-Marne counterattack of July 18–August 6, 1918, pushed back the Germans, as did the St. Mihiel offensive of September 12–16, with fifteen American and five French divisions; eventually both would have only limited success. But the American Expeditionary Forces (AEF), supported by British and French forces, began a major new offensive on September 26 that was sustained and successful, ending only with the armistice of November 11, 1918.

In forty-seven days of combat, the AEF poured 1.2 million men into the conflict. In *For the Common Defense: A Military History of the United States of America*, the authors sum up the American contribution to the war:

> When the war ended, 1.3 million Americans had served at the front in twenty-nine combat divisions. These troops had provided the margin in numbers that allowed the Allies to ground the German army into surrender. In 200 days of combat, the Americans had lost 50,280 men who were killed in action or died of wounds. Over 200,000 more were wounded in action.[20]

Despite these efforts and losses, the other Allies did not consider America's role in the war to be militarily decisive or even significant, contributing to postwar mistrust between the United States and its former wartime partners.

The Home Front

While the Doughboys and Leathernecks were slugging it out in France, George Creel and his Committee on Public Information were waging the publicity wars on the home front, keeping American support for the war at full throttle by selling the story of the war as a great crusade for freedom and democracy. Included in these efforts was an attempt to counter, or at least soften, the public phobia against all things German or even foreign. The silly changing of the names of "Frankfurters" to "Liberty Dogs," "Sauerkraut" to "Liberty Cabbage," "Hamburgers" to "Salisbury Steaks" and "Dachshunds" to "Liberty Pups" was harmless enough but such phobias also included actual physical attacks on individuals and establishments with German names. In some neighborhoods with large German immigrant populations, trees were cut down so that the occupants of the houses could be more closely watched. As Creel himself wrote about this fight, "A wave of national feeling might carry us into the war and national passions and hatred might whip us on, but froth and dregs would be the ultimate result."

One of Creel's strategies was to work closely with foreign-born Americans through their own organizations and societies. Chief among these groups were the Scandinavians, Poles, Yugoslavs, Moravians, Slovaks, Serbs, Romanians, Bohemians, Lithuanians, Hungarians, Greeks, Dutch, Italians, and even Germans. At a special Fourth of July celebration in 1918, President Wilson addressed representatives of thirty-three nationalities at Mount Vernon, George Washington's Virginia home on the Potomac River. After the great Irish (now American) tenor John McCormack sang "The Battle Hymn of the Republic" and "The Star Spangled Banner," the President called those present "Americans by choice."[21]

The work of Creel and the Committee was not without opposition within the United States. Some Americans still sang "I Didn't Raise My Boy to Be a Soldier" and while their opinions were in a decided minority, they would swell to a majority in the disillusionment following the Great War.[22]

The End of the War

The fall of 1918 was a time of triumph for the Allied cause. On September 12 Bulgaria signed an armistice, followed by Turkey on October 30. The Austro-Hungarian Empire, with its subject peoples now establishing their own small nations, signed a ceasefire with Italy on November 3. The headline in the European edition of *The New York Herald* of November 2, 1918, reads: "Great Allied Drive Resumed from Coast to Verdun." The Central Powers had ceased to exist and now only Germany was left. The end came swiftly with Germany threatened not only by military defeat at the front, but revolution at home. On November 10, Germany's ruler, Kaiser Wilhelm II, fled to Holland for asylum, abdicating the throne and ending the Second German Reich on November 28, formally acknowledging what had been in effect since November 9; a new German Republic that would sign an armistice with the Allied Powers.[23]

On the eleventh hour of the eleventh day of the eleventh month—11:00 A.M. on November 11, 1918—the guns of August 1914 finally fell silent. "The War to End All War" was over. The German thought they had signed an armistice, not a surrender, and anticipated negotiations based upon President Wilson's "Fourteen Points" that would be fair to all sides. But the Allies saw in the armistice a victory. The European edition of *The New York Herald* of November 12, 1918, proclaimed in a bold front-page headline: "The War Is Won!" The Allies had won the war, in fact, if not yet in words. The words of victory and defeat would come with the June 28, 1919 Versailles Peace Treaty that would prove to be neither just nor lasting.

The Fourteen Points

A political idealist, reluctant warrior, and perhaps the most naïve official in his administration, President Wilson believed that since America had entered the war on the side of the Allies without self-interest, she should also act as an honest broker at war's end who could reconcile both sides. What he didn't understand about European politics and politicians would prove to be vast.

President Wilson proposed a plan for a just and lasting peace centered on Fourteen Points, which he outlined in an address to Congress on January 8, 1918. They called for "Open covenants of peace openly arrived at," freedom of the seas, equal trade, disarmament, impartial adjustments of all colonial claims with some concern for the native populations, German withdrawal from conquered territory in Belgium and Russia, the restoration of Alsace-Lorraine to France, readjusting Italian frontiers based on nationality, autonomy for the peoples of Austria-Hungary, self-determination for the peoples of the Balkans, the Ottoman Empire, and Poland, and a "league of nations" to guarantee political and territorial integrity. Not surprisingly, both the Allies and the enemy powers were quite cool to Wilson's proposal. What strikes the reader, even today, is how clear and reasonable these Fourteen Points seem. Perhaps, if the Allies had been truly committed to pursuing them, a decent and lasting peace could have been achieved, possibly averting Russian Communism, Italian Fascism, German Nazism, and the Second World War.

As defeat became a reality, Germany accepted the Fourteen Points as the basis for negotiations. However, the Allies had their own scores to settle and fully intended to humiliate and punish Germany and Austria-Hungary for the war. Even in the United States, many of President Wilson's fellow citizens were calling for harsher treatment of Germany than promised by the Fourteen Points. The tiger had been roused and now could only be satisfied with blood.

President Wilson had made a classic marketing blunder. He had promised what he could not deliver because he did not have control over the essential elements involved in the war. When he failed to deliver the promise, he lost credibility not only with the Allies and the enemy but, eventually, with the American people. In his idealistic hubris, he had rendered himself vulnerable to his enemies in Congress. He and the Democratic Party would pay dearly for that failure.

For most Americans, the Great War was over. The president and the Committee on Public Information had won both the war of battles and the war for the hearts and minds of the American people. Now, the time had come to deliver the peace promised by the sacrifices of war. In his autobiography, George Creel quotes President Wilson's prophetic observation about the difficulties performing on the promises:

> "It is a great thing that you have done, but I am wondering if you have not unconsciously spun a net for me from which there is no escape.... People will endure tyrants for years, but they tear their delivers to pieces if a millennium is not created immediately. What I seem to see ... is a tragedy of disappointment."[24]

The promises spelled out by the Fourteen Points were noble but would prove impossible to keep. In America, the euphoric high of wartime sacrifice and patriotism soon gave way to a depressive hangover that would linger for two decades.

The Great War was a war filled with diplomatic and military blunders that sacrificed lives needlessly, but perhaps the greatest blunder was the war itself. In addition to the millions of military and civilian deaths, the war had bankrupted most of Europe, toppled four empires, weakened France and Great Britain, and laid the foundations for communism in Russia, fascism in Italy, and Nazism in Germany. Ironically, it had not even solved the problems in the Balkans that had triggered the conflict in 1914, and which continue to this day.

The president, who had kept America out of war in 1916, led America into war in 1917 and to victory in 1918, now urged Europe to negotiate a peace that justified the sacrifices. The goal was clear, but hidden dangers awaited President Wilson at home and "Over There."

DEFEAT IN PEACE—THE VERSAILLES TREATY AND THE LEAGUE OF NATIONS

Winning the Peace

American and Allied successes on the battlefields had validated the Committee on Public Information's goals and strategies. General Pershing and the American Expeditionary Forces had delivered on the promise to win the war in Europe. But there was trouble at home. Immediately after the armistice on November 11, 1918, Congress effectively ended operations by the Committee on Public Information. Democratic and Republican senators and Republican-friendly newspapers openly attacked Creel and the Committee, charging them with censorship during the peace conference.[25]

In Europe, President Wilson was hailed by the public as a savior; he fared less well with the leaders of France, Great Britain, and Italy. French Premier Georges Clemenceau, noted for his quip that "War is much too serious a matter to be left to the military," obviously believed that peace was much too serious to be left to an American President. He dismissed President Wilson's Fourteen Points, joking that "The good lord had only ten." Clemenceau was not about to throw away France's chance for revenge and retribution for her defeat and humiliation in the Franco–Prussian War, fought four decades before, and her sacrifices in the Great War. Also, Prime Minister David Lloyd George of Great Britain was not going to miss this hard-won opportunity to keep Germans from ever again challenging Britain's rule of the waves. Baron Sidney Sonnino, representing Italy, was intent upon reclaiming territories that "rightly" belonged to the Italian people, guaranteed by the secretly negotiated Treaty of London.

Despite President Wilson's efforts, the Treaty of Versailles signed on June 28, 1919, by the Allied Powers and Germany in the same Hall of Mirrors where the Second German Reich had been proclaimed on January 18, 1871, was the result of threat rather than reason. The Germans were forced to admit full guilt for the war and the damage caused to civilians and property; to make economic reparations; to accept drastically reduced armed forces; to return Alsace-Lorraine, taken in the Franco–Prussian War of 1870, to France; to allow international control of the industrial Saar Basin; to cede other parts of Germany and all overseas colonies to the victors and the new League of Nations; and to allow French troops to occupy the Rhineland as a guarantee against future German aggression. The new German Republic, with its capital relocated from Berlin to Weimar, was burdened not only with war guilt and economic hardships but also with a constitution that was viewed by many conservative Germans as being imposed from without by the Allies. The Treaty of Versailles planted the seeds of the Second World War (1939–1945); these seeds would be cultivated, nurtured, and harvested by a then obscure Austrian, Adolf Hitler, who had served as a lance corporal in a Bavarian regiment during the Great War.[26]

Selling the Peace

In the United States, President Wilson tried to sell the Versailles Treaty and its attached League of Nations (one of his own Fourteen Points) to the American people and the U.S. Senate, which has the duty of ratifying all treaties. Beginning with the elections of 1918, which returned forty-nine Republicans and forty-seven Democrats to the Senate, the President suffered a series of political setbacks culminating with the Senate's rejection of the Treaty on March 20, 1919, by a vote of 49 to 35, short of the two-thirds majority vote needed for ratification. As *The New York Herald* of March 21, 1919, noted: "Treaty Is Rejected by Democrat Votes: Sent Back to Wilson." Creel called a campaign to gain public support for the treaty "a failure of advertising," believing that salesmanship in print could find buyers for a good product.[27] He may have had a point: if the Committee on Public Information had been allowed to sell the peace as it had sold the war, the outcome could have been a triumph for the president and the internationalists.

How We Advertised America

In the aftermath of war, those who had fought the war of words and images took to print to defend or to criticize their own efforts. George Creel's *How We Advertised America* (1920) was a popularized version of his final report to Congress on the work of the Committee on Public Information. It is defiant, defensive, and boastful in revealing the strategies and tactics used to sell the war to America. One of Creel's aides was Edward L. Bernays, who made himself famous afterward as "the Father of Public Relations" with such books as *Crystallizing Public Opinion* (1923), *Propaganda* (1928), and *The Engineering of Consent* (1955). In *Public Relations* (1952), Bernays summed up his view on the work of the Committee on Public Information:

[E]ngineering of consent on a mass scale was ushered in in the 1914–18 period.... ideas and their dissemination became weapons and their words became bullets...from 1914 to 1918 it was the government of the United States that was the number one factor in public relations. President Wilson and various government agencies mobilized every known device of persuasion and suggestion to sell our war aims and ideas to the American people.... [28]

Disillusionment challenged these positive views on advertising the war. Walter Lippmann's *Public Opinion* (1922) and *The Phantom Public* (1925) warned a generation of Americans of the power of mass manipulation through the press and advertising. Gustav LeBon's warnings in *The Crowd* (1895) of a "mass mind" shaped by the popular press gained new life as a theme for scholars and critics of popular culture. Perhaps no writer put it more bluntly or with greater self-disgust than the journalist and critic George Seldes in 1935:

> I now realize that we were told nothing but buncome, that we were shown nothing of the realities of war, that we were, in short, merely part of the great Allied propaganda machine whose purpose was to sustain morale at all costs and help draw unwilling America into the slaughter.[29]

The American people came to distrust both the messenger who sold the war and the war itself. "The war to end all war" was now viewed as one more cynical example of might masquerading as right as the European victors claimed territorial and colonial spoils. As the American public came to distrust the messages and the war itself, they began to question the credibility of the messengers. In marketing terms, President Wilson and the Committee on Public Information had sold a product they could not deliver; they had failed to perform the promise in the peace that followed the war. In short, they had violated a cardinal rule of marketing: they made the initial sale but lost the customer by not assuring that the customer continued to feel satisfied about the purchase decision.

In *On War*, Clausewitz stressed that war is never an isolated event but a complex mixture of combat and politics, of morale and material, of emotion and reason, of policy and chance. In separating the war from the peace that followed, President Wilson and the Committee on Public Information failed to win sufficient support for the peace that followed as they had for the war. This failure began with the president himself, with his idealistic belief that nations could be guided by "open covenants, openly arrived at." This belief ran into the real-politic of European diplomacy perhaps best characterized by Otto von Bismarck's famous aphorism: "It is best not to look too closely into the making of sausages or treaties." Among his fellow Allied leaders, the President was an innocent abroad, an idealistic scholar in a den of political lions and tigers.

President Wilson believed that he could either sway his fellow leaders or appeal directly to the citizens of the Allied countries, but he lacked both the political sophistication and the propaganda apparatus to sway either the Allied leaders or influence public opinion in Europe as British propagandists had done so effectively in America prior to the U.S. government's decision to enter the war. Without the Committee on Public Information behind him, the president was at the mercy of the governments and the press of the Allies. Perhaps, if Wilson had the flair and charisma of a president like Teddy Roosevelt, he might have succeeded in winning their hearts and minds. Roosevelt knew how to manipulate audiences at home and abroad, using emotional appeals to sell American control of Puerto Rico and the Philippines as a blessing for the native peoples there and control of the Panama Canal as a blessing for all mankind.

Ironically, the one country that desired a peace based upon the Fourteen Points was the defeated Germany. The subsequent failure of the Versailles Peace Treaty to bring a just and lasting peace to Europe would encourage bitterness and hatred in Germany toward the Allies, and toward those whom the Nazis would call "The November Criminals" for signing the armistice in 1918 as well as those who signed the Treaty of Versailles in 1919. In postwar Germany, Adolf Hitler and the National Socialist German Workers Party would make political capital out of their hatred for, and opposition to, the Versailles Treaty and all those connected to it. The program of the Nazi Party adopted on February 24, 1920, had as its second point: "We demand equality of rights for the German people in its dealings with other nations, and the revocation of the peace treaties of Versailles and Saint-Germain."[30]

At home, President Wilson found himself losing favor with the public. A trend toward isolationism in America returned. In popular culture, the war became a setting for personal tragedy, disenchantment, and lost ideals. The postwar films like *The Big Parade* (1925), *What Price Glory?* (1926), *Wings* (1927), and *Dawn Patrol* (1930) celebrated individual heroism and sacrifice, but the war itself was not celebrated. In 1930, the Hollywood film version of Erich Maria Remarque's *All Quiet on the Western Front* presented a sympathetic and pacifistic view of ordinary German soldiers in the war not as hated Huns but as fellow victims of politicians and propaganda.

What is clear from examining the propaganda to market the Great War to America is that the Allies were highly successful in making a sale in the United States. The American people bought the story that this was a fight against tyranny despite the fact that Russia was a despotic dictatorship and the other Allies held overseas colonies that exploited their indigenous populations. The Allies sold America a war to end war and Americans bought the package.

From the American declaration of war on April 6, 1917, to the armistice on November 11, 1918, Americans overwhelmingly supported involvement in this European War. Volunteers and draftees went "Over There" to make the world safe for democracy by saving Europe from what they believed were persuaded was the savage German hordes whose own Kaiser had compared the German Army to the Huns of Attila, the scourge of Western civilization in the fifth century. Americans saw themselves engaged in yet another crusade to save civilization from chaos and savagery. The Committee on Public Information did an excellent job of selling the war, and the American people became not only eager buyers but happy customers until the war's end.

The Flawed Peace

In the flawed peace that followed the conflict, President Wilson failed to perform on his promises to assure a lasting peace. The Treaty of Versailles and the League of Nations had neither logical nor emotional appeals for the American people. The Republican Party exploited the public disenchantment with the war and the flawed peace, sweeping to victory in the presidential elections of 1920, 1924, and 1928. In the wake of these events came Prohibition and isolationism. The very slogans that helped send Americans "Over There" were now viewed as cynical manipulations to sell a war that people neither understood nor had needed. The antiwar isolationism of the 1920s and 1930s hindered any efforts to raise public concern over the very real threats to America later posed by Fascist Italy, Nazi Germany, and Imperial Japan.

In public relations terms, President Wilson and the Committee on Public Information performed well in analyzing the situation and defining their goals. They identified key target audiences and employed effective strategies and tactics to reach these audiences. Their creative strategies and executions were clear, concise, and reinforced through repetition. They made extensive and adroit use of all available media. They succeeded in the short term but failed to provide a just and lasting peace.

In mobilizing public opinion to support the war, the president and the Committee promised what ultimately could not be delivered—world peace. On the battlefront and the home front, the war was won but the peace was badly planned. The iron law of successful marketing was violated in President Wilson's failure to perform the promise.

The legacy of the selling of World War I was an America distrustful of any leader selling war, an America unwilling and unprepared to defend itself and its interests. It would take a dramatic propaganda of the deed—the Japanese attack on Pearl Harbor on December 7, 1941—to awaken America from its false dream of peace and safety over here.

3

The Good War—World War II

PRELUDE TO WAR

The Marketing Environment

It is a fundamental rule of marketing that if a customer doesn't believe his initial purchase decision of a product was as gratifying as the seller had promised, it will be extremely difficult to sell that customer the product a second time. This was exactly the marketing dilemma facing President Franklin Delano Roosevelt in 1940 as once again war clouds formed over Europe, threatening to draw America into another war twenty years after American troops had fought in the First World War. Adding to the president's dilemma, he anticipated that the United States would have to engage in a new armed conflict with Imperial Japan as both countries battled for economic supremacy in the Pacific region. The product he was trying to sell to the American public—U.S. rearmament in anticipation of fighting a war against the Axis Powers (Germany, Italy, and Japan)—had little appeal to most Americans at that time.

In the years following World War I, the so-called "War to End All Wars," the American public had become deeply disillusioned and demoralized: first, by the diplomatic failures of the Versailles Treaty negotiations and then by the Great Depression, following the collapse of U.S. financial markets in 1929.

Following World War I, most Americans wanted nothing more to do with foreign entanglements. The majority of Americans supported isolationist policies reflecting their bitterness about the promises not kept, and a feeling of detachment and security provided by the two great oceans separating the United States from Europe and Asia. Despite incumbent President Franklin D. Roosevelt's personal belief that the United States would have to fight the Axis Powers sooner or later, he felt compelled to reassure his audience at a political rally in New York on the eve of the 1940 presidential elections: "I have said this before, but I shall say it again and again and again: Your boys are not going to be sent into any foreign wars."[1] This was a perfect echo of President Woodrow Wilson's empty promise to the United States electorate twenty-four years earlier, shortly before American troops were committed to fight in Europe.

The Second World War could more accurately be called "The Great War, Part II," for, in fact, it was an inevitable continuation of that 1914–1918 European calamity that reshaped modern Europe and the Middle East. This time, the conflict would embroil not only Europe and the Middle East, but most of the world.

The immediate cause of the war was the German invasion of neighboring Poland on September 1, 1939, provoking Poland's allies, France and Great Britain, to declare war on Germany. However, the seeds of the war had been sown earlier with the flawed Treaty of Versailles following the First World War and the rise of totalitarian governments in Italy and Germany in the 1930s. Also, in Asia, Japan was seeking to expand its empire through military action in China and Mongolia, and was eyeing other parts of Asia in terms of its economic expansion. Representatives of Germany, Italy, and Japan met in Berlin on September 27, 1940, to sign the Tripartite Pact which certified German and Italian domination in Europe and Japanese control of Greater East Asia. Their union was called the Axis Powers, leading a sinister overtone to *axis* that would be exploited by politicians in the future.[2]

Despite President Roosevelt's unprecedented third-term reelection in 1940, the country remained committed to an America first, the last and only policy. Even the President's own Democratic Party was deeply divided between internationalists and isolationists.[3] A Gallup Poll in 1935 revealed that 70 percent of Americans agreed that American involvement in the First World War was a mistake. Reflecting the isolationist sentiment prevailing in 1938, Congress restricted the military planning for combat to the defense of the United States and the Western Hemisphere.[4] The 1940 election would include antiwar slogans like this one from Roosevelt's Republican opponent, Wendell Wilkie's campaign: "No Foreign War with Wilkie." Nevertheless, the American voters trusted Roosevelt to lead the country for four more years.

The Nazis Strike Across Europe

In 1940, Germany quickly overran Belgium, Holland, and France. Norway, Denmark, and Luxemburg also were swiftly conquered by the Nazi forces. Public opinion in the United States now shifted enough to allow the President to provide Britain with fifty aging destroyers in exchange for eight naval bases in the Western Hemisphere.[5] Following the British Army's hasty evacuation from the beaches of France on May 30 and the French surrender to the Germans on June 22, a reluctant U.S. Congress passed the two-ocean Navy bill, providing funds for an expanded fleet.[6]

The Battle of Britain and the Beginning of the U.S. Propaganda Campaign

The Nazi air campaign to bomb the British into surrender or negotiation, called the Battle of Britain, lasted from July 10 to October 30, 1940. It resulted in the first German reverse of the war as the Royal Air Force successfully shielded Britain from the Luftwaffe attacks.[7] For the first time, Americans began hearing live and recorded radio reports from the scene of the battle. The Columbia Broadcasting System (CBS) had reporters like William L. Shirer, Larry LeSueur, Eric Severeid and, above all, Edward R. Murrow providing Americans with their first "living room war." Murrow's on-the-spot broadcasts began on August 24 and continued until the Blitz fizzled out. His first words were simple and dramatic: "This ... is Trafalgar Square." The program, *London after Dark*, included reports from CBS newsmen across the British capital.[8]

Later, Murrow would open each broadcast with a slightly altered text: "This ... is London." These reports did much to increase American sympathy and respect for the courageous British people, and reduce the isolationist sentiments that still prevailed in the country. Murrow himself was clearly on the side of the British, as was evident in his broadcast of September 7, 1940: "We are told today that the Germans believe Londoners, after a while, will rise up and demand a new government, one that will make peace with Germany. It's more probable that they'll rise up and murder a few Germans pilots who come down by parachute."[9]

The growing sympathy of Americans for the British cause was being effectively fostered by a covert propaganda organization based in New York called "British Security Coordination," that was working under the auspices of the British Secret Intelligence Services. This clandestine agency distributed pro-British and anti-German stories to the mass media in the United States, according to an August 19, 2005, article in *The Guardian* by William Boyd. This program was similar to the efforts undertaken by British propagandists to win the support of the American public in the period leading up to the U.S. entry into World War I on the side of the Allies.

In September 1940, Congress passed the Selective Service and Training Act, conscripting 600,000 draftees to an Army already expanded by the federalizing of almost 300,000 National Guardsmen. The Army of the United States could field a force of 1,200,000 soldiers by the summer of 1941; unfortunately, it was an army that was untrained, ill-equipped, and untested.[10]

On June 21, 1941, the Nazi armies invaded the Soviet Union, requiring the Germans to fight a two-front war as they had during World War I. That same day, the American Army ordered that the National Guard be kept on active duty indefinitely.[11] America was mobilizing but the process was a slow one, in a country still deeply divided over possible involvement of the United States in the European War and still deeply disillusioned by its experiences in the First World War.

Hollywood

Radio brought the war into American living rooms and would play an even larger role reporting the war and bolstering morale once America became involved. But it was Hollywood that, once again, was recruited by the U.S. government to support its efforts to sell this war to its citizens and prepare the country for the coming conflict. Although the studios were cautious about offending moviegoers and government officials in Spain, Italy, Germany, and Japan, they began producing films about the overseas conflicts that clearly sided with the antifascists in Europe and with the Chinese who were then fighting the Japanese in Asia.

Hollywood and the World

The Spanish Civil War of 1936–1939, in which Nazi Germany and Fascist Italy aided Francisco Franco and his Falangist rebels against the loyalist Republican government, was a victory for fascism. America remained neutral, but American volunteers fought for the loyalist side in the George Washington and Abraham Lincoln Brigades. While the Roman Catholic Church supported Franco's forces, the American Left sided with the Loyalists. Among the American supporters of the Spanish government was Ernest Hemingway, America's leading novelist of the day and a war correspondent whose reports clearly favored the Loyalists. In 1937, Hemingway would serve as the writer, narrator, and chief fund-raiser for Juris Ivens' film, *The Spanish Earth*.[12] Hemingway also wrote a play, *The Fifth Column* (1938), and a novel, *For Whom the Bell Tolls* (1940), that would be made into a major motion picture in 1943, starring Gary Cooper and Ingrid Bergman. Other films that dealt with the Spanish Civil War were *Last Train from Madrid* (1937) and *Blockade* (1938). All were sympathetic to the Loyalists.

Italy was spared any prewar film treatment, but Germany received some attention. The 1930 film version of Erich Maria Remarque's *All Quiet on the Western Front* presented such a clear antiwar message that the Nazis banned it soon after they came into power in 1933. In 1940, *Four Sons* portrayed the evil effects of Nazism on a German family in Czechoslovakia, *The Mortal Storm* explored the destruction of a Germany family of mixed heritage, *Escape* dramatized the rescue of a mother by her American son, and Charlie Chaplin's *The Great Dictator* satirized, and offended, both Adolf Hitler and Benito Mussolini. *Man Hunt* (1941) was a Fritz Lang thriller about a British big game hunter battling Nazi agents and stalking Hitler. In July 1941, *Sergeant York* premiered, starring Gary Cooper as the Tennessee farm boy turned hero in World War I. In September, Tyrone Power was *A Yank in the RAF*, doing his bit to help win the Battle of Britain. All of these films were pro-Allies and anti-Nazi.

The Japanese were presented as ruthless conquerors in such films as *The Good Earth* (1937), based upon Pearl S. Buck's best-selling novel about Chinese peasants, and *Barricade* (1938), which portrayed an American Christian mission hospital in China under attack by Japanese soldiers.

The Home Front

The home front provided the settings for a number of Hollywood films about the military. The War and Navy Departments encouraged and cooperated with Hollywood studios on these films, provided they contained no antiwar or antimilitary messages. In 1938, American audiences saw *Duke of West Point*, about cadet life at the U.S. Military Academy, *Navy Blue and Gold*, about midshipmen at the Naval Academy, *Submarine Patrol*, about the "Silent Service," and *Wings of the Navy*, about naval air training. In 1941, the films in this genre included *Buck Privates* with Bud Abbott and Lou Costello, and *Caught in the Draft*, with Bob Hope and Dorothy Lamour—both comedies about the peacetime draft. Other films released in 1941 were *Dive Bomber*, a fact-based story of Navy fliers and doctors, *I Wanted Wings*, a story of young men learning to fly in the Army Air Corps, and *Parachute Battalion*, a look at the Army's newest combat arm.

In producing these films, the studios risked losing box office receipts in countries offended by negative portrayals of their leaders and positive support for American military preparedness. However, the growing political and diplomatic differences between the United States and the Axis Powers would inevitably have resulted in the loss of box office revenues in those countries regardless of the contents of American film.[13] These anti-Axis and pro-American rearmament films were also criticized at home, especially by those still preaching isolationism. Two leading isolationist U.S. senators,

Gerald P. Nye of North Dakota and Burton K. Wheeler of Montana, denounced Hollywood as a den of internationalists led by Jews and Europeans. These isolationist voices in Congress, in the press, on radio, and among the public would continue to protest against America becoming involved in foreign wars until the Japanese attack on the American fleet at Pearl Harbor silenced them.[14]

To support President Roosevelt's "Good Neighbor Policy" aimed at improving relations among all the Americans, Hollywood served up a fiesta of musical comedies: *Down Argentine Way* (1940), *That Night in Rio* (1940), and *Weekend in Havana* (1940).

Yankee Doodle Dandy

If one film best exemplified a reawakened American patriotism and a willingness to assume the American mythic role of the reluctant but decisive warrior, it was *Yankee Doodle Dandy* (1941). It was a rather fanciful biographical tribute to that great Broadway song-and-dance man and producer, George M. Cohan. Most of the film is told in flashback as Cohan recounts his life to President Roosevelt in a private meeting upstairs at the White House where he is to receive a civilian Congressional Medal of Honor "For his contributions to the American spirit." In the movie, President Roosevelt says to Cohan (played by James Cagney): "'Over There' was just as powerful a weapon as any cannon, any battleship we had in the First World War. Today, we're all soldiers; we're all on the Front. We need more songs to express the American spirit. I know you and your comrades will give them to us." Cohan tells the president not to worry about America, that "We've got this thing licked."

As Cohan leaves the White House, after dancing down the main staircase, he joins a column of marching soldiers as he and they sing "Over There," that great anthem from the last war and now a symbol of America's commitment to not "come back till it's over over there."

God Bless America

But not all expressions of popular culture were so pro-war before Pearl Harbor. Perhaps the song that best expressed the shelter of America's isolation from the troubles of the world was Irving Berlin's 1939 hit, "God Bless America." While the second stanza became almost a second national anthem during World War II and continues to be a major musical response to all of America's crises and challenges, it was the first stanza that reflected the popular opinion of the majority of Americans at that time:

> While the storm clouds gather far across the sea,
>   Let us swear allegiance to a land that's free,

Let us all be grateful for a land so fair,
As we raise our voices in a solemn prayer.

Clearly, this was a tribute to America's continuing as a neutral nation at peace and even the second stanza is no call to arms but rather a prayer that begins "God bless America, my home sweet home."

Preparing the People

President Roosevelt knew that war with Germany and Japan was inevitable and on January 6, 1941, he said in his address to Congress

> No realistic American can expect from a dictator's peace international generosity, or return of true independence, or world disarmament, or freedom of expression, or freedom of religion—or even good business. Such a peace would bring no security for us or for our neighbors. Those who would give up essential liberty to purchase a little temporary safety, deserve neither liberty nor safety.[15]

What Roosevelt advocated was a worldwide acceptance of Four Freedoms: "... of speech and expression ... to worship God ... from want ... from fear...."[16] Roosevelt followed up this speech with his famous "Fireside Chats" on the radio that further sold his view of the crisis in Europe to the U.S. public.

In 1941, tension with Japan over its conquests and future ambitions in the Pacific, and with Germany over the freedom of the seas increasingly challenged American neutrality. Despite his 1940 campaign promise that Americans would not die in any "foreign" wars, Roosevelt knew that events would soon force the issue. The United States had broken the Japanese diplomatic and naval codes with their cryptographers' Magic interceptions and knew that the Japanese naval forces were preparing to strike against the U.S. Navy somewhere in the Pacific. By December 6, it was clear to the President that war with Japan was unavoidable and imminent. When one of his chief aides, Harry Hopkins, suggested that America conduct a preemptive first strike against the Japanese, President Roosevelt replied: "No, we can't do that. We are a democracy and a peaceful people."[17]

In accepting the Democratic Party's nomination for a second term in 1936, President Franklin Roosevelt spoke as a prophet: "To some generations much is given. Of other generations much is expected. This generation of Americans has a rendezvous with destiny...."[18]

WAR COMES TO AMERICA

Rendezvous with Destiny

At 7:49 A.M. (Hawaii Time) on Sunday, December 7, 1941, planes from Japanese aircraft carriers struck American military bases at Hickam Field, Schofield Barracks, and the Pacific Fleet anchored in Pearl Harbor. A second strike occurred at 9:00 A.M. In less than two hours, the Japanese destroyed 200 U.S. aircraft, sank 5 battleships and 3 other naval vessels, and killed 2,500 American soldiers, sailors, and Marines.[19] The December 8 front page of *The New York Times* proclaimed: "Japan Wars on U.S. and Britain; Makes Sudden Attack on Hawaii. Heavy Fighting at Sea Reported." The Japanese losses were minimal: 29 planes, 5 midget submarines, and less than one hundred killed. The United States had been caught by surprise and the price to be paid was steep. The prelude to war was over. War had now come to America. Pearl Harbor would prove to be the propaganda of the deed that moved American public opinion from neutrality and isolationism to powerful patriotic support for a war with Japan.

There has been considerable conjecture by historians in later years about whether President Roosevelt deliberately chose not to alert the commanders of the U.S. Pacific Fleet to the imminent danger of attack in the hours before the bombing began to allow the outrageous assault to occur in order to better mobilize stronger public support for war. However, no evidence has ever been produced that the poor communication between the White House and the naval forces anchored at Pearl Harbor was based on anything other than the limitations of the electronic technology at the time and incompetence.

The New York Times of December 8 printed the text of Emperor Hirohito's declarations of war as picked up and translated by the National Broadcasting Company (NBC). The first and last paragraphs are worth quoting:

> We, by grace of Heaven, Emperor of Japan and seated on the throne of a line unbroken for ages eternal, enjoin upon thee, our loyal and brave subjects. We hereby declare war upon the United States of America and the British Empire .... We rely upon the loyalty and courage of our subjects in our confident expectation that the task bequeathed by our forefathers will be carried forward and that the sources of evil will be speedily eradicated and an enduring peace established in East Asia, preserving thereby the glory of our empire.[20]

Emperor Hirohito's words and images would be used throughout the war to symbolize the enemy and reveal his evil intentions. *The Times* editorial that day was an open call for a dedication of war:

The United States has been attacked. The United States is in danger. . . . We go into battle in defense of our land, of our present and our future, of all that we are and all that we still hope to be, of a way of life which we have made for ourselves on free and independent soil, the only way of life which we believe to be worth living.

The Manifest Destiny of the United States was now to defend not only America but the American way of life itself.

Source Credibility

Like Woodrow Wilson in the First World War, President Franklin D. Roosevelt would become the central voice in selling war to America. But, unlike Wilson, Roosevelt shared with his distant cousin, Teddy Roosevelt, a preference for action rather than reflection, a willingness to gamble in place of caution, and rhetoric well suited to a call to arms. As he stood before a joint session of Congress on Monday, December 8, the president, leg braces locked to hold him erect to belie the crippling effects of polio, was not defeated but defiant. He called upon Congress to regard what he termed the "dastardly" attacks of December 7 as acts of war:

Yesterday, December 7th 1941—a date which will live in infamy—the United States of America was suddenly and deliberately attacked by naval and air forces of the Empire of Japan.

He then listed a litany of additional attacks against Malaya, Hong Kong, Guam, the Philippines, Wake Island, and Midway Island. While acknowledging the American losses, Roosevelt was confident and upbeat at the end:

With confidence in our armed forces—with the abounding determination of our people—we will gain the inevitable triumph—so help us God. I ask that Congress declare that since the unprovoked and dastardly attack by Japan on Sunday, December 7, 1941, a state of war has existed between the United States and the Japanese Empire.

The response from Congress was quick and almost unanimous (with only Congresswoman Janette Rankin, Republican of Montana, casting a nay vote); in only thirty-three minutes of debate, Congress declared war on Japan.[21] "Remember Pearl Harbor" quickly became the rallying cry of a newly aroused nation, encompassing in one simple slogan the only justification most Americans would need to buy this war with Japan. It took its place with other slogans from the part: "Remember the *Maine*" from the Spanish-American War of 1898 and "Remember the *Lusitania*" from the First World War.

While angered Americans were eager to fight the Japanese for their sneak attacks, the President and his Cabinet were already committed to a "Germany First" policy, correctly predicting that this would be a two-ocean war, with Germany as the main enemy. Fortunately for President Roosevelt, he did not need to sell Americans a war against Germany and Italy since both countries declared war on the United States on December 11 in compliance with the Axis Pact of Steel.[22] President Roosevelt's request for declarations of war against the two other main Axis powers was quickly approved with only Congresswoman Rankin voting a neutral "Present."[23] *The New York Times* front page of December 12, 1941, provides a boxed line-up of the two sides in the war. The Allies were Australia, Belgium, Canada, China, Costa Rica, Cuba, Czecko-Slovakia, Dominican Republic, El Salvador, Free France, Great Britain, Guatemala, Haiti, Honduras, Netherlands Indies, Nicaragua, Norway, Panama, Poland, South Africa, Soviet Union, United States, and Yugoslavia. The Axis Powers were Finland, Germany, Hungary, Italy, Japan, Manchukuo, Romania, and Slovakia. In actually selling the war to America, the main enemies would be Germany and Japan, with Italy a distant third.

Once again, America called forth the image of the reluctant American warrior provoked to defending himself against sudden and dastardly attacks by vicious and unscrupulous enemies. Once again, the "Gunfighter Nation" had been roused from peaceful isolation to tame the savage outlaws who threatened not only America, but world peace. Once again, some evil men needed killing, some evil nations needed defeating, and America was summoned to defend the Frontiers of Freedom.

Side by side with the actual combat and the work in the factories, there was the symbolic struggle to sustain American morale and resolve, both at home and overseas. To totally engage the hearts and minds of America, the government created the theme of the "War between the Slave World and the Free World." As in the First World War, government propagandists had to blur some obvious, but uncomfortable truths about our allies—that China, under former warlord Chiang Kai-Shek was neither free nor unified, that Belgium, France, Great Britain, and the Netherlands still claimed oppressive colonial empires across the globe, and that the Soviet Union, a recent ally of Germany, was a brutal totalitarian state in which "freedom" was more slogan than reality. But, as they say, love, politics, and war make strange bedfellows.

The Fight for Freedom

Following President Roosevelt's lead, Americans enlisted or were drafted into "America's Fight for Freedom." To this fight, the United States committed not only fighting men. It also became the "Arsenal of Democracy," providing the military weapons and supplies needed by our allies in the long fight ahead. In the end, the United States spent more money on the war than any of the other allied or enemy countries but suffered the fewest men killed in action (405,399).[24]

At home, Americans, ordinary citizens, and Hollywood stars, joined in seven massive U.S. Treasury bond drives to secure the money needed to fight the war. Children joined adults in planting "victory gardens" and conducting "scrap drives" to recycle precious metals, paper, rubber products, silk stockings, and other items essential to the war effort. All Americans shared the burden of the rationing of gasoline, rubber, meat, dairy products, and sugar, and the end of automobile production for civilian use in 1942. As in World War I, this was not only a war fought by the American military, but a total mobilization of all citizens, now mustered to serve on the home front. All Americans were encouraged to do their part and almost all did.

Air raid drills, complete with identification tags, patrolling house and block wardens wearing white helmets, and the construction of air raid shelters kept America constantly alert to the possibility of attack on the homeland, although no serious attempts were ever made to bomb the Continental United States. U.S. factories became part of the "Arsenal of Democracy" and workers were encouraged to see themselves as "Soldiers on the home front" and "The men (later women) behind the man behind the gun."

The actual war battles interest us here only as they relate to the selling of the war to the American people. The American defeats at Pearl Harbor, Guam, Wake Island, and the Philippines, coupled with the Japanese victories over the British in Hong Kong, Singapore, Burma, and Malaya, the Dutch in the East Indies and the French in Indochina, had given control of the South Pacific to the Japanese, with invasion threats looming for Australia and New Zealand. Meanwhile, German armies penetrated deeply into Russia and overran the British forces at Tobruk in Libya. All in all, 1942 was a year of military defeats and disasters for the Allies.

In terms of tactical or strategic importance, the Doolittle Raid on Tokyo and other Japanese cities by sixteen U.S. B-25 Mitchell Bombers launched from the aircraft carrier *U.S.S. Hornet* on April 2, 1942, might have been little noted nor long remembered. But its impact on the Japanese admiral and generals who saw their samurai honor tarnished by such an attack on the Emperor and its capital city was both profound and disastrous. In response, the Japanese warlords decided to attack the U.S. controlled Midway Island to choke off the key American base threatening Japan's naval defense of the home island.[25] American ingenuity in the breaking of the Japanese codes combined with American courage, technology, and some luck gave the U.S. Navy a small victory in the Battle of the Coral Sea on May 7–8, 1942, and a major victory in the Battle of Midway on June 4—6, 1942. While the Japanese enjoyed clear advantages in the sizes and numbers of ships and aircraft at this point in the war, the Japanese First Air Fleet, including most of its large aircraft carriers, was sunk by the Americans. After Midway, the rising sun on the Japanese battle flag became a setting sun as Japan now reverted from offense to defense.[26]

Hollywood director John Ford, on active duty in the Navy, created a stirring documentary about that battle, shooting some of the film himself and being wounded in an air raid. *The Battle of Midway* would win Ford an Academy Award to go with his Purple Heart and Air Medal for his actions.

In November 1942, American forces landed in French North and West Africa, effectively opening a "Second Front" to relieve pressure on the Soviet Union by drawing Axis troops from the Eastern Front.[27]

The daring of the Doolittle Raid, the tactical and strategic significance of the victories at Coral Sea and Midway, and the Army and Marine offensives in New Guinea and the Solomon Islands gave America renewed confidence that it was on the road to victory. The vengeful slogan "Remember Pearl Harbor" was being replaced with the triumphant "On to Tokyo." The U.S. government's Office of War Information (OWI) was established in 1942 to coordinate all American efforts at selling the war. Its creative strategy was to focus America's attention on the victory to come and less on the American sacrifices being made. In shaping its mission and strategy, the OWI was careful not to repeat the mistakes of George Creel's Committee on Public Information from the First World War that was ultimately perceived by the U.S. public as being misleading and manipulating. At the same time, the OWI hoped to use those strategies and tactics that they believed were effective in mobilizing public opinion and action. Six tenets codified the OWI's efforts:

1. a firm belief in the rightness of our cause;
2. an awareness of the difficulties of the struggle;
3. confidence in ourselves and our leaders;
4. confidence in our allies;
5. resentment against the enemy for starting the war; and
6. belief that military victory will lead to a better world.[28]

Later, as the war progressed, one phrase came to embody American re-solve to defeat German Nazism, Italian Fascism, and Japanese Militarism— "Unconditional Surrender." Every form of communication was enlisted in the propaganda campaign.

Media Go to War

Radio had become the key medium for communication reaching directly into American homes. Virtually every home in the country had at least one radio. In addition to informing people of the latest war news, and providing entertainment to give them respite from the war, radio now became the elec-tronic link between home and the fighting forces scattered across the globe. From the frozen wastes of Alaska, Greenland, and Iceland to the tropical jungles of the South Pacific; from the sands of North Africa to the beaches at Salerno and Normandy; from the cruel seas of the North Atlantic to the vast reaches of the Pacific: radio was there to connect America's fighting forces to hearth and home. And it was *home* more than anything else that the troops overseas wanted most. The Armed Forces Radio Network brought home to the troops overseas through such programs as *Command Performance*, in which celebrities like Bob Hope, Bing Crosby, Frances Langford, Betty Grable, Lana Turner, and other radio and movie stars would meet requests from the military. Sometimes, it was a song, a greeting from a loved one, a piece of comedy—comedians Abbott and Costello's Classic skit, "Who's on First?" was a favorite—or, in one unique case, movie star Lana Turner frying a sirloin steak in a pan while comedian Bob Hope made wisecracks. The overall theme of the show was "Anything for the Boys."

Newspapers and national magazines continued to play their traditional roles of providing news, commentary, and advertising. Throughout the war, the press acted less like the "watchdogs of democracy" and more like cheerleaders for the administration. Even those newspapers hostile to President Roosevelt, like the *Chicago Tribune* and the *Los Angeles Times*, muted their criticisms and supported the war, if not the president himself. National magazines like *Life, Look, Collier's Time, Newsweek*, and *The Saturday Evening Post* mirrored the nation's newspapers in adhering to the guidelines established by *A Code of Wartime Practices for the American Press*, issued on January 15, 1942. All played their parts in the great war effort.

Even the publishers of books joined the war effort. Captain Ted Lawson, one of the pilots on the Doolittle Raid, wrote a best-seller that became a hit film in 1944—*Thirty Seconds over Tokyo*. Richard Tregaskis's *Guadalcanal Diary*, published in 1943, became a popular film that same year. Correspondent Ernie Pyle's newspaper columns won a Pulitzer Prize, became a best-selling book in 1943, *Here Is Your War*, and were ultimately produced as a major motion picture, *The Story of G.I. Joe*, in 1945.

While radio and print media played their parts in the war effort, it would be Hollywood that was cast in the primary role of selling this war to America. Many popular radio performers came from the motion picture industry, and newspapers and magazines regularly covered Hollywood stars doing their bit for the war.

When the Office of War Information (OWI) was created by President Roosevelt on June 13, 1942, it relied upon the Bureau of Motion Pictures (BMP) to oversee the U.S. movie industry's contributions to the war effort. As its operating principle, the OWI was pledged to tell the truth to the American people and required film producers and studios to answer seven questions:

1. Will this picture help win the war?
2. What war information does it seek to clarify, dramatize, or interpret?

3. If it is an "escape" picture, will it harm the war effort by creating a false picture of America, her allies, or the world we live in?
4. Does it merely use the war as a basis of a profitable picture, contributing nothing to the war effort and possibly lessening the effect of other pictures of more importance?
5. Does it contribute something new to our understanding of the world conflict and the various forces involved, or has the subject already been adequately covered?
6. When the picture reaches its maximum circulation on the screen, will it reflect conditions as they are and fill a need at that time, or will it be outdated?
7. Does the picture tell the truth or will young people of today have reason to say they were misled by propaganda?[29]

Clearly, this last question was in response to the public's subsequent backlash against the selling of the First World War by George Creel and his Committee on Public Information. The OWI was determined not to oversell the war this time. Instead, the government intended to perform the promise, to deliver the product as advertised.

The OWI Manual for the motion picture industry categorized films under five headings: *Why We Fight, The Enemy, The United Nations, The Home Front,* and *The Fighting Forces.* As part of the *Why We Fight* effort, General George M. Marshall, the Army Chief of Staff, handpicked Hollywood director Frank Capra to head the U.S. Army Signal Corps Photo Signal Detachment. Capra, who had won Academy Awards for directing such classics as *It Happened One Night* (1934), *Mr. Deeds Goes to Town* (1936), *Mr. Smith Goes to Washington* (1939), and *Meet John Doe* (1941), was assigned the job of producing motion pictures to educate the troops about the causes of the war. Working with Major (later Colonel) Capra were veteran Hollywood actors, writers, directors, cameramen, editors, and a host of others needed for modern motion picture productions. Perhaps their most famous series of films was called *Why We Fight.* The first of these, *Prelude to War* (1942), actually covered all five headings listed by the OWI and used the enemy's own words, deeds, and images, carefully reedited, against Germany, Italy, and Japan, taking its central theme from the Gospel according to St. John: "Ye shall know the truth and the truth shall make you free."

Released to the general American public by presidential order, *Prelude to War* won the Academy Award for best Documentary Feature Film of 1943. It was not a great hit with the public or theater owners, and none of the other six films in the series were shown to the general public. While Capra and his fellow servicemen produced information, training, and combat report films for the military throughout the war, the Hollywood studios they left behind was busily turning out pictures that also met the OWI's five categories.

After the Japanese sneak attack on Pearl Harbor on December 7 and the declarations of war on the United States by Germany and Italy on December 11, 1941, selling the American people the need to fight was largely superfluous, but some films continued to provide background explanations for why we were fighting, including 1942's *Yankee Doodle Dandy* and *Across the Pacific*.

Of all of Hollywood's efforts to explain why America was fighting, perhaps the best was Warner Brothers' *Casablanca*. Released in 1943, the movie was an allegory in which the characters were not individuals but representations of nations and political positions. The setting is Casablanca in French Morocco in December 1941, just days before the Japanese attacks on Pearl Harbor. Much of the action takes place in Rick's Café Americain, a bar, restaurant, and illegal gambling house, owned by Richard C. ("Rick") Blaine, an expatriate American who keeps out of foreign entanglements, identifying his nationality as "drunkard" and "saloon keeper" and insisting, "I stick my neck out for nobody." He is clearly a once idealistic American (who fought the Fascists in Ethiopia and Spain) who now wants only his own separate peace. His isolation is broken by the arrival of Victor Laszlo, a Czech underground leader newly escaped from the Nazis in Europe, and his beautiful wife, Ilsa Lund, a Norwegian refugee who was Rick's lover in Paris when she believed her husband to be dead. Major Heinrich Strasser of the Third Reich has come to Casablanca to prevent Laszlo's escape to America to "continue the fight." Aiding Strasser is the corrupt prefect of police, Captain Louis Renault, representing a France torn between loyalty to the Nazi-installed Vichy government and the Free French forces of General Charles DeGaulle.

An assortment of minor characters represents refugees from such war-torn lands as Germany, Norway, Poland, Romania, and Russia. There is even an Italian military attaché who provides comic relief as the butt of Captain Renault's quip: "If he gets in a word, it will be a major Italian victory."

In one stirring scene, Rick allows Laszlo to lead the band and the customers in a rousing rendition of "*La Marseillaise*," the French National Anthem, to drown out the Germans officers' singing of "*Wacht am Rhein*." Eventually, Rick, while bitter about losing Ilsa, echoing America's "betrayal" by her allies after World War I, does rejoin the fight, helping Laszlo to escape and seeing that Ilsa goes with him to insure that Laszlo's work against the Nazis will continue. Laszlo speaks for Europe to America in his farewell to Rick: "Welcome back to the fight. This time I know our side will win." In the climax, Rick, in standard gunfighter tradition, shoots it out with Major Strasser, outdrawing the villain and restoring order to this new frontier. In the final scene, as Rick and Captain Renault walk off together, heading for a Free French garrison in Brazzaville, Rick (America) says to the captain (Free France): "Louis, I think this is the beginning of a beautiful friendship." The greatness of *Casablanca* lies in its not being perceived as propaganda by audiences, thereby allowing its messages to sink in at an almost subliminal level.

The enemy was portrayed as evil Nazis in such films as *Berlin Correspondent, Hitler's Children, Hitler's Madmen,* and *The Hitler Gang* and as evil Japanese in such films as *Behind the Rising Sun* and *Blood on the Sun.* Italy was spared negative portrays to such an extent that, in *Hollywood Goes to War,* authors Koppes and Black do not even list Italy in the index.

The United Nations were celebrated according to their nationalities: China in *A Yank on the Burma Road, China, China Girl, China's Little Devils, Dragonseed,* and *Flying Tigers*; Britain in *Five Graves to Cairo, Mrs. Miniver, This Above All,* and *The White Cliffs of Dover*; Canada in *Corvette K225, The Forty-Ninth Parallel,* and *Northern Pursuit*; France in *Cross of Lorraine, Joan of Paris, Passage to Marseilles, This Land Is Mine,* and *Uncertain Glory*; Czechoslovakia in *Hangmen Also Die*; Norway in *Edge of Darkness* and *The Moon Is Down*; the Philippines in *Bataan, Back to Bataan,* and *They Were Expendable*; Russia, as the Soviet Union was always called, in *Boy From Stalingrad, Counter-Attack, Song of Russia,* and *Three Russian Girls.* Two films about Russia are especially significant here: *Mission to Moscow* and *The North Star.* The first was a 1943 film version of U.S. Ambassador Joseph E. Daniels' 1941 best-selling book; both were tributes to Josef Stalin, the Communist Party, and the Russian people. The second, based on an original screenplay by Lillian Hellmann, focused on the German invasion of the Ukraine Soviet Republic and the heroic resistance to Nazi brutality. Both films were successful and both promoted improved American public opinion about the Soviet Union.

Office of War Information polls taken in 1942 through 1945 showed an improvement in public opinion toward Russia as rising from 38 percent to level off at 51 percent for the remainder of the war. While this showed improvement, the comparable approval rate for China was 86 percent and for Great Britain 72 percent.

These successes in selling the value of our allies would have a boomerang effect in the Cold War frenzy following the war, when Hollywood was called to answer charges of promoting pro-Soviet and pro-Communist propaganda in these wartime efforts to sell Russia as a liberal democracy.

The home front movies stressed freedom, democracy, and unity in the civilian war effort: financing the war ("Buy a bond, build a bomber"), rationing as fair and patriotic, volunteerism, working women, labor–management cooperation, and self-sacrifice. The final *Why We Fight* film was titled *War Comes to America* (1945) and it is a celebration of American virtues of courage, self-sacrifice, and freedom. Among the Hollywood offerings in this category were the following: *Joe Smith, American, The Human Comedy, The More the Merrier, Stage Door Canteen, Hollywood Canteen,*

The Fighting Sullivans, Pin-Up Girl, Since You Went Away, (which producer/writer David O. Selznick dedicated to "The Unconquerable Fortress— The American Home 1943"), *The Doughgirls, Hail the Conquering Hero, Pittsburgh, Sunday Dinner for a Soldier,* and, in 1946, the postwar *The Best Years of Our Lives,* about the difficulties facing returning servicemen and their families.

The Fighting Forces received the most attention, with each service getting its share. A common theme was the geographic, ethnic, class, and religious multiculturalness of the servicemen shown. Country boys teamed with city slickers, WASPS with Italians, Irish, Greeks, and others, the country club set with the inner-city youth, the Protestant with the Catholic and Jew. Hispanic Americans and Native Americans were shown but African Americans (or Negroes, as they were politely called in the 1940s) rarely appeared except in subservient roles, reflecting the very real racial segregation then in place in the Armed Forces and throughout most of the Southern States. Frank Capra's unit tried to redress this oversight in *The Negro Soldier* (1944), a documentary about the contributions of Negroes to America that somehow managed to omit any mention of slavery. Japanese-Americans fared even worse; despite their shameful internment as suspected threats to Americans, many enlisted in the Army to fight in the Pacific and Europe, establishing a record of bravery and success that belied their status as Americans of questionable loyalties. Hollywood would not acknowledge their contributions until 1951 with *Go for Broke!*

The Army was represented by such offerings as *Bataan, Sahara, This Is the Army, See Here, Private Hangrove, Objective Burma,* and the realistic rendering of Ernie Pyle's dispatches in *The Story of G.I. Joe.* The Army Air Corps (later, U.S. Air Force) received coverage in *Air Force, I Wanted Wings, A Guy Name Joe, Winged Victory, God Is My Co-Pilot, Memphis Belle, Thirty Seconds over Tokyo,* and *The Purple Heart,* the last two about the 1942 Doolittle Raid and its aftermath, especially the torture, trial, and execution of American flyers captured by the Japanese. In *The Purple Heart,* the Americans suffer torture and refuse favors from the Japanese military intent on learning the location from which they attacked Japan. At the close of their trial, the American leader, Captain Harvey Ross, confronts the chief Japanese interrogator-torturer, General Ito Motsubi, and delivers America's answer to Pearl Harbor:

> It's true we Americans don't know very much about you Japanese, and never did and now I realize you know even less about us. You can kill us—all of us, or part of us. But, if you think that's going to put the fear of God into the United States of America and stop them from sending other fliers to bomb you, you're wrong—dead wrong. They'll blacken your skies and burn your cities to the ground and make you get down on your knees and beg for mercy. This is your war—you wanted it—you asked for it. And

now you're going to get it—and it won't be finished until your dirty little empire is wiped off the face of the earth!

Army nurses received special attention with two films about the fall of the Philippines: *Cry Havoc* and *So Proudly We Hail*, which the public loved but which embarrassed and angered the nurses who survived Bataan.[30]

The Navy received its share of Hollywood gloss in films like *Crash Dive* and *Destination Tokyo* (submarines), *The Story of Dr. Wassell* (medical corps), *Wing and a Prayer* (aircraft carriers), *They Were Expendable* (PT Boats), and *The Fighting Seabees* (construction battalions).

The Marine Corps received what the Army and the Navy thought was more than its fair share of celluloid guts and glory in such screen sagas as *Wake Island*, *Gung Ho*, *Guadalcanal Diary*, *The Shores of Tripoli*, and *Pride of the Marines*.

While the Coast Guard, despite its combat services in landings in the Pacific, North Africa, Italy, and France, received no film tribute, the Merchant Marine was honored with *Action in the North Atlantic*.

In 1945, *Hollywood Quarterly* published an article by Dorothy Jones on "Hollywood War Films, 1942–1944" that summarized the movie industry's contributions to the war effort: in 1942, 25.9 percent of all films were about the war; in 1943, the figure was 32.2 percent; in 1944, 28.5 percent.[31] In 1976, Robert Fyne's doctoral dissertation listed a total of 32 Hollywood war films from September 1, 1939, to December 7, 1941, and 168 from December 8, 1941, to August 15, 1945 (the day of the Japanese surrender).[32] Of the films produced during America's participation in the war, Fyne found five themes as most common motivations for why America was fighting: to stop the spread of the Axis Powers; to protect the American Way of Life; "We didn't start this war;" to safeguard religious freedom; and to respect the flag and the country. Our enemies' motivations also had five major themes: to conquer the world; to enslave free people; to rid the world of inferior peoples; to follow a divine calling; and to be evil for evil's sake.[33]

Along with films directly concerned with the war itself were Hollywood comedies, dramas, and musicals designed to boost civilian and military morale by offering a few hours of escape from the realities of war and overtime work in the factories, plants, and shipyards. Hollywood women stars and starlets provided morale boosts in the form of the "The Pin-Up Girl." Among the most popular were Linda Darnell, Betty Grable, Rita Hayworth, Veronica Lake, Hedy Lamar, Dorothy Lamour, Ginger Rogers, Ann Sheridan, Lana Turner, and Esther Williams.

Music and Comic Books

Other parts of popular entertainment also contributed to the war efforts. Songs, as in World War I, not only amused but sent messages; among these were "We Did It Before and We Can Do It Again," "Coming in on a Wing and a Prayer," "Praise the Lord and Pass the Ammunition," "Let's Remember Pearl Harbor," "We're Gonna Have to Slap the Dirty Little Jap," "You're a Sap Mister Jap," "The Japs Haven't Got a Chinaman's Chance," "When Those Little Yellow Bellies Meet the Cohen's and the Kelley's," and "Der Führer's Face" (from the Academy Award winning Disney cartoon short). Love songs also reflected the war in such tunes as "I Left My Heart at the Stage Door Canteen," "White Christmas," "I'll Be Seeing You," "Long Ago and Far Away," and "I'll Be Home for Christmas (If Only in My Dreams)."

Among children, comic books and comic strips in newspapers also went to war with prewar heroes like *Batman* and *Superman* enlisting in the fight against the Axis villains. Soon, they were joined by new, war-created heroes *like Captain America, Daredevil, Blackhawk, Submariner, The Star-Spangled Kid, Captain Courageous, The Human Torch, and Devil Dogs*, and one heroine, *Wonder Woman*, the Amazon princess who left her island home to help America win the war.

The Election of 1944

A clear indication of how the American people felt about Roosevelt's handling the war can be seen in the results of the 1944 presidential election in which Roosevelt, seeking a fourth term, was challenged by Republican Governor Thomas E. Dewey of New York. Not since 1864 had a presidential election been held in wartime. Dewey's slogans promised to deliver victory and peace, but sooner: "Peace and Jobs Quicker with Dewey and Bricker." While the Democrats call upon Americans to "Vote Democratic for Victory And Peace" the Republicans countered with "For Victory and Lasting Peace Vote Straight Republican." Since Dewey and the Republicans did not oppose the war, they could only promise to wage it better and faster. But they were hard-pressed to overcome the appeals like those found in a James Montgomery Flagg poster for Roosevelt. Flagg's famous image of Uncle Sam, used so successfully in World War I and World War II recruiting drives, points directly at the viewer and, says, "I Want *You* F. D. R. Stay and Finish the Job!" A presidential Roosevelt stares out at the viewer with a reassuring gaze. The fighting President easily defeated the prosecutor-turned-governor with 53.5 percent of the votes. The voters had chosen Roosevelt to continue to win the war. Clearly, they approved of both products.

The Allies

By 1945, Americans were fully confident of ultimate victory but the actual price would be high for those bearing the battle. Despite the massive battles fought and won by the Russians at Stalingrad, Leningrad, and Kursk,

Soviet victories rarely figured in American war propaganda or popular culture. As Koppes and Black note, 1943–1944 proved to be the high-water mark for pro-Soviet films from Hollywood, with only one released in 1945—*Counter-Attack*, which portrayed Russian partisans waiting for a Russian advance to drive the Germans from Russian soil.[34]

The British fared only marginally better and they were decidedly not amused by *Sahara* (1943), starring Humphrey Bogart as U.S. Army Tank Sergeant Joe Gunn who leads a United Nations of soldiers in Libya: two American soldiers, a British Army Medical Corps captain from Dublin, two British enlisted soldiers, a French Resistance Fighter now serving with the British, an Australian, a South African, and Sudanese Sergeant Major Tambul; all join Gunn and his two American crewmen of the U.S. tank "Lulu Bell." Although the film ends with reports of the British victory at El Alamein, the film strongly suggests that the victory was made possible by the Alamo-like stand by Gunn and his men that prevented a German Africa Corps battalion from reaching the battle. America's British allies were even more upset with *Objective Burma* (1945), with the dashing Errol Flynn as Captain Nelson who leads an American paratroop mission into Burma to destroy Japanese radar installations in preparation for the big Allied advance. Both films suggest that even when British forces were engaging the enemy, they needed American leadership and example to succeed.

American films about China portrayed China, its leader, Chiang Kai-Shek, and the people as decent, American-friendly, and ready to follow American leadership in such films as *Flying Tigers* and *God Is My Co-Pilot*, both paeans to the famed American volunteer flyers. Despite the failures of Chiang's armies to achieve much success against the Japanese and the friction between Chiang and U.S. General Joseph ("Vinegar Joe") Stillwell, the American liaison who disparagingly referred to Chiang as "The Peanut," the American public only saw positive images of China in the public media and news reports rarely touched on the troubles and failures of the alliance.

America's propaganda, whether in the Atlantic or the Pacific, in Europe or Asia, or on land, sea, or in the air, was turning inward, focusing more and more on America and her own war efforts. Some American generals and admirals emerged as heroes in the press—Army generals like Douglas MacArthur, George S. Patton, Dwight D. Eisenhower, Omar Bradley, and Mark Clark; Air Force Generals like H. H. "Hap" Arnold and James Doolittle; Navy Admirals like Ernest King, William "Bull" Halsey, and Chester Nimitz; Marine generals like Archer Vandergrift and Holland M. "Howling Mad" Smith. However, American propaganda and popular culture largely celebrated the average guy and girl, the G.I. Joe, the ordinary sailor or airman, the down home Marine, the citizen soldiers fighting a just war for the common man. World War II would not be presented as "a rich man's war and a poor man's fight."

President Franklin Delano Roosevelt, as Commander in Chief of the Armed Forces, was the nation's leading cheerleader, happily transforming himself from "Dr. Fix the Economy" to "Dr. Win the War," and using his boundless optimism to reassure the country. Indeed, his January 7, 1942, address to Congress provided the promise of a better world that would be founded upon what he called "The Four Freedoms":

> In future days, which we seek to make secure, we look forward to a world founded upon four essential human freedoms:
>
> The first is freedom of speech and expression everywhere in the world.
>
> The second is freedom of every person to worship God in his own way everywhere in the world.
>
> The third is freedom from want—which, translated into world terms, means economic understandings which will secure to every nation a healthy peacetime life for its inhabitants—everywhere in the world.
>
> The fourth is freedom from fear—which, translated into world terms, means a world-wide reduction of armaments to such a point and in such a fashion that no nation will be in a position to commit an act of physical aggression against any neighbor—anywhere in the world.[35]

In the end, without Roosevelt's leadership, these promises would prove difficult to deliver, but during the war they provided noble and achievable goals that justified the sacrifices then being asked of the American people. For popular consumption, however, the war was still presented from the common citizen's view. Within the military, nothing captured the average G.I.'s attitudes toward the war better than the Willie and Joe cartoons of Bill Mauldin, first published in the Army's *The Stars and Stripes* and later collected into a best-selling book, *Up Front*, in 1945. Mauldin's soldiers are grubby, unshaven, tired, and not given to patriotic rhetoric. Typical captions include: "Must be a tough objective. The old man says we're gonna have the honor of liberating it." Another has Willie saying to Joe while bullets pin them down, "I feel like a fugitive from the law of averages." To an Italian woman looking angry amid the ruins of her house, Joe says, "Don't look at me, lady, I didn't do it." About a clean, properly dressed rear-echelon corporal who has just reprimanded Willie and Joe for their rugged, front-line scruffiness, Willie says, "He's right, Joe. When we ain't fightin' we should act like sojers." Satirizing war films in which celluloid soldiers denounce the enemy for being savages, a cartoon shows Willie and Joe stare with horror at a wine cellar smashed and drained of wine: "Them rats! Them dirty, cold-blooded, sore-headed, stinking Huns! Them atrocity-committin' skunks...." To a medic offering him a Purple Heart for being wounded, Willie says, "Just gimme a couple aspirins. I already got a Purple Heart." About an aggressive-looking soldier in a town, a weary Willie says to an equally weary Joe, "That aint no combat man. He's looking for a fight."

Two officers stand atop a mountain looking at a magnificent view: "Beautiful view. Is there one for the enlisted men?"[36]

In the Pacific, the Battle of Iwo Jima lasted from February 19 until March 26, 1945, thirty-five days and nights of total hell, as 21,000 Japanese troops under Lt. General Tadamichi Kuribayaski sought to kill as many Americans as possible. The capture of Mount Suribachi on D-Day-plus 4, February 23 was only the prelude to thirty-one more days of battle but it produced perhaps the single most-celebrated photograph of men in combat—the raising of the American flag at the summit. The first flag was raised at about 10:00 A.M., captured on film by Marine combat photographer Staff Sergeant Louis R. Lowery. Later that morning, a second, larger flag was raised by five Marines and one Navy Corpsman. This raising was captured by both Marine combat motion picture cameraman Sergeant William Genaust and by Joe Rosenthal of the Associated Press. Rosenthal's shot became an instant classic, providing the image for the Seventh War Loan ("Now All Together"), first-class postage stamps (issued July 11, 1945) which sold more than 150 million, and for the U.S. Marine Corps Memorial in Arlington, Virginia, which was dedicated on November 10, 1954 (the Marine Corps Birthday). Three of the men who raised the second flag (Sergeant Michael Strank, Corporal Harlon Block, and Pfc. Franklin Sousley) would become part of the 6,821 Americans killed taking the island. With 19,217 wounded and 2,648 cases of combat fatigue, the total American casualty list for Iwo Jima would reach 28,688, of which 25,851 were Marines. Of the 21,000 Japanese troops on the island, only 1,083 survived the battle as prisoners.

Among the American survivors were three men who had raised the flag over Mount Surabachi—Privates First Class Rene Gagnon and Ira Hayes and Navy Corpsman John Bradley. On orders from President Roosevelt, the three were brought back to the homeland to help the Seventh War Loan Drive, meeting with the newly inaugurated President Harry Truman on April 20, 1945, to present him with a copy of the Iwo Jima poster.[37]

Seventh Bond Drive

The goal for the Seventh Bond Drive was $14 billion and the three heroes from Iwo Jima traveled from Washington, DC, to New York City, Philadelphia, Boston (where they were joined by Hollywood stars Joan Fontaine and Jane Wyman), Chicago (where they were joined by Humphrey Bogart, Lauren Bacall, and Ida Lupino), Detroit, Indianapolis, St. Louis, Tulsa, San Antonio, Portland, Seattle, El Paso, Houston, Dallas, Phoenix, Charleston, Richmond, Norfolk, and back to Washington for a triumphant Fourth of July celebration. In eight weeks, the Iwo Jima Bond Drive raised $26.3 billion, twice the projected goal and nearly half of the total American National budget for 1946.[38]

Casualties of War

On April 12, 1945, President Roosevelt died of a cerebral hemorrhage in Warm Springs, Georgia. The *New York Post* April 13 edition carried this announcement under "Today's Casualty List":

Army-Navy Dead
Roosevelt, Franklin D., Commander- In-Chief, wife Mrs. Anna Eleanor Roosevelt, the White House.

The leader was gone but the war continued under the new president, Harry Truman, uninformed, uninvolved, and untested in running a war. Fortunately, Truman proved to be a quick learner and he was blessed with continued Allied victories. As the headlines in *The New York Times* of April 13 proclaimed: "President Roosevelt Is Dead; Truman to Continue Policies; 9th Crosses Elba, Nears Berlin." A smaller story lower on the front page notes the continuing Battle of Okinawa (April 1–June 21, 1945) and the Japanese use of *Kamikazes* (divine winds), suicide planes that attacked the American fleet: "Our Okinawa Guns Down 118 Planes." Okinawa would prove to be the last great battle of the Pacific War and the prelude to the atomic bombings of Hiroshima and Nagasaki.

In Europe, Hitler's dream of an empire was crumbling with Allied advances from both East and West. *The New York Times* front page of March 24 tells the tale: "Patton crosses Rhine in a daring drive without barrage, expands bridgehead; Nazis say Russians are moving on Berlin." By April 13, the Americans and the Russian armies met at the Elba River in Germany. In Berlin, Adolf Hitler attempted to continue the war from his Führer Bunker under the Reich Chancellery, celebrating his fifty-sixth birthday on April 20, marrying his longtime mistress, Eva Braun, on April 29, and ending his life in a double suicide with her on April 30.[39] Hitler's death was headline news in *The New York Times* on May 2, 1945. Despite Nazi leadership vows to continue the war, by May 8, it was all over in Europe. *The New York Times* front page of May 8, 1945, tells the tale: "The War in Europe Is Ended! Surrender Is Unconditional; V-E Day Will Be Proclaimed Today; Our Troops on Okinawa Gain."

The final headline reminded Americans that the war was far from over, with the Japanese defending their homeland with total warfare, including the use of suicide planes, the *Kamikazes*, which sank 28 U.S. Navy vessels, damaged 325 more and inflicted 10,000 casualties. On Okinawa, the U.S. Tenth Army, composed of Army and Marine divisions, suffered 10,000 killed in action and 30,000 other casualties while killing more than 100,000 Japanese troops. At least 600,000 Okinawan civilian natives also perished in the battle. The American victory was complete but the price was excessively high.[40]

As the American soldiers, sailors, and Marines prepared for the coming invasion of the Japanese home islands, Operation Downfall, planned for November 1, 1945, few American survivors of the war in Europe and the Pacific had any doubts that the invasion would be worse than any fighting thus far, with the American casualties being calculated at 1 million. Every fighting man now felt like Mauldin's "fugitive from the law of average" and the odds were getting longer by the hour. But D-Day in Japan would not come. A technological miracle would end the war in two stunning attacks. Those who think the atomic bombs ultimately saved lives credit the carnage on Okinawa with persuading President Truman that the A-bombs would spare both American and Japanese lives.[41]

The New York Times front page of August 7, 1945, announced the news of the attack on Hiroshima the day before: "First Atomic Bomb Dropped on Japan." Although Truman warned the Japanese of a "rain of ruin," the United States possessed only one more atomic bomb which was dropped on Nagasaki on August 9. That day's *New York Times* reported the second bombing but gave it only second billing below the Soviet declaration of war on Japan.

The end came quickly with Emperor Hirohito's radio broadcast to the Japanese people on August 15 that asked them to "endure the unendurable and bear the unbearable" but never used the words "surrender" or "defeat."[42] The front page of *The New York Times* for August 15, 1945, has it right: "Japan Surrenders, End of War! Emperor Accepts Allied Rule; M'Arthur Supreme Commander." On September 2, 1945, aboard the *U.S.S. Missouri*, General Douglas MacArthur, the Supreme Commander of Allied Powers in Japan who had performed his promise of returning to the Philippines, accepted the Japanese formal surrender. MacArthur closed the ceremonies with words of hope that "a better world shall emerge out of the blood and carnage of the past—a world founded upon faith and understanding—a world deducted to the dignity of man and the fulfillment of his most cherished wish—for freedom, tolerance and justice."

After three years and nine months since the Japanese attack on Pearl Harbor, America was now at peace. The war had been sold to America as "the Good War," "the Necessary War," a war to free enslaved peoples around the world. Americans had bought the promise and the hope. In all respects, the government, from the president to the Office of War Information, had mobilized both the home front and the citizen warriors to fight a war for democracy. With victory in battle and high morale at home, those who sold the war could claim to have performed the promise; they had delivered the victory that President Roosevelt promised in asking for a declaration of war on December 8, 1941: America had "gained ... the inevitable triumph." America had risen from the Great Depression and the defeat at Pearl Harbor to the triumphs of V-E Day and V-J Day. The Allied policy of "Germany first' had been vindicated by total success first in Europe and then in Asia.

With the war won in Europe and Asia, the time had come to bind up the nation's and the world's wounds, to perform the promises of peace in a more just world, to occupy and demilitarize Germany and Japan, to liberate conquered peoples and punish war criminals, to destroy Fascism, Nazism, and Japanese Imperialism, to prevent economic hardships in Allied and enemy countries, and to restore the former enemies to the world of democratic nations. The great challenge was to turn the deeds of the warrior band of brothers into a brotherhood of man. One significant step toward that dream had already been taken before the end of the war when the U.S. Senate ratified the treaty establishing the United Nations on July 28, 1945.[43]

THE GOOD PEACE

The Price of War

Unlike the end of World War I, this time there was no doubt about who won and who lost. The military leaders of Germany and Japan had no "traitors" to blame for their defeats, no "stabs in the back" to excuse their failures. The total destruction of German and Japanese military forces offered convincing proof of their inability to protect their homelands. This time, the United Nations would not only punish those guilty of "war crimes" and "crimes against humanity" but would oversee the rebuilding of the shattered countries. And shattered they were. While we may never know the exact figures, the fatalities were horrendous: 25 million in the Soviet Union, 15 million in China, 6 million in Poland, 1.5–2 million in Yugoslavia, 4 million in Germany, 400,000 in Great Britain, 300,000 in the United States, a couple of hundred thousand in Italy, and 6 million Jews. Overall, more than 60 million people died in the War, with civilians accounting for two-thirds of the deaths.[44]

Added to these deaths were millions more maimed, homeless, and without hope. The Japanese attack on Pearl Harbor justified the war to most Americans. Only a lasting peace could justify the sacrifices made by so many. With most of the world in ruins and national economies in peril, the United States was now the most powerful economic power on earth, but would be challenged by the Soviet Union for global leadership in economics, politics, and power. In contrast to the aftermath of the last war, the United States did not retreat into isolation following World War II, in part because technological developments during the war—in communication, computers, radar, jet planes, nuclear weapons, and missile delivery systems— made it both unwise and unsafe to ignore the rest of the world. Still, the United States dramatically reduced its armed forces in response to public demands, and placed its trust in the United Nations to preserve peace on earth.

The United Nations and a Changing World

On paper, the plan looked promising with the Big Five Allies of the war—China, France, the Soviet Union, the United Kingdom, and the United States—pledged to work together on the UN Security Council for peace and cooperation. Unfortunately, the new world produced by the peace promised more conflict, not order. In China, the civil war between the Communists and the Nationalists, postponed by the Japanese invasion, again burst into open armed conflict and concluded with a Communist victory and the Nationalists driven into exile on the island of Formosa in 1949. In Europe, the Russians and the West were growing mutually distrustful of each other. As Winston Churchill noted in a top secret telegram to President Truman on May 12, 1945, and elaborated upon it in an address at Westminster College in Fulton, Missouri on March 5, 1946: "From Stettin in the Baltic to Trieste in the Adriatic an iron curtain has descended across the Continent."

While Russian tanks enforced Soviet hegemony over the nations of Central and Eastern Europe, America attempted to shore up Western Europe and contain Soviet expansion. The American government created such strategies as the Truman Doctrine of March 1947 (promising aid to free people to fight "armed minorities or outside pressures"), the inter-American Treaty of Reciprocal Assistance (Rio Pact) of September 2, 1947, and the North Atlantic Treaty Organization (NATO) in April 1949. But perhaps the greatest American weapon for holding the line against communism in Europe was not a weapon at all, but humanitarian aid in the form of the European Recovery Plan, proposed by former wartime Army Chief of Staff and now Secretary of State George C. Marshall in a commencement address at Harvard University on June 5, 1947:

> Our policy is directed not against any country or doctrine but against hunger, poverty, desperation and chaos. Its purpose should be the revival of a working economy in the world so as to permit the emergence of political and social conditions in which free institutions can exist.

Across the globe, change was the only constant, as national borders were redrawn, populations relocated, former colonies voluntarily freed, wars of liberation fought against lingering colonialism, and capitalism threatened by socialist and communist alternatives. In Europe, the Nuremberg Tribunals began the trials of Nazi war criminals, condemning twelve top Nazi leaders to death and six to prison on October 1, 1946.[45] More trials would follow and Germany's division into Western and Soviet zones would harden into separate states—the German Federal Republic in the West and the German Democratic Republic in the East, a division that would last until the reunification of Germany in 1989 as a free and democratic nation. But in the immediate postwar period, Germany would serve as a flash point between

East and West, a place for spies and counterspies, for state security and the construction of the infamous Berlin Wall of 1961.

In Japan, the United States enjoyed total control under General of the Army Douglas MacArthur as Supreme Commander. To politically cleanse the country, twenty-five senior Japanese officials, led by Tojo Hideki, the former prime minister, were tried for "Crimes against peace, conventional war crimes and crimes against humanity." All twenty-five would be found guilty and executed; in total almost six thousand would be tried and over nine hundred executed for their crimes. The samurai code of *bushidro* had brought not warrior honor but criminal guilt and punishment to the leaders of *Dai Nippon Teikoku* (the Great Empire of Japan).[46]

Perhaps echoing Japan's past, General MacArthur acted like a twentieth century *shogun*, forcing change on the Japanese people. Incredibly, this forced "peace and democracy" succeeded, making Japan a stable and economically sound state closely allied to American interests. The overall record may not have been as neat as the propaganda claimed, but the American people bought the story of the chastened and redeemed Japanese.[47]

While Americans were winning hearts and minds in West Germany and Japan, France's attempts to retain its colonial empire in North Africa and Southeast Asia would end in failure and drag America into a quagmire called Vietnam.

Meanwhile, back on the home front, millions of men and women who had served in the war were being discharged, flooding the country with young people yearning for better lives. They used the G.I. Bill of Rights to pay for education, finance new homes, and build new lives. They became what broadcaster Tom Brokaw has termed "The Greatest Generation" for surviving the Depression, winning the war, and building a better America.

One dark cloud now menaced America's bright horizon—Communism. Abroad, the Soviet Union and, later, Communist China threatened armed conflict. At home, communists were suspected of betraying the country. The threat of Communism seemed to be global, directed at capitalism, colonialism, and America. While the reality was more complex, with profound disagreements and distrusts among the various factions within communism, Americans saw the conflict as a replay of the clash between the Slave World and the Free World, this time with Godless Communism threatening God-fearing America. Added to the usual competition between opposing powers were ideological dichotomies involving atheism versus religion, communism versus capitalism, closed versus open societies, wars of liberation versus lingering colonialism, and diametrically opposed views of history and the future.

In the face of communist threats from outside and inside the country, a great fear descended upon the land. With the Soviet development of an atomic bomb (which many people blamed on American traitors like Julius and Ethel Rosenberg) and the Communist victory in China, both in 1949, there seemed to be little distinction to be made between the home front and the war front. In the age of nuclear weapons, everyone—soldier and civilian alike—was a primary target; Hiroshima and Nagasaki had provided ample proof of the destructiveness of these weapons of total war.

Selling a War

From a selling perspective, World War II was a huge success. The Japanese attack on Pearl Harbor had given the U.S. government both a cause and a slogan, "Remember Pearl Harbor," that not only reminded Americans of their frontier heritage ("Remember the Alamo") but silenced the antiwar isolationist voices in Congress and on the streets. Clearly, a sneak attack on unprepared Americans is the best motivation for Americans to support the counterattack. Along with the slogan and the motivation, President Roosevelt had an organization, the Office of War Information, already in place to start selling the war immediately after the declaration of war, enlisting the entire nation in the struggle.

In Aristotelian terms, the time, place, and circumstance of the Japanese attack had provided the proper *context* in which the President and the government maintained their credibility (*ethos*) by military victories; their messages had both logical and emotional appeals; and the American people responded positively to both the speakers and their messages. Every available medium was enlisted in the struggle. Newspapers, magazines, billboards, radios, movies, bond drives, and public rallies and parades all played the parts they were assigned by the Office of War Information. In essence, the selling of World War II was a marketer's best case scenario, with satisfied customers totally committed to the product.

The government's selling of World War II is a perfect example of what modern marketers call Integrated Marketing Communications (IMC). Every vehicle of mass communication was effectively harnessed to play a carefully synchronized role. In best IMC practice, both mass and selected target audiences were chosen to receive messages from the media best suited to reach and persuade them. Creative strategies and executions were carefully developed to assure the most positive and desirable responses. And the distribution of contradictory messages was largely eliminated, through censorship and government regulation, to assure that Americans didn't receive any messages that might dilute the impact of these approved by the U.S. government.

In war, as in marketing, a product that performs the advertised promise satisfies the customers and keeps them buying. Like Coca Cola, World War II was sold like any other product; it satisfied customers and sold itself. Neither during the war nor in the years following have the customers questioned the marketing strategies nor become disenchanted with the product itself. Of course, success in battle was essential for the entire enterprise to succeed.

4

The Forgotten War—Korea

THE COLD WAR TURNS HOT

If President Harry Truman had better understood what marketers describe as "consumer behavior" when the North Korean Army invaded South Korea in June 1950, his marketing communications strategy for positioning the conflict to the American people might have spared him and his administration many problems in the years that followed.

Truman assumed that ordering American forces to immediately confront this unexpected assault was a judgment that would be fully understood and supported by the American people. His decision to send G.I.s into combat won public support initially because most Americans believed that the U.S. military, fighting under the UN banner, would easily rout the communist invaders. However, when American troops began suffering heavy casualties and experiencing major reverses in the early stages of the war, the U.S. public started questioning the president's judgment. We believe that the American people hadn't been sufficiently informed about the nature of the new communist threat to the Free World's security, nor motivated to engage in a new and prolonged global conflict only five years after it was generally thought that an era of peace had begun with the end of World War II.

People's minds are conservative instruments, slow to accept new ideas and equally slow to change them once those ideas have taken root. Understanding what is on the minds of the target audience you are trying to inform or influence before starting to communicate with them is a fundamental axiom of marketing communications. Our modern Aristotelian marketing model characterizes this as the *pathos of the audience.*

Only after discovering the mindset of that audience do contemporary marketers propagate ideas that are compatible with what the audience already believes, or is prepared to believe. To ignore these facts is to court disaster, as President Harry S. Truman ultimately discovered in his failure to effectively communicate and market the Korean War to the American people from the beginning.

The Context

The Cold War between Communism and the Free World suddenly turned hot just before dawn on June 25, 1950, when an army of the Democratic People's Republic of Korea (North Korea) crossed the 38th Parallel border and invaded the Republic of Korea (South Korea). The North Koreans (DPRK), armed by the Soviet Union with tanks and other heavy weapons, swiftly destroyed the defenses of the South Korean (ROK) Army, which the United States had only provided with light defensive military equipment. DPRK troops then began marching on South Korea's capital city of Seoul, only thirty-five miles south of the border separating the two nations. On June 28, the front page of *The New York Times* declared, "Truman Orders U.S. Air, Navy Units to Fight in Aid of Korea; U.S. Council Supports Him; Our Fliers in Action; Fleet Guards Formosa."

Even before World War II ended, the Soviet Union and its former wartime allies had been skirmishing in Europe and Asia over control of conquered territory or countries previously occupied by the Axis powers. The invasion of South Korea by North Korea followed months of mutual threats and provocations, border skirmishes and guerrilla attacks by both North and South Korea. There is ample evidence that U.S. and Korean military intelligence were aware that a large invasion force was building up on the border in North Korea; however, it appears that South Korean President Syngman Rhee and President Harry S. Truman were totally surprised when North Korean troops swept across the border that morning on a broad front.

Prologue to the War

President Harry Truman and his administration were clearly unprepared for this crisis in the Far East when it erupted that early summer day. Two years earlier, President Truman had narrowly won his own election for President of the United States. In June 1950, his grip on political power was still extremely shaky. Under continual attack by political conservatives of both parties, particularly by Right Wing Republicans, he was beset by a variety of domestic challenges, ranging from labor unrest to the repeated accusation that he was "soft on Communism." Using Aristotle's frame of reference, the president's *ethos* (or credibility) was weak in the eyes of the country. With the United States caught in the grip of a "Red Scare," incited by conservative politicians like then-Republican Congressman Richard M. Nixon and Republican Senator Joseph R. McCarthy, public concerns were largely focused on domestic issues. It was in this *context* (combining Aristotle's analysis with modern marketing—the environment in which products are sold) that the American people were struggling to adjust to enormous economic, political, and social changes within the country following the recent end of World War II, and they were generally not inclined to fret about foreign matters. Truman, a former U.S. Senator and Vice President under President Franklin Delano Roosevelt, was a fiscal conservative who was feared by the leaders of the U.S. Armed Services because he had sought drastic cuts in military spending both before and after World War II.

There were 6 million troops serving in the U.S. Army at the end of the Second World War. Bowing to overwhelming public opinion and Congressional pressure to reduce military expenditures and "bring the boys back home," President Truman and his fiscally conservative allies slashed U.S. Army force levels to a little more than a half million men by 1948. The other American military services force levels were also savagely cut and starved of funding, with most American troops stationed in either Occupied Germany or Japan.[1]

Before the North Koreans invaded, senior government officials in Washington had made several public statements that had the effect of assuring North Korea that the United States would not defend South Korea if it was attacked. U.S. Senator Tom Connally of Texas, Chairman of the Senate Foreign Relations Committee, told the press that the Communists were going to overrun South Korea when they were ready, "whether we want it or not."[2] U.S. Secretary of State Dean Acheson further encouraged the North Koreans to attack its neighbor when he neglected to include South Korea in a list of nations the United States would defend if attacked, in a widely reported speech.[3]

THE NORTH INVADES THE SOUTH

Shortly after the North Korean Army invaded South Korea, Secretary of State Acheson sought and won United Nations (UN) support to defend against the North Korean aggression at the direction of President Truman. Three days later, the president ordered U.S. Army, Marine, Navy, and Air Force units, commanded by General Douglas MacArthur in the Far East, to join the battle. Two weeks after that, a unified United Nations command, under General MacArthur, was authorized by the UN. Military units from a number of UN member countries, including France, Great Britain, Turkey, and Greece, began sending troops to Korea to fight.[4]

There is no evidence that President Truman questioned that the American people would back his decision to protect South Korea at that time. Nor is there any indication that he bothered to take public opinion polls on this issue before he acted decisively. A Gallup Poll taken shortly after President Truman committed American troops to battle revealed that 77 percent of those queried said they approved his "decision to send United States military aid to South Korea."[5] The fact is that when the undeclared war started, the president's decision to act by calling on the UN for support and ordering the U.S. Armed Forces into action in Korea did not immediately generate political opposition or disapproval by the American people.[6] Unlike President Roosevelt, who in 1941 went on national radio within twenty-four hours of the attack on the U.S. Fleet at Pearl Harbor to inform the American people of what had happened and to prepare them for the bloody world war that was to come, President Truman waited almost a month before addressing the nation directly on national radio and television.

While Congressional leaders quickly supported his decision to act decisively, President Truman did not immediately seek broad Congressional support or approval for these swift decisions, carefully characterizing the conflict, which was subsequently going to cost many thousands of American lives, as a "Police Action," rather than a war. This was a very big mistake in branding strategy, one that no contemporary brand manager would make. First, by describing the conflict as a "Police Action," Truman failed to comprehend that most Americans' understanding of that phrase suggested nothing more significant than a DUI arrest or the investigation of a burglary. Second, by applying the term "Police Action" to what turned out to be a bloody and prolonged war in Asia, he minimized the importance of an event that would subsequently cause many thousands of American soldiers to be wounded or to lose their lives. It was a classic misrepresentation that would haunt his administration in the months and years to come.

President Truman did not directly address Congress or the American people about his decision to wage an undeclared war in the Far East until the third week in July, more than three weeks after the North Koreans had invaded South Korea and U.S. combat forces had begun fighting. His speech about U.S. involvement in the war to a joint session of Congress and broadcast to the U.S. public was the first national event of major importance covered by all the major U.S. television networks, reaching nearly 30 million Americans.[7]

From the onset of the Korean War, President Truman's military strategy was influenced by his administration's concern about the possibility of direct military involvement of the Soviet Union in the conflict. He was determined not to execute a strategy that might cause the Soviets to further expand the war into Europe and other parts of the world. It may have been that concern that led him to describe the war as a "police action" rather than the major armed conflict it was.

Truman's determination to engage in a limited and regional armed conflict rather than positioning it as a much broader battle between global communism and the forces of the Free World would ultimately lead to a dramatic confrontation between the president and General MacArthur, who openly espoused the pursuit of a more aggressive military strategy. The incompatibility of their divergent views would ultimately result in the general's dismissal from his post as Far Eastern Commander.

America Joins the Battle

In the 1950s, the neo-Aristotelian *use and control of public media*, defined in contemporary terms as understanding and manipulating political advertising, media planning, and public relations tactics, were still in their infancy in the United States. In that era, the obsessive analysis of overnight public opinion polls had not yet become a governing influence determining every White House policy decision. This scrutiny of what impact policy decisions might have on existing public opinion (understanding what is in the mind of the public to assure a positive outcome before taking any significant action), an examination of what neo-Aristotelians call the *effects of the persuasion*, today rules the behavior of almost every American politician. While President Truman did not seem to be concerned about the state of public opinion at the beginning of the Korean Conflict, his most senior general in the region, General MacArthur, was far more sensitive to the American public's views. In fact, throughout World War II and in the ensuing years that he reigned as the Viceroy of postwar Japan, General MacArthur unceasingly used the U.S. news media as a powerful vehicle to maintain a positive public image of himself in the minds of Americans. Charismatic and articulate, he carefully crafted a mythic image in the public's eye as a wise and omnipotent leader over the years, manipulating the *logos of the messages*, or message content, to assure that all his public communications appeared clear and reasonable, while exploiting the emotional mindset of the American public. Where Truman was prickly and impatient with newspaper and magazine reporters, MacArthur was endlessly charming. His skill with the "sound bite" was legendary, as was his sense of the "perfect photo op." MacArthur had nurtured this public persona since early in his military career, much as contemporary marketing executives nurture and protect the brand identities entrusted to them, like Coca Cola or IBM.

The Media

There was little press coverage of the Korean War in its early days. Those few Western news correspondents who managed to get to South Korea during the first week of battle witnessed the total collapse of the ROK Army. Seoul was quickly overrun and broken elements of ROK military units were being driven further and further south into the southern tip of the Korean Peninsula. The correspondents retreated with them, flying back to Japan with their news dispatches because electronic transmission facilities were unavailable to them in Korea.[8]

At first, the American public confidently assumed that North Korean troops would break and run on first contact with the leading elements of the American Army that were being hurriedly ferried into the Pusan Perimeter Beachhead from their bases in Japan. But when news stories began appearing in American media reporting that American troops were being battered by the North Korean Army and were retreating, questions began to be raised by the public and critics of the administration in the United States. Only five years after the Axis powers surrendered unconditionally to the Allies, the American public could not comprehend that the most powerful military force in history had been reduced to a shadow of its former strength and military resources. These reverses baffled the American people, not acknowledging that the majority of Americans had demanded a rapid dismantling of our military forces at the conclusion of World War II.

In the early weeks of the war, there was no official press censorship. However, when dispatches began appearing in American newspapers describing, "whipped and frightened GIs," MacArthur's headquarters in Tokyo branded the correspondents who had filed these stories as traitors, who were guilty of "giving aid and comfort to the enemy." Even without official censorship, Army officials in Korea and Japan began to pressure the journalists to use more restraint in reporting what they saw. Six months later, a more formal censorship system was introduced, but throughout the three-year war, U.S. Army commanders did everything in their power to stifle the free flow of information to the American people about actual conditions at the front. With the exception of Vietnam, this has been the pattern of media–military relationships ever since. In many cases, MacArthur cultivated the top executives of mainstream American news organizations, trusting that his charm would insure a more friendly coverage than that generated by their correspondents in the field. Three months after the initial North Korean attack, MacArthur invited the senior executives of the four major U.S. news agencies to join him as special guests on his flagship during the successful amphibious assault on September 15, 1950, at Inchon off the east coast of South Korea. Field correspondents covering the assault were crowded into special press boats and held offshore, unable to report on the actual fighting firsthand. Many of them didn't get ashore until three days later, long after the beachhead had been secured.[9]

Following the extraordinary success of the amphibious landing at Inchon, and the subsequent encirclement of North Korean forces trapped below UN forces in the north and other elements of the UN Command in the south, American public opinion on the handling of the war became much more positive. A Gallup Poll taken shortly after the Inchon landing revealed that 66 percent of the country believed the United States had not made a mistake in deciding to defend South Korea.[10] A fickle American public now regarded General MacArthur, who had conceived this seaborne assault on the North Korean Army's exposed flank, as a military genius. This shift in public opinion relieved President Truman of some of the hostile political pressure he had been receiving from conservative members of Congress and in the news media.

Prior to the successful Inchon invasion, President Truman had been content to simply drive the North Korean army across the border and out of South Korea. However, Secretary of State Dean Acheson and other advisors in Washington began encouraging him to contemplate a bolder military strategy—moving north across the 38th Parallel with the determination of toppling the North Korean regime itself.[11] Eighty-one percent of Americans polled now supported pursuit of total victory against North Korea,[12] and Truman, trying to demonstrate to the country that he was not "soft on Communism," believed that embracing this aggressive military strategy would offer dramatic evidence that he was as hawkish as MacArthur.[13] Further, there was a prevailing belief in Truman's administration in Washington and in MacArthur's headquarters in Japan that the Communist China, which bordered on the north with North Korea, was still too weak militarily to present a significant danger of intervention to UN forces.[14]

President Truman decided to meet personally with General MacArthur in mid-October, 1951. They had not met previously. Truman's decision was based on his concern about the political and public relations "end runs" that MacArthur had previously made around the White House in his attempts to directly influence American public opinion. Truman also decided to meet with MacArthur because he thought he could capitalize on his relationship with the military hero who was now being lionized by the American people, thereby strengthening his own shaky relationship with the voters. Using updated Aristotelian analysis joined with modern marketing strategy that deals with the *ethos* of the source, he was borrowing credibility from MacArthur because Truman believed the general was more revered by the public than he was.

President Truman met with MacArthur on tiny Wake Island in the middle of the Pacific Ocean, ostensibly to discuss future military strategy. During this meeting, MacArthur assured Truman that North Korean resistance would collapse by Thanksgiving and that Red Chinese military posed no major threat to his UN forces. He expressed the hope that he could withdraw his U.S. Eighth Army to Japan by Christmas. Truman flew back to Washington assured that MacArthur was in complete support of administration policies and would soon deliver victory in Korea in time to help Democratic Party candidates win an off-year U.S. election in November.[15]

Truman's satisfaction lasted only a week and a half. He was informed then that shortly after MacArthur returned to his Far East Command in

Tokyo, he had ordered his generals to aggressively press the attack north until UN troops reached the Chinese border, without bothering to seek White House approval. MacArthur and Truman did not yet know that Chinese Army "volunteers" in the tens of thousands had already started covertly advancing south across their common border into North Korea to confront the advancing UN forces.[16] It was another colossal military intelligence failure.

Truman was now caught between the proverbial rock and a hard place. Right wing politicians were flailing the Truman administration with loud public accusations about his mismanagement of the Government's Far East policy. They were accusing him of allowing communists to infiltrate the U.S. government. Fearing political repercussions from his domestic critics, Truman was still reluctant to bring his rebellious military commander to task. MacArthur was the hero of the Right Wing of the Republican Party, and was already being mentioned by many Republicans as a possible presidential candidate. Truman knew that openly confronting MacArthur or forcing him to resign at this time would allow his political enemies in the United States to weaken the winning chances of every Democrat running for election, possibly resulting in the loss of Democratic control of Congress. American public opinion had already been powerfully influenced by the dramatic rhetoric of demagogues like Republican Senator Joseph McCarthy. The country was becoming obsessed with the "Red Menace of Communism." Like so many U.S. presidents before and after him on the eve of closely contested elections, Truman chose the course of discretion over valor and allowed MacArthur to continue his advance northward, attempting to halt the Chinese Army's infiltration by bombing the bridges over the Yalu River separating North Korea from China.[17]

Truman's timidity didn't help the Democrats politically. Following the November 1952 elections, the Republicans gained five seats in the U.S. Senate and twenty-eight seats in the House of Representatives, critically narrowing Truman's and the Democrats' control of Congress.

Fighting grew more intense between the UN forces and growing numbers of Communist Chinese troops pouring into North Korea. Finally forced to go on the defensive, the UN forces began retreating south. The retreat turned into a total rout as first South Korean, and then U.S. Army units broke and fled before the Communist onslaught. Hundreds of thousands of Chinese soldiers were now attacking UN troops on a broad front as the ferocious Korean winter set in. UN troops retreating down narrow roads through the mountains of North Korea were now besieged on all sides.

As news reports of this military disaster began appearing in U.S. news media, the American people were stunned. For months, the U.S. government had been assuring them that UN forces, under the leadership of General MacArthur, were destroying the North Korean Army. They also were told that the end of the Korean War was near, resulting in a total victory for the American military in its first open combat with Communist forces. Harry Truman heightened national fears at this time by inferring, at a Washington press conference, that he would possibly authorize the use of the atomic bomb against the Chinese if he judged its use necessary. This presidential statement shocked the American people and the world.[18]

General MacArthur chose this time to make a series of public statements which were extensively covered in U.S. media, blaming the Truman administration for a number of strategic blunders which he suggested had sabotaged the chances for total military victory. MacArthur had aligned himself with those Republican Conservatives who believed that the United States should provide support for the exiled forces of Chiang Kai-Shek, driven by the Communists from Mainland China and now based on the nearby island of Formosa (now called Taiwan). General MacArthur and his political supporters sought to encourage Chiang's Army to invade the mainland of China, relieving pressure on the embattled UN forces. MacArthur's efforts to move UN troops up to the Chinese border were thought by many to be a prelude to launching an all-out assault on China, in coordination with Chiang Kai-Shek's Army.

MacArthur began challenging President Truman's political competence through a series of interviews he granted to news organizations and sympathetic columnists that he had been cultivating for years. Once again, President Truman backed away from a direct confrontation with MacArthur, fearful that sacking the general would further erode his and the Democratic Party's political strength. Opinion polls taken at the time revealed that the American people's support for the war in Korea had dropped precipitously— from a 66 percent approval rating in July to 39 percent approval rating just six months later. By March 1951, polls indicated that President Truman's public approval rating was at an all-time low of 26 percent as UN casualties rose to 228,941, of which 57,120 were American.[19]

Without confronting General MacArthur directly, President Truman issued a series of presidential directives ordering that all government officials "reduce the number of public speeches appertaining to foreign or military policy" and to obtain prior clearance from Washington before issuing them. Clearing intended to muzzle MacArthur, the directives further ordered Defense Department officials overseas to "refrain from direct communications" with newspapers, magazines, and other media.[20] MacArthur responded by issuing a series of communiqués and holding several press conferences in which he flagrantly challenged President Truman's directives, and openly questioned the administration's overall strategy in Korea and the Far East.

The confrontation between General MacArthur and his Commander in Chief reached a climax in April 1951, when a letter written by MacArthur to the House of Representatives Republican Minority Leader Joseph W. Martin, Jr., was released to the press. Taking aim at President Truman's efforts to reach a negotiated end to the Korean War, MacArthur's letter insisted that "there was no substitute for victory" and called for Chiang Kai-Shek's Chinese Nationalist forces to invade the Chinese mainland. The contents of this letter, which clearly was challenging the policies of the American President, made for headlines across the United States and around the world.

President Truman fired MacArthur a few days after the general's letter became public. A *New York Times* front-page headline on April 11, 1951, stated, "Truman Relieves M'Arthur of All His Posts; Finds Him Unable to Back U.S.-UN Policies; Ridgeway Named to Far Eastern Commands."

The reaction of the American public to the president's act was one of outrage. Republicans in Congress and much of the conservative press attacked the President in angry tones, calling for his impeachment and demanding MacArthur's reinstatement. The legislatures of four states voted to condemn the president's action. President Truman's sacking of General MacArthur crystallized the sense of dissatisfaction that most Americans had come to feel about this limited war with no victory in sight. Republican Senator Joseph McCarthy charged that Truman's decision to fire MacArthur had been influenced by "bourbon and Benedictine." Republican Senator Kenneth S. Wherry began calling it "Truman's War," and that pejorative term caught on with a large segment of the American public. A national poll at that time indicated that 69 percent of the country was backing General MacArthur.[21] MacArthur returned to the United States after a fourteen-year absence, a national hero. Huge parades were staged honoring him on both coasts.

President Truman and his administration hunkered down and decided to wait until the storm of public and political protest waned. And wane it finally did, after ten weeks of Congressional hearings about the handling of the war sputtered out. While the American public was still held in sway by the almost mythic image of General MacArthur, they largely agreed with the administration's policy of limiting the U.S. commitment to Korea and the Far East. Public opinion was further mollified when it became apparent that General Matthew Ridgeway, General MacArthur's replacement in the Far East, was doing an excellent job of stabilizing the front in Korea and holding the Communists at bay.[22]

The Beginning of the End of the War

The beginning of the end of the Korean War was initiated by the Soviet Union, acting as an intermediary for the People's Republic of China. At this point, China had superceded the North Koreans in such matters and was largely dictating political and military strategy. After a series of political exchanges between the United States and the UN on the one hand, and the Soviet Union, China, and North Korea on the other, peace talks were initiated in July 1951. However, the fighting was to continue sporadically for another two years as each side tried to weaken or out-negotiate the other at the conference table. Militarily, a stalemate developed roughly along the 38th Parallel, the original border dividing the two Koreas. Each side continued to jab at each other, sometimes with artillery exchanges and sometimes with fierce combats that cost both armies heavy casualties but did not fundamentally change the terrain each army controlled. It took another year and a half for the guns to grow completely silent.[23] During that time, UN forces suffered an additional 60,000 casualties; 20,000 of them were American.[24]

President Truman was growing increasingly determined to end the conflict in Korea as the 1952 national elections approached. His standing in public opinion polls was still extremely poor and the Democrats were trying to get the war behind them as quickly as possible. After the resounding and irrefutable victories that the United States had achieved at the end of the Second World War, the American people were tired of waging a war they couldn't win, or even resolve by any other means. Most Americans, in fact, did not feel that there was a genuine war being waged. Recognizing that he could not overcome the negative feelings that the voters had about him and his inability to end the conflict in Korea, President Truman announced that he would not run for reelection.

Dwight D. Eisenhower, then Supreme Commander of NATO forces in Europe, retired from military service in May 1952 and soon began a successful campaign as the Republican candidate for president. While already enormously popular, he virtually assured his election when he told the voters that if elected, "I will go to Korea." After he became president-elect, Eisenhower kept his promise and visited Korea for three days, conferring with American generals and South Korean President Rhee. However, on his return to Washington, Eisenhower announced that he was going to continue the Truman's administration strategy for seeking peace, rejecting the more extreme strategies proposed by General MacArthur and the Republican Right Wing that would have enlarged the war into the Chinese mainland.[25]

The fighting officially ended in Korea in the early morning hours of July 27, 1953, more than three years after it commenced. A front-page headline in *The New York Times* on that day reported, "Truce Is Signed, Ending the Fighting in Korea; P.O.W. Exchange Near; Rhee Gets U.S. Pledge; Eisenhower Bids Free World Stay Vigilant."

The war ended with neither victory nor defeat for either side. In America and in other countries allied with it, the cease-fire was greeted largely with relief. Nearly 1,820,000 men were killed or wounded during the protracted conflict, 1,420,000 or 78 percent of them Communist soldiers. There were 16,000 UN allied casualties. The American toll was 33,629 dead and 103,284 wounded in battle.[26]

CEASE-FIRE AND THE AFTERMATH

At war's end, America was a deeply divided country. General MacArthur's challenge to the civilian authority of the U.S. government and the consequences of his extremely effective public relations campaign to win the support of the people at the expense of President Truman's administration split the nation politically. Public confidence in the U.S. government's ability to effectively conduct foreign affairs was severely weakened, and the attacks on anyone vaguely considered liberal or leftist reached new levels of acrimony as the Republican Right Wing continued its harassing tactics.[27]

Perhaps most difficult for the American people to comprehend or accept was the concept of a limited war. Americans had become conditioned to fighting wars and achieving total, unconditional victory, not a negotiated peace. At the very beginning of the conflict in June 1950, President Truman shrank from calling it "a war." Instead he described it as a "Police Action," a phrase that initially confused Americans and ultimately came to be used in a depreciatory way. Throughout the Korean War, President Truman studiously avoided acknowledging that the United States was in fact fighting a war. He consistently referred to it as a "Police Action" or "conflict."

If the United States was not in a war, then the usual patriotic themes used to motivate emotional and physical commitment by the American people could not be used effectively. Nor could naysayers be as easily silenced as in a formally declared war. Questions were raised about exactly whom we were fighting and why? Once the North Koreans were defeated militarily, the UN was confronted by the Communist Chinese on the battlefield. Many Americans wondered why American and UN forces did not immediately attack this new enemy's homeland, as they had done in other wars. This more aggressive strategy was essentially what General MacArthur and the Right Wing of the Republican Party were demanding of the Truman administration. The American public asked: If the American military was fighting under a UN flag, why were the vast majority of the soldiers fighting and dying in combat mainly Americans? Why weren't other UN member armies showing up to fight and die in equally large numbers?[28] Similar questions were raised fifty years later when President George W. Bush insisted that U.S. forces were only one component of a "Coalition of the Willing" in Iraq.

The Korean War was the first American war to be covered by television. Still in its infancy in 1950, 30 million Americans were estimated to have watched President Truman address the U.S. Congress three weeks after the war started. Most Americans tuned into this event by radio, which was still the only mass electronic medium covering the entire country at the time. However experienced Harry Truman may have been as an old-fashioned, backroom politician, he did not understand how to control and exploit the *use and control of public media*, using the power of national mass media to gain public support for his policies and programs. It was his misfortune that General MacArthur understood far better than President Truman how to exploit the U.S. news media to get his message across to the American people.

Truman was generally accessible to reporters in the White House and held frequent press conferences, but he was generally suspicious of the press, and frequently hostile to the many newspaper columnists and publishers of news magazines who were then wielding enormous influence on American public opinion. His cantankerous and blunt comments did little to endear him to the news media at the time. In the years that have passed, however, his biographers and White House historians have come to retrospectively regard those same qualities of blunt candor with respect and admiration.

POPULAR CULTURE—TELEVISION, HOLLYWOOD MOVIES, MUSIC, TOYS, COMIC BOOKS

Television

The U.S. television industry was still in its infancy in 1950. The medium was primarily regarded as a new source of entertainment, and to a lesser extent sports coverage. There were less than 4 million homes with television sets in the United States at that time, less than 9 percent of total U.S. households.[29] Television, however, had already habituated millions of Americans into regularly watching comedians like Milton Berle on "Texaco Star Theater" and Sid Caesar on "Your Show of Shows," popular western series like "The Lone Ranger" and "Hopalong Cassidy," and the top-rated musical variety show, "Arthur Godfrey's Talent Scouts."[30] Network TV news was of negligible importance to most Americans who in 1950 still depended on their local newspapers and radio stations to learn what was happening of importance. The Truman administration did collaborate with the NBC Television Network in August 1950 to produce a weekly series, "Battle Report, Washington," whose purpose was to counter negative reports about U.S. battlefield reverses and put a more positive spin on the war effort.[31]

Hollywood Films

While a number of Hollywood films dealing with the Korean War were produced during those years, there is no evidence that the Truman administration made any attempts to persuade their producers to present a sympathetic picture of U.S. involvement with the war, or to motivate the public to support the administration's policies concerning it. Shortly after U.S. troops went into action in Korea in 1950, a group of senior executives representing Hollywood's largest studios met with President Truman to offer the motion picture industry's support in the war effort. In a statement, they said, "We are at your service, at the service of the country and the United Nations."[32] However, the government never formally asked the heads of the major Hollywood film studios to mobilize the resources of their industry in support of the war effort as had been done so effectively during World War II.

While the government virtually ignored the morale building potential of patriotic war films like those commonly produced during World War I and World War II, the Hollywood studios did independently exploit the theme of the Korean War for commercial purposes, producing a number of low-budget action and battlefield romance dramas, most of them filling the bottom half of double bills at movie theaters around the U.S. writer-director Samuel Fuller's *Fix Bayonets* (1951), the bleak story of an infantry platoon covering the withdrawal of a larger unit of American soldiers, was well received by the critics, but this action movie had little to do with persuading Americans to support the war effort or provide them with reasons why America was fighting in Korea.

A series of less memorable, inexpensively produced action or romantic dramas followed, simply using the Korean War as a setting. All were shot on Hollywood sound stages or on California locations, not in Korea itself. Among them was *A Yank in Korea* (1951), *Retreat, Hell* (1952), *One Minute to Zero* (1952), starring Robert Mitchum and Ann Blyth, *Battle Zone* (1952), *The Glory Brigade* (1953), starring Victor Mature and Lee Marvin, *Mission Over Korea* (1953), and *Battle Circus* (1953), starring Humphrey Bogart and June Allyson.

In the years following the cessation of hostilities in Korea, a number of Hollywood films dealing with the Korean War were also produced. Notable among them was *The Bridges at Toko-Ri* (1954), starring William Holden and Grace Kelly, *The Manchurian Candidate* (1962), starring Frank Sinatra, *Pork Chop Hill* (1959), starring Gregory Peck, and *M*A*S*H* (1970), directed by Robert Altman (on which the later successful TV series was based). Almost all of the films produced during and after the war dealt with the travails of either the individual U.S. fighting man or of small unit actions, and were devoid of any inspirational or "Why We Fight" themes of World War II. None of them reflected the Truman administration's concerns about the necessity of fighting a limited war in order to keep the battle between the United States and the Soviet Union from spreading to other parts of the world.

The most proactive cinematic effort the U.S. government did make in this realm was to sponsor a film documentary called *This Is Korea* (1951) by noted Hollywood film director and retired Navy officer John Ford. The film, commissioned by the U.S. Navy, depicted combat in Korea in a relatively objective but impersonal manner. It made no attempt to examine the root cause of why America was fighting in this Asian country. *This Is Korea* was distributed to U.S. theaters by Republic Pictures, but was unsuccessful, both at the box office and as a propaganda vehicle. It was pulled back from distribution soon after it was released.[33]

The U.S. government also sponsored crude propaganda films that were produced by the U.S. Defense Department about various aspects of the war. Regular military personnel, unlike the extraordinary professional Hollywood civilian talent that had been recruited to produce motivational films supporting the war effort during World War II, created these films.

Half-hour documentaries, like the U.S. Army's series, *The Big Picture*, were designed to present the activities of the armed forces in a totally favorable light and to reinforce the necessity of militarily confronting the Soviet Union and its client states throughout the world in order to stop the spread of communism. These documentaries were provided free to local television stations around the United States, and were usually broadcast in fringe time slots (e.g., early Saturday morning) in fulfillment of local stations' public service requirements. They inevitably had limited viewership.

Popular Music, Toys, and Comic Books

Unlike World War II, which produced many popular and patriotic tunes, no songs about the Korean War ever were embraced by the American people. This lack of patriotic sentiment was further evidence of the disconnection between the average U.S. citizen and the bloody war that was being waged by American soldiers in Korea. On the other hand, with the onset of hostilities, the U.S. toy industry capitalized on the opportunity to promote its war-like product lines aimed at young male American children. Several U.S. toy manufacturers, notably Hasbro, successfully marketed "G.I. Joe" and similar action figures equipped with replicas of weapons and clothing based on those actually being used by U.S. forces in Korea. Since virtually all of these weapons and clothing were the same as those used by U.S. forces in World War II, no great degree of research and retooling was necessary. The publishers of comic books like Marvel Comics and DC Comics, targeted at boys and young men, also took immediate advantage of the Korean War by producing dozens of new titles depicting heroic American soldiers killing barbaric North Koreans, and later Red Chinese soldiers. These toys and comic books did not attempt to synchronize with the U.S. government's war themes, but were largely designed to gratuitously gratify the psychological and entertainment needs of young, male American children. Nor is there any evidence that the government ever attempted to harness the creative energies of these industries to support their propaganda goals.

Although Americans fought valiantly in Korea and many received medals for bravery, none achieved the public recognition given to military heroes in the two world wars, like Sergeant Alvin York in the First World War and Audie Murphy in the Second World War. And while comedian Bob Hope and a few other entertainment industry celebrities continued the tradition of staging U.S.O. Christmas show tours in Korea, the commitment of film studios, radio networks, and most other popular culture stars were decidedly less than in those two previous conflicts. No U.S. bond drives were needed; no rationing was imposed; no calls to mobilize the home front were issued. In short, the Korean Conflict never captured the attention or deeply involved the American people.

ANALYSIS

In marketing terms, the Truman administration never sold the public on the need for the United States to engage in a prolonged war. Truman never called for the comprehensive sacrifices that were demanded of the people during World War I and World War II. By describing the conflict as a "Police Action," he trivialized the war and gave the public reason to believe it was likely to be of short duration, requiring limited sacrifice. Unlike Franklin Delano Roosevelt, his predecessor in the White House, Truman never mastered the role of the communicator, disdaining regular broadcast talks with the American public, and maintaining an adversary relationship with the news media.

By 1952 Americans were frustrated with the U.S. military's inability to win a clear victory, and the long-term stalemate along the 38th Parallel that had ensued. They wanted to pursue their own lives and their own interests. Most were not psychologically prepared or motivated to engage in the long conflict between world communism and the Free World that began almost immediately after victory was achieved over the Axis powers. Modern practitioners of marketing could have predicted that human behavior problems would arise when the U.S. public was asked to radically alter what it had been previously led to believe by the government. The new theme, "We must fight global communism" had suddenly replaced "We defeated our Axis enemies, and Americans can now enjoy a world at peace." Modern marketers know that the average person does not usually develop a fixed idea about another person, product, or idea immediately. It takes time for perceptions to develop. This is because the average person already has preconceptions about a wide variety of things. The more a preconception has been positively reinforced, the more difficult it is to dislodge that conception in place of another. This is essentially the difficulty that the Truman administration experienced with American public opinion during the Korean War.

President Truman, without consulting the American people, announced that America was going into battle to protect one Far Eastern country (South Korea) from another (North Korea) for reasons that were not clearly understood or accepted. Unlike the unexpected attack by the Japanese on our military forces in the Pacific that largely destroyed our fleet at Pearl Harbor, there was no immediate opportunity for the government to exploit the nation's outrage at the onset of the Korean War.

On the other hand, there was little consternation expressed by the U.S. public in the beginning because Americans generally have felt that they are "the good guys," and have responsibilities for protecting the weak from "the bad guys." Besides, most Americans incorrectly assumed that once a few units of the previously omnipotent American military arrived in Korea, the battle would be over. Few Americans had any idea that the North Korean attack was part of a global communist strategy directed by the Soviet Union that had already been acted upon in other parts of the world, notably in Greece and Central Europe. The U.S. public also did not comprehend how weak America's military power had become in the years following World War II.

When American troops went into combat and increasing numbers of GIs began to be wounded, captured, and killed as they were forced to retreat, American public opinion was totally unprepared for this eventuality. The public's negative attitudes about supporting the war were exacerbated by the fact that President Truman did not call for total mobilization of the U.S. military and civilian population, as U.S. presidents had done at the onset of World War I and World War II. It was difficult for most Americans to justify significant numbers of U.S. casualties while participating in a "Police Action." While President Truman did call up military reserves to active duty and accelerated the military draft, the concept of every American being involved in this fight was not invoked by the administration as it had been in previous wars. The American people remained emotionally detached from the war in Korea, focusing primarily on domestic issues in the United States and getting on with their own lives.

In the aftermath of the cease-fire, few Americans took note of another battle that had been going on in South East Asia since shortly after the end of the World War II—between Communist guerrillas under Ho Chi Minh in the north and French military forces in the south who were attempting to recolonize Vietnam after the occupying Japanese Army had surrendered. Even before the conflict started in Korea in June 1950, the American government was providing the beleaguered French Colonial Forces with military supplies.[34] The definitive Battle of Dienbienphu—in which Communist Viet Minh forces overwhelmed the cream of the French Colonial Forces —was fought only four months after the guns had grown quiet in Korea in July 1953.[35]

5

The Domino Theory War—Vietnam

AMERICA AFTER THE KOREAN WAR ENDED

The Gap between the Generations

Today, marketers would consider it unthinkable to launch a promotional campaign targeted at the American public without first conducting a SWOT analysis (Strengths, Weaknesses, Opportunities, and Threats) that examines, among other things, every aspect of a target audience's cultural and economic environment that might influence their consumer behavior.

Unfortunately for Presidents Truman, Eisenhower, Kennedy, and Johnson, in the 1950s and early 1960s these now commonly applied marketing insights about the *pathos* (as articulated by Aristotle) of the new American generation that was emerging were not available to them and their administrations. They were obliged to make fateful and flawed decisions about the country's foreign policies in Southeast Asia that were to ultimately rip apart the fabric of American society in the late 1960s and early 1970s more than any time since the Civil War.

The Cultural Divide

A clear dividing line exists in American cultural history between those born in the period between the middle 1940s and the late 1950s, and those who began life in earlier decades. The culture of the "Baby Boomer" generation was radically different from the "Greatest Generation" or the "Silent Generation" it followed. And those differences produced a social and political environment that led to disastrous consequences for America during the Vietnam War, both domestically and in Southeast Asia.

Born after the Second World War ended, the Baby Boomers were not influenced by the specter of the Great Depression and the world war that followed, as were earlier generations. This was "the first generation to be concerned with being happy," says historian Steve Gillion.[1] America's involvement in the Vietnam Conflict was incompatible with the Baby Boomers' philosophy.

Domestic Issues Prevail

When the fighting in Korea ended in 1953, America was caught in a political maelstrom. The hunt for domestic Communists in government and elsewhere in the United States by Senator Joseph R. McCarthy and his right wing allies had intensified. Fear of Communist infiltration within American society and the expansion of global communism were ceaselessly promoted by these political factions as a dire threat to the nation. Even President Dwight D. Eisenhower and his Republican administration were put on the defensive as ultra-anticommunists challenged his domestic and foreign policies, accusing him of "failing to fight Communism effectively."[2]

Most Americans did not question the policies of their government in the late 1940s and early 1950s. They were essentially disengaged. The group coming of age at this time was termed "The Silent Generation" by *Time*, although its passive behavior was shared by a large majority of the U.S. public.[3] This then was the *context* in which succeeding U.S. administrations formed foreign policy aimed at thwarting the spread of global communism.

The style of President Eisenhower and his administration was a reflection of this era, conducting the business of government at a "slow, soporific, conservative tempo" that "deflated anxiety, bringing reassurance."[4] Eisenhower continued the foreign policies initiated by President Truman intended to halt the spread of communism, which like his predecessor's were heavily focused on preserving the unity of those America's allies in Western Europe composing the NATO alliance. A cornerstone of the Eisenhower administration's foreign policy was the formulation of the "Domino Theory," a political proposition suggesting that if one nation in a region fell to the Communists, all the others in the surrounding area would follow. "You have a row of dominoes set up, and you knock over the first one, and what will happen to the last one is the certainty that it go over very quickly, so you have the beginning of a disintegration that would have the most profound influences," President Eisenhower said.[5]

How American Involvement in Vietnam Began

America's descent into the bloody quagmire that became the Vietnam War was prompted by the Japanese surrender to the Allies, concluding the Second World War. Only weeks after hostilities ended in early August 1945, British Commonwealth troops accepted the surrender of Japanese forces in that region and occupied the southern part of Vietnam. The Allied Command asked Chiang Kai-Shek and his Chinese military forces to cross the common border between the two countries and temporarily retake control of the northern part of Vietnam from the Japanese.

From that point forward, the misconceived and badly executed policies of five successive U.S. presidents over the next four decades contributed to the military debacle in Vietnam that ultimately resulted in America losing its first war. The U.S. government's woeful attempts at justifying its ever increasing involvement in Vietnam were to provide future U.S. presidents with a textbook case on *how to avoid* similar problems in persuading the American public to support the wars they wanted to wage.

The United States Helps France to Recolonize Vietnam

While the U.S. government was generally pursuing a postwar policy of encouraging national independence of former colonized nations, its English and French allies were reluctant to give up their former colonial possessions when World War II was over. Shortly after the British troops arrived, they freed French colonial troops previously captured by the Japanese and rearmed them so that they could reestablish sovereignty over Saigon and all the other parts of Vietnam which they had formerly ruled. A brief battle then was fought between the French and the insurgent Viet Minh troops led by Ho Chi Minh over control of Saigon. The Viet Minh soldiers were pushed out of the city into the surrounding countryside. This was the opening battle of a nine-year war between the French Colonial Army and the Vietnamese followers of Ho Chi Minh that continued until the catastrophic military defeat of French forces at Dien Bien Phu on May 8, 1954.[6]

One of the great unknowns is whether Ho Chi Minh was a Vietnamese nationalist who was driven into the arms of the Communists by U.S. indifference to his early pleas for assistance in establishing an independent Vietnam, or a committed Communist from the beginning who worked to impose a Marxist form of government on Vietnam. It cannot be questioned, however, that Ho Chi Minh's fight to establish a government controlled by the Vietnamese ultimately resulted in his total embrace of the Soviet Union and its Communist allies who were happy to provide him and his forces with weapons and material to sustain effective combat. This decision placed Ho on a collision course with a U.S. foreign policy resolved to prevent global communism from establishing a beachhead in Southeast Asia.

Aftermath of the Korean War

At the end of the Korean War, U.S. foreign policy established by President Eisenhower was driven by the fear that the Soviet Union in Europe and the People's Republic of China in Asia would attempt to further expand their spheres of influence into surrounding nations. The U.S. government chose to support the French government as it recolonized Vietnam, considering any alternative to a communist takeover a more desirable scenario. So the U.S. began to provide funding and noncombat military assistance to the beleaguered French Colonial Forces who were fighting against Ho's Viet Minh army in the north, as well as trying to suppress communist guerrilla resistance against the French and their anticommunist Vietnamese allies in the south.

By the time the warring parties concluded a peace accord in Geneva in 1954, resulting in the French agreeing to a cease-fire and the surrender of North Vietnam to the Communist Viet Minh, the United States already had 700 military advisors in South Vietnam.[7] *The New York Times* of July 21 ran this front-page headline: "Indochina Armistice Is Signed; Vietnam Split at 17th Parallel; U.S. Finds It Can 'Respect' Pact." By now, financial aid provided by the U.S. government was accounting for 80 percent of French expenditures in Indochina.[8] That commitment was only the start of the Americanization of the Vietnam War.

American Involvement in South Vietnam Begins to Escalate

Both before and after the signing of the Geneva Accords, the United States was supporting military efforts against communist forces by the South Vietnamese Government under the weak leadership of Emperor Bao Dai. However, it wasn't until June 1954 when U.S. Secretary of State John Foster Dulles and other influential U.S. leaders endorsed an ardent anticommunist Vietnamese exile named Ngo Dinh Diem as Bao Dai's Prime Minister that America began displacing the French as the primary sponsor of the South Vietnam government. Commenting on why Diem was endorsed for the job by the United States, Dulles said, "We knew of no one better."[9] Within five months, the United States announced that it was "planning to take over the training of South Vietnam's national army from the French."[10] By the fall of 1955, Diem had deposed Emperor Bao Dai in a disputed referendum vote and installed himself as the South Vietnamese Chief of State.

Democratic President John F. Kennedy replaced Republican Dwight D. Eisenhower in the White House in 1961, but the "Domino Theory" aimed at containing global communism expansionism remained a fundamental element of America's foreign policy. President Kennedy lauded the Diem regime as "the cornerstone of the Free World in Southeast Asia," and Vice President Lyndon Johnson "hailed Diem as the reincarnation of Winston

Churchill," following a visit to his country in 1961.[11] Despite U.S. support, however, Diem's army failed to defeat the communist forces facing them.

Determined to keep this news from reaching the American public, Diem tried to censor U.S. correspondents' reports of his army's failures, as well as those reporting on the increasingly active role that U.S. military advisors were playing in actually fighting Vietnam's battles. The Kennedy administration supported him in this policy. On January 15 1962, President Kennedy was asked at a White House press conference if American soldiers were fighting in Vietnam, he said flatly, "No."[12] Untruthful statements like this and by others in the Kennedy administration began to erode the *ethos,* or source credibility, of the Government's communications with the American public.

In February 1962, the United States took further steps to support Diem's attempts to stifle the U.S. press covering the war in Vietnam. The American Embassy in Saigon issued a directive advising members of the U.S. Mission in Vietnam that "it is not . . . in our interest . . . to have stories indicating that Americans are leading and directing combat missions." In an early attempt at spin control, Secretary of State Dean Rusk warned the U.S. Mission not to permit reporters to go along with U.S. troops "whose nature [is] such that undesirable dispatches would be highly probable."[13] Concerned that the American people were not being properly informed about the war, "a number of U.S. military officers . . . expressed concern because they [were] being muzzled by the South Vietnamese government with the support of the United States government."[14] Reporting the truth of the situation to the American people was turning out to be an inconvenience for U.S. officials who preferred to conceal the fact that our main ally in Vietnam was seemingly incapable of defeating the Communists.

Although Diem remained in power for nine years, his arrogance, corrupt administration, and incompetence as head of state finally exhausted the patience of President Kennedy and his advisors, who were seeking the reform of the South Vietnamese government. Henry Cabot Lodge, jr., then U.S. Ambassador to Vietnam, tried to persuade Diem to leave the country, warning that the American public was growing critical of his repressive policies and that the U.S. Congress might not approve a new appropriations bill for Vietnam if he didn't comply. Diem refused, convinced the United States needed him as a bulwark against communist expansion. Diem told Lodge that he (Lodge) should be responsible for persuading Congress to continue providing financial assistance to his country. "If American opinion is in the state you describe," Diem said, "then it is up to you, Ambassador Lodge, to disintoxicate American opinion."[15]

Unable to persuade Diem to leave, Lodge encouraged a group of Diem's generals to depose him and put a new head of state in power. On November 1, 1963, the South Vietnamese military staged a coup in Saigon, during which Diem was killed.[16]

Three weeks later, John F. Kennedy was assassinated in Dallas, Texas. There is no evidence of a connection between these two assassinations.

LYNDON B. JOHNSON BECOMES PRESIDENT: U.S. ENGAGEMENT IN VIETNAM GROWS

There were only 12,000 U.S. military advisors and support personnel in Vietnam when Lyndon B. Johnson was hurriedly sworn into office as president in Dallas on November 22, 1963, following the death of John F. Kennedy. A public opinion poll conducted at that time indicated that 63 percent of Americans were paying "little or no attention to the situation" in Vietnam.[17]

While the U.S. public was still largely unaware and unconcerned about American military involvement in Vietnam in 1963, President Johnson was worried that it would become an increasing problem for his administration. Shortly after taking office, he had begun pressing for new legislation in Congress aimed at eliminating racial discrimination and poverty in the United States, a crucially important new initiative in his administration.

Determined not to allow America's growing involvement in Vietnam to become a distracting issue with Congress and the electorate, Johnson's Secretary of Defense, Robert J. McNamara, issued a directive to the U.S. Military Mission in Vietnam aimed at discouraging news correspondents in Saigon from filing negative stories that might affect U.S. public opinion. It said, "Indoctrination of military personnel in the importance of suppressing irresponsible and indiscreet statements is necessary" and warned American military advisors to restrict their conversations with reporters.[18] President Johnson and Robert McNamara's misguided understanding of the *use and control of public media* that led to their clumsy attempts to "spin" the news coverage emanating from Vietnam clearly set the pattern for a growing antagonism between the administration and news organizations in Washington and, especially, in Saigon.

Following the overthrow of the Diem Regime, a South Vietnamese general took control of the government, to be overthrown a few months later by another general, and yet again by a third. Reports by U.S. correspondents about the inadequacy of the South Vietnamese military and the instability of its government became increasingly negative, affecting American public opinion. A national public opinion poll indicated that the Johnson administration's handling of the conflict in Vietnam had dropped from an earlier approval rating of 57 percent to 43 percent by the end of March 1964.[19]

President Johnson, perhaps more than any of his predecessors in the White House since Franklin D. Roosevelt, understood the importance of maintaining the support of Congress and the American people if he was to accomplish his domestic agenda. While public concern about America's involvement was still relatively limited in early 1964, he understood that a deeper U.S. engagement in Vietnam resulting in growing casualties could sharpen the public's misgiving.[20] President Johnson was as deeply committed to the support of a U.S. foreign policy guided by the "Domino Theory" as Presidents Kennedy and Eisenhower had been before him. At the same time, he was facing the upcoming presidential elections of 1964 in which he would be running against Barry S. Goldwater, a hawkish Republican Senator who was an outspoken advocate of taking a more aggressive U.S. strategy against the communists in Vietnam.

To tighten control over the news that the public was receiving, President Johnson's administration established a centralized system for the dissemination of information concerning Vietnam in June 1964. In Saigon, an experienced U.S. Information Agency public affairs officer, Barry Zorthian, was named a public relations "czar," with overall authority "to marshal whatever resources he needed ... to move reporters to the positive side of the story."[21] He worked in collaboration with General William C. Westmoreland, soon to be named Commander of the U.S. Military Assistance Command in Vietnam.

Zorthian placed particular emphasis on having "the Defense and State Departments to ensure that information released by officials in Washington coincided with the word from Saigon." In addition, they "began to push for a program to bring editors, businessmen, and other American opinion leaders to Saigon, where they could be exposed to the importance of what the United States was accomplishing. Returning home, those dignitaries and celebrities could then make special appearances to talk about what they had seen."[22] This was a brazen scheme to exploit seemingly neutral third parties with no apparent vested interest in championing American involvement in Vietnam whose *source credibility* would be regarded with less suspicion by the American public than more biased government officials. Criticizing this scheme, Malcolm Brown of the Associated Press and other correspondents based in Saigon said the free junkets for stateside celebrities and journalists put the recipients under a psychological obligation to follow the official line.[23]

The "Visit Vietnam" program was a basic strategy of the United States Information Agency (USIA), whose leadership believed in identifying the "politically or culturally elite ... opinion leaders and individuals" in a position to influence others rather than appeal to the masses directly. Leo Bogart quotes a USIA report that stated, "We should think of our audiences as channels rather than as receptacles" and "It is more important to reach one journalist than ten housewives or five doctors."[24] In modern marketing terms, the program was designed to generate "third party endorsements" of U.S. policy in Vietnam. This technique is based on the principle that seemingly disinterested U.S. citizens with credible reputations would have a more powerful influence on positively swaying American public opinion if they endorsed the government's Vietnam policy than if Johnson administration representatives expressed positive statements about it. The technique re-called George Creel's creation of the "Four Minute Men" of World War I who were trained to give seemingly impromptu talks in support of the war.

During Lyndon Johnson's 1964 presidential campaign for reelection, he positioned himself as a peacemaker and labeled Goldwater a warmonger. President Johnson repeatedly stated that "the United States seeks no wider war" and dismissed the idea of further bombing and blockading of North Vietnam's ports as "no solution."[25] At the same time, he succeeded in largely neutralizing right wing criticism of his platform when on August 4, 1964, he ordered U.S. forces to bomb targets in North Vietnam in retaliation for what he alleged were two attacks by North Vietnamese torpedo boats on American destroyers cruising in the Gulf of Tonkin off the coast of North Vietnam. A front-page headline in *The New York Times* that same day said, "U.S. Planes Attack North Vietnam Bases; President Orders 'Limited' Retaliation After Communists' PT Boats Renew Raids." The day after he ordered these attacks, both Houses of Congress almost unanimously passed a resolution granting President Johnson authority "to take all necessary measures to repel any armed attack against the forces of the United States and to prevent any further aggression."[26] In later years, this incident in the waters off the coast of North Vietnam was judged by many to be an invented provocation justifying the administration's determination to escalate direct U.S. combat involvement in Vietnam.

In November 1964, American voters gave Lyndon Johnson a landslide victory over his Republican opponent Barry Goldwater. "He had deflected Goldwater's early attempts to rally right wing sentiment against him, and his readiness to bomb North Vietnam had immunized him against charges of being 'soft' on Communism."[27] Three months after his inauguration in January 1965, President Johnson ordered the increased and continuous bombing of North Vietnam and began dispatching more U.S. troops to South Vietnam.

A Marketing Blunder—Promising the Consumer What You Don't Deliver

More than any of the American presidents who preceded his involve-ment in the Vietnam Conflict, President Johnson violated one of the most basic of marketing principles—promising the consumer a product that you don't deliver. The bond of credibility on which successful marketing depends is based on the expectation that you never make a promise to your consumer audience you can't or won't perform. Yet this is precisely what President Johnson did when he persuaded the American people that if elected presi-dent he would end the war in Vietnam without the commitment of American combat troops or an extension of the bombing campaign in North Vietnam. In his desperation to defeat Senator Goldwater, he promised the electorate that he wouldn't escalate American involvement in the Vietnam War, although he knew he would be unlikely to be able to deliver on this promise. In doing so, he initiated a foreign policy that would inevitably cause an increasing number of Americans to feel he had betrayed them. It ultimately lost him the trust of the country and the opportunity to be reelected in 1968.

Controlling the Flow of Information

When Lyndon B. Johnson became U.S. president in 1963, he shared the late President Kennedy's concerns about the impact that news media reporting from Vietnam would have on American public opinion. Soon after taking office, he addressed these concerns with his advisors who proposed that he approve a public relations campaign designed to "educate the American people" as the United States continued to escalate its military presence in the country. President Johnson, a wily politician, was initially reluctant, concerned that "educating the public was simply another way of preparing the country for a wider war in Vietnam. I think if you start doing it," "they're going to be hollering, 'You're a warmonger.'"[28] However, he agreed to proceed, instructing the State Department to develop "a broad program to bring to the American people a complete and accurate picture of the United States involvement in Southeast Asia."[29]

In the years that followed, the Johnson administration and later the Nixon administration found themselves increasingly in conflict with the news media in Vietnam and in the United States. As public opinion turned against them and their conduct of the war, both Presidents Johnson and Nixon inevitably blamed the news media for their predicament. In 1980, seven years after the last U.S. combat units were evacuated from South Vietnam, President-elect Ronald Reagan continued this refrain when he said that Vietnam had been a "noble cause" and that the war had been lost only because of American "self-imposed restraints."[30]

Television Changes American Politics

In 1950, when President Truman ordered American military forces to fight in Korea, less than 10 percent of the country's households owned a television set, and U.S. television broadcasters had not yet established national capability. A coast-to-coast television connection did not occur until September 1951, when President Truman gave an address that was carried by ninety-four stations, reaching 95 percent of the country's television homes, with an audience estimated at about 1 million. By the time President Johnson ordered American warplanes to start bombing North Vietnam in 1964, 92 percent of the nation's 52 million homes owned at least one television set. The average viewer was spending almost five and a half hours each day viewing television in their homes. The three major television networks were regularly broadcasting nightly news shows distributed by 526 affiliated stations simultaneously from coast to coast.[31]

"Extensive television coverage of national events in the early 1960s caused Americans to start considering network television their primary source of immediate information. . . . Regular network television news coverage was dramatically expanded as all three networks increased their evening news shows from fifteen minutes to the half-hour format that presently prevails."[32]

Vietnam was the first war in which television became the primary news medium for most Americans and has often been characterized as "television's war." Until the early 1960s, the U.S. public depended on the print media and, to some extent radio, to tell them what was happening in the world. During the Korean War, television news programs did broadcast newsreel-like film clips of the combat, but in the early 1950s most Americans still relied on the older forms of news media for their news.

But by 1964, television news in the United States was having a powerful impact on the ways the country regarded both its government and the war in which America was becoming progressively more engaged in Southeast Asia. Filmed reports from television correspondents like CBS's Morley Safer were being carried nightly on network television news shows, causing viewers to experience the fighting in a more intense and immediate way than in previous wars. The use of lightweight film and sound equipment allowed television news teams to get closer to the action, and the accelerated delivery of filmed reports to the United States on jet aircraft reduced the time delay between the moment the event occurred and when it appeared on the nation's TV screens. The introduction of color television in the early 1960s further heightened the public's sense of the war's bloody reality. By the late 1960s, when the Vietnam War was at its bloodiest, there were 100 million televisions in the United States; at the time of the Korean War there were only 10 million.[33]

President Johnson Escalates the War in Vietnam

In early March 1965, President Johnson decided to escalate American involvement in the war without acknowledging this fact to the American public. He ordered a fleet of U.S. Air Force bombers, accompanied by South Vietnamese aircraft, to attack North Vietnamese military facilities in retaliation for previous attacks on U.S. installations. His Secretary of Defense, Robert J. McNamara, described the bombing attacks as "a means of communication. Bombs were metaphors meant to win the North Vietnamese to a recognition of America's inevitable victory, and American planes dropped what came to be known as 'bomb-o-grams' on civilian as well as military targets, less for tactical than for rhetorical reasons."[34]

A few days later, the force level of U.S. troops in Vietnam—23,500 by this time—was increased when 3,500 U.S. Marines landed at the American air base in Da Nang. This was the first U.S. infantry unit to enter the war, although their initial mission was ostensibly to protect the American air base. Shortly after the Marine battalions arrived, they began combat operations in the surrounding region.[35] When President Johnson ordered Secretary of Defense Robert J. McNamara to send the Marine combat units to Vietnam, he also advised him to "minimize the announcement."[36] Frank Rich of *The New York Times* observed that vintage film clips show Mr. McNamara "promoting good news and suppressing the bad as the war turns sour...."[37]

President Johnson's decisions were driven by the conviction that it was vital to America's strategic interests to stand fast in Vietnam against Communist domination or face the ultimate loss of all of Southeast Asia to global communism. He was also burdened by the tendency to personalize any criticism of his Vietnam policies, whether by members of Congress, the news media, or the American people. These beliefs led him to continually accede to the requests by General William Westmoreland (now Commander of all U.S. Armed Forces in Vietnam) for additional American combat units while concealing from the U.S. public the changed nature of the war. General Westmoreland, like most of the senior officers in command at that time, was also uncomfortable with the idea of too freely sharing information with the public. He was quoted as saying, "Vietnam was the first war ever fought without any censorship. Without censorship, things can get terribly confused in the public mind."[38]

It was not until June 1965, that President Johnson finally acknowledged to the American people that he had sent U.S. combat units into offensive operations in Vietnam. By the end of that year, 180,000 American troops were serving in South Vietnam.

Protests against the War Begin in the United States

Until early 1965, most Americans supported Johnson administration policies in Vietnam. But shortly after the first Marines waded ashore at Da Nang, those sentiments began to change, starting on U.S. college campuses. The first "teach-in," an all-night protest against the war by professors and students, occurred at the University of Michigan on March 24, 1965. "I think the students of the universities are coming out of a long sleep," said one professor. "The silent generation may have given way to the stirred-up generation."[39]

Opposition to the war began to be voiced by students in Washington, DC, as well. On April 17, 1965, a crowd of more than 15,000 demonstrators, organized by Students for a Democratic Society (SDS), joined to protest against the war in front of the Capitol Building. By mid-May, professors and students on 122 college campuses were involved in a nationally broadcast radio debate about the war.[40] Many potential draftees tore up or burned their draft cards in front of induction centers, leading to the passage of federal legislation providing severe penalties for the destruction of military draft registration cards.[41]

The White House sought to neutralize campus protests, first by publishing and widely distributing a State Department White Paper on Vietnam "intended to prove that the war in Vietnam had been forced on the United States which now had the moral responsibility to support the government in South Vietnam." The Johnson administration then dispatched an Inter-Departmental Speaking Team on Vietnam Policy that included two lieutenant colonels who had served in Vietnam to present its case at a number of midwestern college campuses. According to *Time*, "the reception of the 'truth team' was chilly where it was not downright hostile...."[42]

The administration continued its public relations campaign, with senior government officials making speeches accusing those opposed to U.S. involvement in Vietnam of being appeasers. This triggered a harsh rebuttal from U.S. Senator Wayne Morse, an outspoken critic of the administration's Vietnam policy. Speaking on the floor of the Senate, he said, "I warn the American people that a propaganda drive has been started by spokesmen for the Johnson administration to interfere with one of their most precious, fundamental liberties and freedoms, namely the right of free men to criticize the government."[43]

The public controversy over President Johnson's handling of the war broadened when a former administration ally, Democratic Senator William Fulbright, Chairman of the powerful Foreign Relations Committee, held Senate hearings to critically examine President Johnson's Vietnam policies in early 1966. The president attempted to neutralize the negative impact of these hearings on public opinion by seizing the headlines at a hastily arranged conference in Honolulu with the South Vietnamese head of state, Nguyen Cao Ky, at the same time the hearings were taking place in Washington. Following these hearings, however, President Johnson's approval ratings for his handling of Vietnam plummeted from 63 percent positive to 49 percent positive, with a growing number of Americans expressing the belief that America should withdraw from Vietnam.[44]

The Johnson administration's PR campaign to win the support of the American people for his Vietnam policies was dealt another severe blow late in 1966 when *The New York Times* published a series of stories written in North Vietnam by Pulitzer Prize winning journalist Harrison Salisbury. He confirmed North Vietnamese claims that the United States was bombing civilian areas of Hanoi. The Defense Department initially denied, but subsequently acknowledged, the probability of unintended destruction of civilian areas. Salisbury, who was assistant managing editor of the *Times*, was accused of disloyalty by a senior Pentagon official who sarcastically said he was writing for "*The New Hanoi Times.*"[45]

In 1967, U.S. civil rights leader Martin Luther King joined those opposing the war. In a speech titled, "Declaration of Independence from the

War in Vietnam," King condemned the expanding American presence in Vietnam, largely because he believed it would drain away resources from vital social programs in the United States. "...I knew that America would never invest the necessary funds or energies in rehabilitation of the poor so long as Vietnam continued to draw men and skills and money like some demonic, destructive suction tube."[46]

By this time, President Johnson was seriously apprehensive about the antipathy of the American people toward the war. He ordered General Westmoreland to collect hard data demonstrating that progress in Vietnam was being made. "When he [President Johnson] encountered an extremely optimistic appraisal of the situation in the II Corps Zone, for example, he insisted that the commanders of the other three corps write similar reports so that he could use them in his dealings with the press."[47] Michael J. Arlen noted in *Living Room War* that the American public "wants and needs hard news, something concrete amid the chaos....The public also presumably wants and needs a sense of progress."[48] By generating statistics showing an increasing number of Viet Cong body counts, the administration hoped to fulfill that need for demonstrable progress in the war. "All they ever cared about was body counts," said former Gunner's Mate Gus Kerkoulas, then manning a .50 caliber machinegun on a U.S. Navy patrol boat in the Mekong Delta region. "We were told to shoot at anything that moved on the river banks."[49]

Concerned that his credibility was wearing thin with the public, the news media, and members of Congress, President Johnson ordered General Westmoreland to return to the United States and testify before the House of Armed Services Committee. General Westmoreland told the committee "that American forces were gaining the upper hand in South Vietnam and they would begin to turn the fighting over to the South Vietnamese within two years."[50] This was a classic marketing application of borrowing credibility from a well-respected source (*ethos*), to support your own less credible reputation with the audience you are trying to influence. It is a common practice of consumer marketers to employ respected celebrities like basketball icon Michael Jordan or golf champion Tiger Woods to endorse their products, thereby enhancing their brand's image.

Early in the morning on January 31, 1968, North Vietnamese Army and Viet Cong guerilla forces launched a coordinated surprise attack on towns and cities throughout South Vietnam during the traditional cease-fire period of Tet, the Vietnamese New Year. The U.S. Embassy and General Westmoreland's headquarters in Saigon were also targets of these well-coordinated attacks.

This was a devastating blow to President Johnson's campaign to rally American public support for his administration's efforts to wage the war in Vietnam. Although most of the attackers were killed or driven off throughout South Vietnam, communist forces occupied the ancient imperial city of

Hue for more than three weeks before they were either killed or ousted. As images of the fighting flooded television screens in American homes each night, public support for President Johnson's leadership faded. "The country's trust in his authority had evaporated. His credibility—the key to a president's capacity to govern—was gone," said Stanley Karnow.[51] After CBS Network news anchor Walter Cronkite told his viewers that it was time for the United States to get out of Vietnam, President Johnson reportedly said, "It's all over."[52] At this point, there were more than a half million American troops in Vietnam.[53]

HOLLYWOOD FILMS AND POPULAR SONGS

Films

Hollywood motion pictures produced during the Vietnam War reflected the cultural and political shifts that were taking place in the United States during the late 1960s and early 1970s. Just as during the Korean War, the U.S. government made no effort to influence the Hollywood studios to support White House foreign policy by producing films about U.S. involvement in the Vietnam War, except for *The Green Berets*.

In 1968, the year that *The Green Berets*, a Hollywood action/adventure movie about the Army's Special Forces starring John Wayne premiered, U.S. forces in Vietnam were at the most intensive stage of combat against the Communists. Totally pro-war in its sentiment, the action film was produced on location at Fort Benning, Georgia (headquarters of the Special Forces) with the encouragement and cooperation of the U.S. government. "This picture is naturally from the hawk's point of view," said John Wayne, who was also the film's director.[54] When the film opened, *The New York Times* critic described it as "sick ... an outrage ... a travesty."[55]

The Green Berets was hailed by supporters of U.S. military involvement in Vietnam and attacked by those with antiwar opinions. Demonstrations—and even the bombing of movie theaters—accompanied its screenings in the United States and in other countries. *The Green Berets* was the only major motion picture about the Vietnam War that was produced while American troops were engaged in combat that championed the U.S. government's position on fighting the war. It was also the only commercially produced motion picture during that period that was actively endorsed by the U.S. government, which also provided the filmmakers with significant technical and logistical support.

Hollywood had produced two major motion pictures about Vietnam before American combat troops began fighting there. They were Joseph L. Mankiewicz's *The Quiet American* (1957), from the Graham Greene novel of the same name, and *The Ugly American* (1963), starring Marlon Brando.

Both films, produced by Universal International and United Artists respectively, supported the view that America was trying to help the Vietnamese people and that the communists were attempting to subjugate them.

Hollywood studios also distributed a number of inexpensively produced action/adventure films about Vietnam before major American military involvement began. The first to use Vietnam as a setting was Paramount Pictures' *Saigon*, a 1947 action film about soldiers involved in a robbery, starring Alan Ladd and Veronica Lake. It was followed in 1952 by Columbia Pictures' *A Yank in Indochina*, about American fliers in a guerilla war; Warner Bros.' *Jump into Hell*, (1955), depicting French paratroopers' struggle at the ill-fated siege of Dien Bien Phu; 20th Century Fox's two Cinemascope productions, *China Gate*, (1957), and *Five Gates to Hell* (1959), an action film involving American nurses, starring Gene Barry, Angie Dickinson, and Nat King Cole.[56] While these films largely focused on action, they all characterized the communists as oppressors trying to dominate the people of Vietnam.

As American troops in Vietnam began engaging in combat, and U.S. casualties started mounting in the mid-1960s, more socially conscious motion pictures began being produced by Hollywood that dealt with the war resistance movement. These films responded to the sensibilities of younger, more rebellious audiences as well as reflecting their growing sense of alienation and anger against the traditional values of American society, as well as the war that was now intruding into every aspect of American culture. Almost without exception, these films reflected a hostile attitude toward the American government's policies in Vietnam that was strongly tied to younger Americans' concerns about the burgeoning military draft. There is no evidence that the U.S. government ever attempted to influence the content of these films as they had done so directly during World War II.

Brian de Palma's *Greetings* (1968), starring Robert De Niro, was the first major Hollywood motion picture made during the war that dramatized the growing war resistance movement. Three films with similar themes were released in 1969. Arthur Penn's *Alice's Restaurant* depicted the attempts of folk singer Arlo Guthrie to avoid military service. *Hail, Hero!*, starring Michael Douglas, presented the problems of a pacifist soldier returning from Vietnam. And Haskell Wexler's *Medium Cool* portrayed a television news cameraman's transition from an uninvolved observer to a participant in the antiwar movement. Richard Rush's *Getting Straight* (1970) starred Elliott Gould as a returning Vietnam veteran on a college campus who fails to successfully adapt to civilian life. It is almost impossible to judge the specific impact that the release of these films had on influencing American public opinion during that time, but it is reasonable to assume that they played some role in deepening the divisions that already existed concerning the country's military involvement in Vietnam.

Many Hollywood films, such as Martin Scorcese's *Taxi Driver* (1976), Michael Cimino's *The Deer Hunter* (1978), Francis Ford Coppola's *Apocalypse Now* (1979), Oliver Stone's *Platoon* (1986) and Stanley Kubrick's *Steel Metal Jacket* (1987) were produced after U.S. troops were withdrawn from Vietnam. They are not dealt with here because they had no impact on American public opinion during the years when American forces were fighting in Vietnam.

Songs

Popular songs became the anthems of both the pro-war and antiwar movements in America during the late 1960s, as well as for many of the troops fighting in Vietnam. In at least one case, Peter Yarrow's song "Puff the Magic Dragon" was transformed from an "apparently innocent childhood fantasy sung by leading antiwar folksingers, into both the nickname of the deadliest of all gunships [used by the United States in Vietnam] and a sly celebration of marijuana," according to H. Bruce Franklin. Another song popular with American troops in Vietnam, Eric Burdon's rock song, "We Gotta Get Out of This Place," became such a matter of concern to the U.S. Military Command in Saigon that Armed Forces Vietnam Network was ordered to ban it from its radio broadcasts.[57]

Folksinger and antiwar activist Pete Seeger's "Waist Deep in the Big Muddy" became the focus of national attention in 1967 when the CBS Television Network demanded that the performer drop one verse of the song's lyric in a performance he had taped as part of the then popular *The Smother Brothers Comedy Hour*. Mr. Seeger refused and that song was cut from the broadcast by CBS, possibly because CBS executives feared the wrath of the White House. The lyric, "Now every time I read the papers, That old feelin' comes on, We're waist deep in the Big Muddy, and the big fool says to push on," was considered by CBS Management to be a parable about President Johnson's escalation of U.S. military involvement in Vietnam, and which might have caused a political furor. Mr. Seeger publicly accused CBS of censorship, further fanning the flame of controversy.[58]

Another powerful challenge to the U.S. government's Vietnam military policy was the 1964 rock hit, "I-Feel-Like-I'm-Fixin'-to-Die Rag," performed by Country Joe and the Fish, which became one of the most popular songs of the antiwar movement, as well as with the troops fighting in Vietnam.[59]

Supporters of the pro-war government policy were equally committed in their choice of songs. One of the most popular tunes in this genre was U.S. Army Special Forces Sergeant Barry Sadler's "Ballad of the Green Berets," a patriotic paean to the soldiers of this Special Operations branch of the Army. Sergeant Sadler wrote the tune while recuperating from wounds suffered in Vietnam. By early 1966, the song had sold almost half a million copies in the

United States.[60] According to H. Bruce Franklin, the song, distributed as part of an RCA Victor album, was actively promoted by "the Pentagon, other corporations, and pro-war columnists." It was at the top of *Billboard's* ratings charts for five weeks and was the biggest-selling single record of 1966. John Wayne used it as the theme song of his film, *The Green Berets* in 1968.[61]

Other pro-war songs were particularly popular in the more rural parts of the country where military service was a long and honored custom and traditional values were more respected than in U.S. urban areas or on college campuses. Kris Kristofferson's "Viet Nam Blues," "I Told Them What You're Fighting for" and Merle Haggard's "Okie from Muskogee" received extensive play on the hundreds of country and western radio stations throughout the United States. That song and Haggard's "Fightin' Side of Me" became enormous hits and were regarded as "hard hat" anthems during the era when antiwar protests were at their height. The songs rejected "prevailing cultural forces in the 60s—leftist values and hippie ideals at the pinnacle of the Vietnam War. . . . "[62]

In 1971, a defiantly pro-war song called "Battle Hymn of Lt. Calley," which extolled the virtues of the officer held responsible for the My Lai Massacre, sold more than a million records in the United States.[63] The role that pro- and antiwar popular songs played in rallying the opposing factions of the public and articulating their feelings about the war was a powerful element in the divisions that sundered America in the late 1960s and early 1970s.

PRESIDENT JOHNSON DECLINES TO RUN FOR REELECTION

Demoralized by his lack of public support and challenged by fellow Democrats, President Johnson surprised the nation on March 31, 1968, when he announced that he would not run for reelection in November and would order a de-escalation of bombing in North Vietnam to allow negotiations to be reinitiated. Five days before the presidential elections, he ordered a complete halt to the bombing. President Johnson's unexpected announcements had a dramatic effect on his public approval rating, which jumped sharply upward.[64]

In November 1968, Richard Nixon was elected President of the United States. *The New York Times* front-page headline of November 7, 1968, reported, "Nixon Wins by a Thin Margin, Pleads for Reunited Nation."

THE NIXON YEARS

During his campaign to win the presidency, Richard Nixon abandoned all talk of winning the war in Vietnam. Instead, he claimed that he had a "secret plan to get the United States out of the Vietnam War if elected in

1968."[65] The Republican presidential candidate confided to a number of journalists that if he became president, "he would (1) arrange a summit meeting with the Soviet leaders to gain their help in ending the Vietnam War, and (2) seek to de-Americanize the Vietnam conflict."[66]

"Nixon promised what the public wanted: to end the war and win the peace," said Daniel Hallin. "He lowered the cost of the war while at the same time presenting himself, in contrast to his domestic opponents, as the one who would stand firm against the Communists and achieve peace with honor."[67]

Now, more than ever, the North Vietnamese and the United States were engaged in a propaganda campaign to win over public opinion in the United States and around the world. The North Vietnamese and their communist allies regularly trumpeted stories of alleged atrocities committed by U.S. troops against innocent Vietnamese peasants or the bombing of civilian targets in North Vietnamese cities. Since the North Vietnamese leadership imposed total censorship of news reports emanating from their country, objective reporting of these events was impossible.

On the other hand, the U.S. military in Vietnam was handicapped by its unwillingness to impose censorship and its inability to influence the frequently negative, but factual, news stories emanating from Saigon about the progress of the war that were being filed by United States and correspondents of other nationalities. In desperation, General Westmoreland resorted to heavy-handed attempts to cosmeticize the language that the U.S. Command was using to describe its combat operations. "Aware that the phrase *search and destroy* had come to connote indiscriminate violence against hapless civilians, he replaced the term in his command's lexicon with neutral phrases such as *spoiling attack* and *reconnaissance in force*."[68] A skeptical press ridiculed these PR ploys.

In the months following the inauguration in January 1969, the American public initially supported the new president, but began losing patience with him and his administration as little progress was made either in winning the war or securing a peace. In March 1969, the Gallup Poll reported "that the lack of progress in the war had begun to polarize American public opinion. Twenty-five percent of those responding to a recent survey favored escalation of the war, while another 21 percent opted for withdrawal." Fifteen percent wanted the United States to keep fighting as negotiations between the two sides sporadically continued; another 15 percent wanted the war to cease as quickly as possible.[69]

The Silent Majority Speech

The country became more and more divided about U.S. involvement in Vietnam as American combat casualties mounted. In mid-October 1969, the antiwar movement held a series of large rallies in Washington and other

U.S. cities and on college campuses across the country. Called "The Moratorium," the demonstrations were extensively covered by the news media, further undermining the President's attempts to maintain a strong military posture in Vietnam.[70] They were followed a month later by even greater protest demonstrations in Washington and other U.S. cities.

In early November 1969, President Nixon delivered his most notable speech about Vietnam to the nation, calling on the "great silent majority" of Americans to rally round him in opposition to those who disagreed with his administration's policies. He said that "the more support I can have from the American people, the sooner that pledge [of ending the war] can be redeemed. For the more divided we are at home, the less likely the enemy is to negotiate.... "[71] After delivering this speech, President Nixon's approval rating with the U.S. public jumped twelve points, indicating that a meaningful percentage of Americans still supported his Vietnam policy. But his subsequent policy decisions on Vietnam hampered his ability to sustain the support of the country.

Nixon Expands the War

In March 1969, President Nixon authorized American air attacks on communist sanctuaries in Cambodia and ordered U.S. troops into Cambodia soon after. For a time, administration spokesmen in Washington and Saigon refused to acknowledge that the United States had enlarged the war in a neighboring country in Southeast Asia even as a growing number of news outlets in the United States and elsewhere accurately reported the story based on information provided by anonymous sources within the U.S. Military Command. "With government institutions hardening to the press, official spokesmen were doing less than ever before either to sell the war to the American public or ensure that the news media had the information they needed to construct a rounded picture of events."[72]

Stung by news reports critical of President Nixon's handling of the war, senior administration and military officials struck back. Speaking to various influential U.S. audiences, they accused the news media of writing stories that were "inaccurate and misleading." Another said, "Bad news too often attracts the headlines.... In my opinion, we sell ourselves short by... focusing on the bad, the bizarre, and the big."[73] The administration arranged for Nixon supporters to celebrate an "Honor America Day" in Washington on the Fourth of July, 1969, demonstrating "Silent Majority" support for President Nixon's strategy. Administration spokesmen appeared on television talk shows, and the president's supporters "spent $100,000 on a major radio campaign."[74]

While a majority of Americans were still supporting President Nixon's decisions, he was determined to gain greater public approval of his policies by accelerating his program to bring U.S. troops back home. He also decided to make promotional capital out of this military policy. When the first U.S. Army Brigade returned to Seattle in midsummer, 1969, the troops were ordered to parade through the city. They were cheered by many, but were also jeered by demonstrators waving antiwar signs. U.S. media coverage of the event was limited and most of what did appear was negative.[75] The administration staged no more parades of troops when they returned home from Vietnam.

As the protests spread, the administration attempted to deprecate the antiwar movement. Vice President Spiro Agnew denounced the movement as "an effete core of impudent snobs," as he attempted to belittle it. Launching an all-out attack on those U.S. news media outlets that were not openly supporting the president, Agnew criticized "a small band of network commentators and self-appointed analysts" for expressing "hostility" to the administration's Vietnam policy.[76] The vice president "began assailing the news media as a small and unelected elite [that] do not . . . represent the view of America."[77] In the coming years of the Nixon presidency, these attacks were to become more strident and direct, particularly against the broadcast media.

The My Lai Massacre

Late in November 1969, *The New York Times* and other major newspapers broke the story of the killing of hundreds of unarmed civilians in the South Vietnamese village of My Lai by an American Army platoon in 1968.[78] Soon after the stories ran, the army charged and ultimately convicted the platoon's leader, First Lieutenant William Calley, for premeditated murder. The story of the My Lai Massacre had a major impact on the American public and contributed even greater impetus to the U.S. antiwar movement, not only in the United States, but around the world.

The Kent State University Killings

By early May 1970, antiwar protests were sweeping U.S. college campuses. During a protest rally at Kent State University in Ohio on May 4, Ohio National Guardsmen retreating under a shower of rocks, began shooting. Four students were killed.[79] Referring to the killing of the students shortly after the incident, President Nixon said that "when dissent turns to violence, it invites tragedy."[80]

In the aftermath of the Kent State killings, "more than four hundred universities and colleges shut down as students and professors staged strikes, and nearly a hundred thousand demonstrators marched on Washington. . . . "[81] A commission chosen by President Nixon to study the disturbances in American universities and colleges concluded that "the country was 'so polarized' that campuses might again explode in a fresh cycle of violence and repression, which would jeopardize 'the very survival of the nation.'"[82]

Incursion into Laos and the Pentagon Papers

President Nixon's approval ratings on Vietnam continued to slide as opponents of his policy in Congress, much of the news media and an increasingly vocal electorate voiced their disapproval of his actions. While continuing to withdraw U.S. ground troops from Vietnam, he expanded the war in Southeast Asia into Laos with a bombing campaign aimed at stopping North Vietnamese incursions from the north. By early June 1971 his approval rating on Vietnam had dropped to 31 percent, with almost three quarters of those polled saying that they favored setting a deadline for ending American involvement in Vietnam.[83]

In June 1971 the government's attempt to bolster public support was further undermined when *The New York Times* and other major American newspapers published a series of articles on a secret study made by the Pentagon of American participation in the Vietnam War. A front-page headline in the July 1, 1971 edition of *The New York Times* said, "Supreme Court, 6-3 Upholds Newspapers on Publication of the Pentagon Report; Times Resumes Its Series, Halted 15 Days." Termed the "Pentagon Papers," they were leaked to the newspaper by former Defense Department analyst Daniel Ellsberg who strongly disagreed with the policies being pursued by the U.S. government in Vietnam. Among other things, these articles revealed that President Johnson had been increasing the U.S. military presence and preparing for the opening phases of a sustained bombing campaign in North Vietnam in 1964 at the same time that he was assuring the American people that he would seek "no wider war."[84] The Nixon administration attempted to legally stop the publication of these documents but the U.S. Supreme Court ultimately ruled that the government could not suppress them in advance of publication. The revelations of the Pentagon Papers bolstered the suspicions of many Americans that the policies of the White House lacked credibility.

Nixon vs. the News Media

Beginning in 1971, a consensus developed in the Nixon White House that the antiwar movement had been co-opted by communists. The president also became convinced that he was surrounded by government officials who were leaking confidential information about the war to the press. To plug the leaks, "he ordered illegal wiretaps and surveillance of White House and State Department officials, as well as reporters."[85]

Convinced that a hostile U.S. press was distorting his message and hampering his ability to effectively communicate with the American public,

President Nixon launched a public relations campaign to overcome these obstacles. He demanded and was granted an opportunity to have two hours of the NBC Television Network's top-rated morning program "Today" devoted exclusively to his appearance; he arranged to have extensive interviews conducted on the other major television networks' highest rated news shows by popular newscasters like Walter Cronkite and Howard K. Smith; his daughter Tricia's wedding received extensive live network TV coverage, demonstrating the human side of the president. According to James Reston, a columnist for *The New York Times*, these efforts to increase President Nixon's public support were doomed to failure:

> His support on the conduct of the war is not falling because people don't like him or the venomous press is hostile to him or he isn't effective on television . . . but because he has not persuaded the people that the sacrifices in blood and money are going to achieve the "generation of peace" he talks so much about. . . . the Administration has advertised and dramatized its worst products, but they don't sell. . . . They are passing judgment, not on personality but on policy, and they obviously don't like what they see.[86]

In addition to his overt public relations efforts to win the support of the U.S. public, President Nixon also used covert methods to intimidate the broadcast media. Information about these activities only came to light with the later publication of memos and transcripts of tapes released by the National Archives, of conversations that were recorded during his administration in the White House.

The president's clandestine strategy was targeted primarily at the three television networks, ABC, CBS, and NBC, whose news programs and commentary were considered to be most influential on American public opinion. And the vehicle he used was the threat of a possible Justice Department antitrust suit aimed at their near monopoly of prime-time entertainment with their own programs. A *Washington Post* article reporting on the content of one of the White House tapes said

> a presidential aide named Chuck Colson told the President how NBC had readily agreed to a carry a prime-time special about the wedding of Nixon's daughter, Tricia, just days after all three networks had covered the June 12, 1971, White House wedding live. Colson had organized a nationwide network of Republicans and then prompted them to inundate NBC with telephone calls demanding a reprise of the wedding. Colson had then persuaded Gulf Oil Co. to sponsor the broadcast.[87]

Acting as President Nixon's point man in this realm, Colson met with each of the network presidents, and in a memo to the president noted the "obvious fear" the networks displayed. In another memo to the president's

Chief of Staff, H. Robert Haldeman, Colson wrote, "[The networks] are very much afraid of us and are trying hard to prove they are 'good guys.'" The tapes revealed that Mr. Colson particularly pressured the CBS Television Network, accusing them of "slanting the news." House of Representatives investigators subpoenaed CBS President Frank Stanton after his network aired a critical expose of Defense Department public relations activities called, "The Selling of the Pentagon." Mr. Stanton asked the White House for help. According to Mr. Colson, the CBS president "acknowledged the White House had been badly treated and at one point said he would be taking 'several steps to correct the situation.'" The issue of the CBS program was subsequently buried in a House legislative maneuver.[88]

U.S. print media judged to be hostile to President Nixon were also targeted for coercion. A memo written by Haldeman said, "The president feels very strongly that we need to develop a 'Letters to the Editor' and 'Calls to Broadcasters' program somewhere within the administration. . . . The president wanted a thorough and efficient Nixon network whose task will be to really raise hell with the people who unfairly take us on, and pour praise on those who take a more productive viewpoint." Through the Republican National Committee, a plan was developed to generate letters "on a moment's notice to either national publications or to the networks as soon as word came from the White House."[89]

The United States Withdraws from Vietnam

By early 1972, more than 400,000 U.S. troops had been withdrawn from Vietnam and American deaths in combat had been reduced to less than ten per week. At this point, U.S. public opinion polls credited President Nixon with an approval rating on his handling of the war of almost 60 percent. While he later ordered the mining of North Vietnam's principal port and intensified U.S. air attacks on the country, he won the presidential election of 1972 by a large margin. *The New York Times* front-page headline of November 8 stated, "Nixon Elected in Landslide. . . ." As Stanley Karnow notes, "The public response in the United States was relatively muted; with almost all the American troops home, the war had ceased to be a national torment."[90] According to Karnow, "The American public had been aware of the war in Vietnam in proportion to the number of American combat troops involved and the level of casualties they suffered. President Nixon's policy became, therefore, steadily to withdraw these troops, to pass the ground war over to the Vietnamese, to order the remaining GIs to fight as little as possible, and to switch the weight of the American attack to the air. Since the bombing campaign was not very evident to the American public, the war seemed to fade away."[91]

The peace accord was signed in Paris on January 27, 1973, after which the president said, "We have finally achieved peace with honor."[92] *The New*

York Times front-page headline on January 28 stated: "Vietnam Peace Pacts Signed; America's Longest War Halts." The newspaper described the war as "the longest, most divisive foreign war in America's history." On that same day, U.S. Secretary of Defense Melvin R. Laird announced the end of the military draft saying, "The armed forces henceforth would depend exclusively on volunteer soldiers, sailors, airmen and marines."[93]

Fifty-five thousand Americans soldiers died in Vietnam. More than 20,000 of them died after President Nixon assured the U.S. public in 1968 that he had a "secret plan" to end the war. More than 200,000 South Vietnamese soldiers died in combat. The combined war deaths of the North Vietnamese Army and the Viet Cong were believed to be about one half million. Two million Vietnamese civilians died in both the north and the south.[94]

VIETNAMIZATION FAILS AND THE COMMUNISTS TAKE OVER SOUTH VIETNAM

The North Vietnamese government released the last acknowledged U.S. prisoner of war in March 1973. But the fighting continued for two more years as the U.S.-supplied army of South Vietnam, now without American air support and U.S. military advisors, continued its struggle to contain the Viet Cong in the south and stop the North Vietnamese Army advancing from the north. By this time, President Nixon was deeply enmeshed in the Watergate scandal. He finally resigned from office August 9, 1974, rather than face the likelihood of impeachment proceedings. *The New York Times* front-page headline of August 9, 1974, reported, "Nixon Resigns."

The South Vietnamese Army began to collapse early in 1975 as North Vietnamese Army units accelerated their attacks. By the end of March, Communist forces were marching on South Vietnam's Capitol, Saigon. On April 23, 1975, U.S. President Gerald Ford, who had replaced the disgraced Spiro Agnew as vice president in 1973 and subsequently replaced the disgraced Richard Nixon in the White House, signaled the end of U.S. involvement in Vietnam. In a speech in New Orleans, Ford said, "Today, Americans can regain the sense of pride that existed before Vietnam. But it cannot be achieved by refighting a war that is finished. . . . These events, tragic as they are, portend neither the end of the world nor of America's leadership in the world."[95]

On the night of April 29, 1975, the last Americans were evacuated from Saigon by helicopter to U.S. Navy ships cruising off the South Vietnam coast. The next day, North Vietnamese troops invaded the city and accepted the surrender of General Duong Van Minh, South Vietnam's last Chief of State. *The New York Times* front-page headline in the April 30 edition said, "Minh Surrenders, Vietcong in Saigon; 1,000 Americans and 5,500 Vietnamese Evacuated by Copter to U.S. Carriers."

MARKETING LESSONS LEARNED FROM THE VIETNAM WAR

For students of marketing, the bitter lessons learned from America's involvement in Vietnam are instructive.

Six American presidents, beginning with Harry Truman and ending with Gerald Ford, played some role in transforming a trusting and cohesive U.S. public into a nation divided by age, ethnicity, earning power, and beliefs. America's young, minorities, the poor, and the ideologically unsophisticated who went to fight and frequently die in the war, suffered the most. At war's end, they were also its most alienated citizens. Decades would pass before the American people would return to a semblance of the national unity that existed before more than one-half million U.S. troops were dispatched to fight in Southeast Asia.

With the benefit of hindsight, what are some of the marketing lessons that these American presidents could have learned to avoid the painful consequences of this war?

First, these presidents should have done what every marketing manager does before launching a new program—Do a Risk/Reward Analysis to determine if the financial, physical, and human investment they are about to chance is justified by the likely rewards to be won. In the case of Vietnam, this was never done. Starting with Harry Truman, no American president who was in office during those decades was sufficiently knowledgeable about the cultural/political/economic/military environment in which he was planning to wage war before he made a decision to proceed with his plans.

Right from the beginning, Presidents Truman and Eisenhower were influenced by their determination to contain global communism, particularly in Western Europe. That regional fixation led them to blindly support France, helping it to reestablish its colonial power in Vietnam. This policy was totally contradictory to the American government's previously stated pronouncements encouraging national independence of former colonized countries. When the French could no longer maintain control, the United States reflexively took their place without questioning the long-term viability of the political leadership of South Vietnam and its inability to rally the support of its citizenry. Presidents Kennedy, Johnson, and Nixon automatically continued this commitment without acknowledging that the personal and political flaws of each successive South Vietnamese government leader made it less and less likely that the country could withstand ultimate North Vietnamese domination.

Second, they should have been totally honest with the American people as the U.S. foreign policy in Vietnam started to unravel. You can deceive most people once, but it becomes progressively more difficult to do so when people realize that they have been tricked into compliance. Credibility, once diminished, is almost impossible to restore. Marketing textbooks are filled with the case histories of misguided product promoters who made elaborate promises in order to achieve immediate short-term sales, but who ultimately failed because they concealed the truth about their offerings' deficiencies.

All of the American presidents who were in office during the most active phases of the Vietnam War routinely attempted to hoodwink the U.S. public about the U.S. military's progressively more intense involvement and the deficiencies of the South Vietnamese leadership. And each American president suffered a loss of credibility when it was eventually revealed that they had concealed vital information about their military decisions in Vietnam. The net result was the American public's lack of trust in the presidency that culminated in diminished support for its programs.

Third, since there is no possibility in a democracy of effectively limiting the public's access to the unfavorably reported war news, it was essential that Presidents Kennedy, Johnson, and Nixon understood that they needed to maintain the best possible rapport with the U.S. news media (no matter how they personally felt about the media's coverage of their administrations' war policies). Yet each of these American presidents actively attempted to thwart the news media's efforts to report what their correspondents believed was actually happening in South Vietnam, and in so doing, contributed to further deterioration of their own and their administrations' respective credibility.

In a complex and open society like the United States, all citizens depend on the news media to inform them about the issues that are important to them, as well as to provide an interpretation of those issues that help them better understand these issues. Both in Saigon and Washington, the administrations of Presidents Kennedy, Johnson, and Nixon allowed their relationship with the American news media to deteriorate and become polarized, with an *us against them* attitude ultimately prevailing. This was particularly true of the misguided policies of the U.S. Military Mission in Vietnam that routinely withheld information and deceived the press corps at the nightly press briefings (derisively referred to by journalists as the 'Five O'clock Follies'), as well as in their other routine contacts.

Initially inclined to follow a patriotic line dedicated to supporting the government's policies in Vietnam, the news media became increasingly skeptical and aggressive in seeking information outside the control of the U.S. Military Mission. By the time the United States began withdrawing its forces from the country, much of the news media had become openly hostile in its reporting of South Vietnamese and U.S. military actions.

Fourth, Presidents Kennedy, Johnson, and Nixon drew on traditional political marketing methods to communicate a message out to the public. They relied heavily on making nationally televised speeches to sell their Vietnam policy, encouraging the news media to interview them, as well as maneuvering in Congressional cloakrooms to maintain control of the U.S. Legislature.

President Nixon directed his administration officials to go far beyond these practices, pursuing Machiavellian tactics that would provide him with greater control of the message (*logos*) he wished to disseminate. For instance, his administration organized grassroots letter writing campaigns from influential Republicans to the top management of print and broadcast media companies demanding "fairer" treatment of their coverage of the President. These campaigns appeared to be generated spontaneously, and only came to light after the President's tapes were made public.

President Nixon's aides would also direct his supporters to stage special patriotic events, like "Honor America Day," in various parts of the country as a counterbalance to rallies opposing his policies in Vietnam. He also encouraged his supporters to raise money to fund advertising campaigns that would provide greater media attention in support of his policies.

Beginning with the presidency of Ronald Reagan, many of these marketing insights were absorbed by future U.S. presidents whose administrations put them to effective use in selling the wars that they subsequently chose to fight.

American presidents are all basically salesmen. Their sales success is measured by their ability to persuade the news media, the public, and the Congress to "buy" their proposed policies and to support the subsequent wars they wish America to wage. The Vietnam War was a textbook example of a war that was badly sold, in which a succession of U.S. presidents ignored the most basic of marketing realities.

In the final analysis, it is bad policy to try to sell a useless war regardless of how slick or sophisticated the marketing techniques used. In short, don't sell Americans a war they do not understand, do not need, and do not want. That Americans supported U.S. involvement in Vietnam through four presidencies is less a tribute to the marketing skills of the Eisenhower, Kennedy, Johnson, and Nixon administrations than to the core beliefs Americans have in their own inherent goodness and in the regenerative powers of armed conflict in support of such abstractions of freedom, democracy, justice, and peace.

From a marketing perspective, the Vietnam War was conceptually flawed (there was no subsequent "Domino Effect"), poorly executed ("hearts and minds" were not won and the enemy was not "bombed into submission") and incompetently sold to the American people (no clear goal for the war was ever established). In the aftermath of the American defeat, a Vietnam Syndrome haunted the nation. Politicians learned to avoid antiwar protests by eliminating military conscription and not asking Americans to make tangible sacrifices in support of future conflicts. The American military learned to distrust unfettered news media and to fight only those wars that were winnable by using overwhelming military might (the Colin Powell Doctrine). And the American people learned, but only for one generation, to be skeptical of government marketing strategies selling foreign conflict entanglements as essential to protecting America's national security and the American way of life.

But as surely as one generation passes away and another rises up, the bitter lessons of Vietnam were neither noted nor long remembered by the generation that followed. Instead, the Gunfighter Nation Syndrome and the Myth of the Frontier remained resonant in the American ethos. In the new age of global marketing, Americans would continue to buy wars if the packaging came wrapped in the American flag and the price was hidden from most of the buyers.

6

Operation Desert Storm—The Persian Gulf War

THE U.S. GOVERNMENT LEARNS TO HARNESS THE NEWS MEDIA IN WARTIME

Public relations practitioner and theorist Edward R. Bernays described modern public relations as "the engineering of consent," a phrase which increasingly describes the communications policies of every American president since the Vietnam War in their efforts to enlist public support for the wars they want to fight.

Public Relations is generally regarded by nonprofessionals as a superficial activity, primarily aimed at getting someone's name in the newspaper or on television. In reality, it has become the most powerful of contemporary marketing communications vehicles, at a time when traditional marketing techniques like media advertising have lost their previous credibility and ability to persuade the public to buy products, services, or *ideas*.

In the history of America's wars, no time was ever more dominated by marketing and public relations practitioners using state-of-the-art techniques than the period prior to and during the Persian Gulf War. Strategists trained in modern PR methods who were employed by the government were able to win Congressional and popular support for U.S. involvement in that war by utilizing sophisticated marketing and propaganda techniques. Later, they were able to define America's perception of what was happening in the Persian Gulf War zone and at the conclusion of the war. Previous presidential attempts at orchestrating American public opinion to support putting U.S. armed forces in harm's way seem crude and amateurish in comparison.

In any modern society, people only comprehend what is happening in time of crisis by learning about it from the news media. The U.S. government's ability to manipulate and screen the primary sources of news in the media at the onset of the Persian Gulf War and during the conflict deprived the American public of a chance to form opinions based on full access to all the available information. It was a classic spinning operation, built on the lessons learned in the aftermath of the Vietnam War, and the U.S. military ventures in Grenada and Panama City.

Lessons and Preludes—Images of the Vietnam War Become a Cautionary Tale

Following the signing of the Paris Peace Accords in January 1973, the subsequent retreat of U.S. forces from South Vietnam later that year, and the surrender of South Vietnam to North Vietnamese forces in May 1975, the American military and government officials were almost unanimously of one mind. They were convinced that the war could have been won if only the U.S. news media hadn't poisoned the minds of the American public against our military engagement in that South East Asian country. Those who believed (and still believe) in this theory directly attributed the public's demoralization and diminishing public support for U.S. involvement in the war to hostile reporting and negative interpretation of the news about Vietnam War that appeared in America's leading newspapers, magazines, and on major television network news programs. This was to have a profound influence on the way the U.S. government and the military handled America's engagement in future military conflicts.

In senior U.S. military colleges and in the Pentagon, the public relations "mistakes" committed during the years of the Vietnam War were carefully reviewed. New public relations, propaganda, and marketing strategies were devised to assure that in future wars, the American people would be more supportive of the U.S. government's actions.

The first successful application of this new communications strategy aimed at mobilizing positive public opinion in support of America's wars that occurred in 1983 when U.S. military forces invaded the tiny eastern Caribbean island of Grenada to rid it of its Marxist government. By the time U.S. forces went into action in the Persian Gulf War in 1991, these more sophisticated strategies and techniques involving manipulation of the news media and limiting the American public's ability to acquire an objective understanding of what was happening on the battlefield in real time were executed like a well-oiled machine.

GRENADA

The goodwill and excellent rapport that had existed between the military leadership and the news media in World War II actually began dissipating during the Korean War when General MacArthur's heavy-handed policies of censorship and repression of independent media voices reporting from the frontlines began to have an effect. By the time America's misadventure in Vietnam had ended a decade later, U.S. government and military leaders had almost universally grown to distrust all journalists and the news media they were employed by, regarding them as an enemy. In keeping with this generally held view, the U.S. government officials initiated new and more constraining public relations policies when the country's armed forces invaded the Caribbean island of Grenada on October 25, 1983. This time, President Ronald Reagan and his administration were determined that the American public would learn only *what* the government wanted them to know about the invasion, and *when* it wanted the public to know it.

President Reagan decided to invade Grenada because the Left-leaning prime minister of the island had been assassinated, and an openly Marxist group had taken control of the government by force. Administration officials in Washington also believed that large caches of Soviet supplied weapons were being stockpiled in Grenada. In addition, the communist government of Cuba was building an unusually large airport on the island for the Grenadian government which the U.S. military believed might ultimately be used by the Soviets as a military staging base in the Caribbean region. However, the initial reason offered by the White House as a justification for the invasion of Grenada was the U.S. government's concern for the safety of American citizens on the island and, secondarily, the restoration of a legitimate government.

The White House controlled the flow of news about this event, codenamed "Operation Urgent Fury," so well that even President Reagan's own press office and the Pentagon press office were not informed about the invasion until it was actually underway. As American Air Force, Army, Marine, and Navy units converged on the island in the eastern Caribbean Sea, the story inevitably began to leak as the news media began to learn what was happening from independent sources. Speaking with an innocence born of their ignorance about what actually was occurring, White House and Pentagon spokesmen assured reporters that these stories were not factual. Skeptical about these denials, hundreds of journalists began converging on the eastern Caribbean region, trying to reach Grenada by whatever means were available. This dilution of source credibility, or the *ethos of the source*, began the process of alienation between the media and President Reagan's administration.

At one point, 400 correspondents were waiting on the nearby island of Barbados for an opportunity to reach the site of the battle. As the invasion proceeded, frustrated correspondents attempted to land directly on the Grenada beaches from privately chartered boats. The U.S. military fired warning shots over their heads, and the reporters were forced to turn back.[1] One particularly intrepid reporter who actually was able to reach the island was seized by the U.S. military and confined on a Navy vessel until the action ended. According to an article by Richard Reeves in *The New York Times*, it was at this time that "the modern U.S. military was first able to use force—pointing its guns at American reporters and cameras—to totally control what Americans knew about a military action."[2]

No correspondents were allowed to reach the actual scene of the invasion until two days after the invasion had commenced. At that time, a hastily organized media pool of fifteen correspondents who were expected to provide written and photo coverage to all of the news organizations that had not been given access to Grenada was permitted to land on the island after they had agreed to accept military censorship. Until then, all reports of the action on Grenada were being provided exclusively by the U.S. military. It was not until October 30, five days after the invasion started, that the press was given full access to report directly from the island. By that time, all armed opposition to the attack on Grenada had ceased.

President Reagan's White House had now established a new precedent in controlling the flow of news from the battlefield where American troops were engaged in combat. And it proved to be extremely successful. The American people learned about what happened only through the filter of government-controlled information sources or through the reports that a small pool of closely supervised correspondents could relay to their own and other news organizations.

In the wake of the successful invasion, Les Janka, the Deputy White House Press Secretary for Foreign Affairs, resigned because he felt that he had been put in a position of disseminating news to the media that the White House knew wasn't true. It was reported that White House senior spokesman Larry Speakes threatened to resign for the same reason.[3] The American news media organizations protested loudly against this new policy of secrecy and fabrication, but U.S. government officials insisted that the policy was dictated by concerns about military security as well as the need to protect the press from harm, even if the press didn't ask for such protection. Many journalists believed that this policy was more likely based on President Reagan's judgment that extensive public debate about invading Grenada before military action was taken might have had a negative impact on the prospects for his reelection.

Following the invasion of Grenada, U.S. public opinion did not reflect any sense of concern about the administration's preemptory military actions, apparently demonstrating confidence in President Reagan's aggressive foreign policy approach. A significant majority of the American public, who embraced the military's conviction that the news media had behaved irresponsibly in Vietnam, agreed with the Reagan administration's decision to exclude the press from the area of the military operation. This broad segment of the public enthusiastically supported the president's decision to invade Grenada to replace the communist government that had taken power.[4]

Government officials had successfully judged that the *pathos*, or state of mind of the American people had dramatically changed since the conclusion of the Vietnam War. With an all-volunteer military, the issue of draftee casualties was removed. There was now no fear among the country's youth that they might be conscripted into service. Further, there was a general feeling in the nation that the U.S. military's defeat in Vietnam was an anomaly; this overwhelming attack on a small and virtually defenseless island was a demonstration that the United States had returned to its victorious military traditions.

It would appear that the lesson learned from this military adventure by President Reagan and those presidents who followed him into the White House was to move swiftly with minimal disclosure of the government's plans to the news media and the public, to keep the number of American casualties small, to swiftly announce a victory, and to then go home. This new procedure for handling the news media and the flow of information to the U.S. public in time of war had now been tested and proved effective. It became the public relations template for future U.S. military operations.

Following the Grenada invasion, the continuing complaints of major U.S. news media about the military's practice of denying reporters access to combat zones led to the formation of a commission to formulate new rules for press coverage of America's future wars. This commission, headed by Army Major General Winant Sidle, proposed that a national news media pool composed of a select group of correspondents be formed to provide coverage for all the other news media whenever the military decided that full media access was not practical.

This new pool system suited the military very well. It permitted very limited news coverage of a military operation while assuring tight control of the few correspondents permitted into the war zone.[5] According to this agreement, the preselected journalists would be provided with government transportation to the battlefield and given access to the areas where the fighting was taking place. The correspondents would then file stories or television coverage on behalf of the entire news media industry that was not represented in the pool. Inherent in this plan which the major U.S. news organizations docilely agreed to abide by, was acceptance of the idea that the military would determine when it was safe to allow the press pool access to the field of battle, and where they could pursue their stories. Since each

National Media Pool member was to be accompanied by specially trained public affairs officers, it was safe to assume that every effort would be made to steer them toward combat situations that would reflect well on the military's activities, usually after the fight was concluded. Equally important to the government was the likelihood that correspondents in the pool would be deflected away from more negative aspects of the war which might upset the American public or cause the public to think less enthusiastically about the wisdom of the U.S. government's foreign policies.

Three years after the Grenada invasion ended, Clint Eastwood starred in a Hollywood-made movie as a U.S. Marine sergeant leading his troops to victory in that military operation. *Heartbreak Ridge* (1986) was a very successful motion picture in the United States, offering an extremely positive depiction of the U.S. military's role in that action. A film critic observed that the film "takes longer to play out than the real-life invasion of Grenada it depicts."[6]

PANAMA CITY

The new media pool coverage arrangement was first put to the test in December 1989 when President George H. Bush ordered the American military to invade Panama City, the Capital of Panama, six years after the United States had invaded Grenada. Even today, the reasons why the United States decided to invade Panama City remain extremely murky. They revolved around the complex relationships that successive American administrations had maintained with Panamanian President Manuel Noriega since the 1970s, including his possible employment by the CIA when George H.W. Bush was its director. Threats to American investment in the Canal Zone and national security considerations also played a role.

By the time President George H.W. Bush was in the White House in 1989, it was clear to his administration that the previous cordial relationship that Noriega had enjoyed with the United States had turned sour. With Noriega accused of a variety of crimes, from trafficking in drugs to subverting the Panama Canal Treaty, President Bush called for him to be deposed and for a new Panamanian government friendlier to the United States to be installed. This direct U.S. Government involvement in the affairs of Panama continued to be a tradition begun when Columbia resisted U.S. plans to build a canal through the narrow isthmus bridging the Atlantic and Pacific Oceans. In 1903, President Theodore Roosevelt, then in the White House, conspired with forces in opposition to that government to carve out a new nation called Panama at the site of the planned construction that would be more amenable to U.S. plans.

President Bush's official explanation was largely the same as President Reagan's was at the onset of the invasion of Grenada: primarily protecting American citizens from harm; removing Manuel Noriega from power and reestablishing a democratic form of government in Panama were secondary objectives.

It is recognized in the marketing industry that creating an appropriate and appealing brand name for a product is essential in assuring its successful launch in the marketplace. By selecting "*Operation Just Cause*" as the brand name of the operation that led to the U.S. invasion of Panama, the Bush administration chose well. The catchy and upbeat name was immediately embraced by the news media. Subsequent media references to the invasion of Panama were rarely referred to by the U.S. news media as anything but "*Operation Just Cause.*" And future U.S. military operations all bore equally dramatic and positive brand names.

Activating the national media pool system, the U.S. Department of Defense flew designated pool correspondents from the United States to Panama City where they were then placed under the authority of the U.S. Southern Command. "The Pentagon did not get the 16-person pool to Panama City until four hours after the fighting began, and reporters were unable to file dispatches until six hours after that. Overall coverage improved as hordes of other reporters arrived, but the original pool remained under tight military control and contributed little."[7]

In the days that followed, many print and broadcast journalists from the United States attempting to fly into Panama City on chartered aircraft were refused permission to land by the U.S. military command. Again, as in Grenada, the military gave as its justification the concern for the safety of the journalists. The only perspective that the American people were receiving about what was actually happening in Panama City during the fighting was being almost exclusively sanitized and filtered through the U.S. military's communications channel.

President Bush's popularity rating rose to 71 percent favorable, significantly improved over his favorable rating before he initiated the invasion. Almost three-quarters of those Americans polled believed that the invasion of Panama City was the right thing to do.[8] Republican political insider Lee Atwater described President Bush's decision to launch the invasion a political "jackpot."[9]

The invasions of Grenada and Panama City served as useful prototypes for the U.S. government's public relations strategies and tactics in the wars that were to follow. With virtually all objective news coverage of the battle in Panama City that might disagree with the official White House version of the facts being stifled, the public would inevitably accept the government's version as the truth, lacking any other contradictory input. The subsequent deluge of entertainment and unrelated news media messages bombarding the American public on a daily basis would severely dilute the impact of any stories there were at odds with the government's version of the news that might be disseminated later.

Virtually no other news coverage reached the American people until the fighting in Panama had ended. In manipulating the *use and control of public media*, the White House had assured that no negative or discordant messages were being communicated to the public during the battle that would contradict those messages that were being provided by the government. It adhered to one of the most fundamental rules of effective propaganda, minimizing "static," or messages that question the credibility and/or disagree with your message, so that only your version of events is effectively presented to the public.

An axiom of modern marketing that derives from this principle says that it's easy to persuade the target audience of the desirability of choosing your product if you can manage to limit or shut down your competition's ability to appeal to this same audience. A totalitarian government like the one in North Korea has little trouble controlling the flow of information through the mass media since these regimes closely supervise their output and make certain that nothing is presented to their publics that disagrees with the government's point of view. In the cases of both Grenada and Panama, the success of the U.S. government's program of limiting the news media's access to the combat zone, and to prevent the news media from reporting to the American people in a timely way, was evidence that this axiom could be applied very effectively in even a democratically elected political system. It also provided the U.S. government with a useful template for its next war in the Persian Gulf.

THE PERSIAN GULF WAR

Former Ally Saddam Hussein Invades Kuwait and Becomes a U.S. Enemy

When Iraqi dictator Saddam Hussein's troops invaded neighboring Kuwait on August 2, 1990, the American political and military response was swift and forceful. President George H. W. Bush quickly decided that the Iraqi invasion threatened American access to Kuwait's huge oil reserves, and was therefore a threat to U.S. national security. As American, British, French, and other troops that formed the coalition of military forces began pouring into neighboring Saudi Arabia, preparing to battle Hussein's army and liberate Kuwait, President Bush's administration simultaneously started implementing an elaborate public relations campaign. According to a *New York Times* story, the PR plan, which was called "*Annex Foxtrot*," was designed to assure that the American people totally supported the campaign to drive the Iraqis out of Kuwait. U.S. political and military leaders, having learned well the successful public relations lessons during the invasions of

Grenada and Panama, initiated this operation determined to avoid the mistakes they believed had ultimately contributed to the defeat of U.S. forces by the communists in Vietnam.[10] In that war, the news media could go anywhere and report anything at any time without fear of censorship. In this war, they were determined not to allow the press to have this freedom.

As in the earlier military conflicts in Grenada and Panama, the government operated under the assumption that the news media, left unsupervised, were a menace to military security and possibly to their own personal safety as well. Unsaid, but implicit in the minds of most military and government leaders, was the conviction that journalists could not be trusted to convey the news "constructively" without official guidance. So the National Press Pool procedure was once again activated by the Department of Defense. A small number of journalists, representing both print and electronic media, were chosen by the U.S. government to report back to the huge contingent of other press covering the story in rear areas of the Persian Gulf outside the fighting zone, or back in the United States. This policy was not only used to contain the press, but also to give the U.S. government far greater control over information disseminated about the war in the United States and in other countries.[11]

While all journalists suffered from this restrictive policy throughout the Persian Gulf War, television news crews were the most seriously hampered because of the insatiable nature of the video medium for new imagery. The TV crews all were obliged to use the same limited footage shot during daily briefings and in carefully managed "photo-op" expeditions to the front lines. This army of reporters and camera crews (more than 1,000 in number) had no choice but to cool their heels at the Dhahran International Hotel waiting to be selected by military press officers for a coveted spot in one of the limited number of press pools designated to join combat units.[12]

Not all of the corps of correspondents complied with the U.S. military's system of control. Determined to avoid these restrictions, CBS correspondent Bob Simon and three other CBS crewmembers went off on their own to report on the story. They were captured by an Iraqi patrol on the Kuwaiti border before the United States started its ground attack and held in an Iraqi prison for six weeks before being released. In his memoir, *Forty Days*, Simon later complained about the way the Pentagon and the U.S. news media collaborated on the coverage of the war, stating that the military's high command, "claimed security" when "the motivation was political. The war was to appear clean, safe, and sanitary; no blood, no pain, no body bags."[13] While a small handful of correspondents continued to report outside the control of the U.S. military, most complied with the Pentagon's rules throughout the rest of the war.

Of course, this was exactly how the U.S. government wanted the news coverage to be. Unlike Vietnam, where journalists could communicate views of the war that differed from those of the military command, "*Operation*

Desert Storm," as the Coalition military operation was branded, allowed only one view of the battle: the one authorized by the military. Like tourists, their military handlers led the correspondents from their buses. The network TV crews were then given an opportunity to videotape the "panoramic vista" before them, and then were whisked to the next officially authorized destination. No independent opportunities for press inquiries were permitted. *The New York Times* inserted an advisory to alert its readers about these restrictions. Under a headline, "Censors Screen Pooled Reports," the entry read:

> The American-led military command in Saudi Arabia has put into effect press restrictions under which journalists are assembled in groups and given access to military sources. The pool reporters obtain information while under military escort and their accounts are subject to scrutiny by military censors before being distributed. Some of the information appearing today on American military operations was obtained under such circumstances.[14]

This policy was in sharp contrast to the way combat was covered during the Vietnam War. In that war, "A correspondent in Saigon could hop aboard a helicopter heading for Pleiku or Danang or Hue, wherever the action was that day, then accompany the troops on search-and-destroy missions into the deepest rain forest, all the while interviewing officers and foot soldiers who, routinely, were happy to have press notice," says Neil Hickey, now a *Columbia Journalism Review* editor who covered the Vietnam War and other wars for *True Magazine* and *TV Guide*. "That all ended in the Persian Gulf War," he adds, "where the military virtually closed down journalistic enterprise in favor of guided tours of the front by public affairs officers who led pools of obedient, unhappy journalists on brief visits to fighting units, and then reviewing their dispatches for possible mischief."[15]

Correspondents' Complaints Ignored

Many correspondents assigned to cover the action protested mightily during the war in the Persian Gulf. But as in Grenada and Panama, there was no ground swell of American public opinion pressuring the government into supporting the media's demands for greater freedom to operate independently. In fact, surveys indicated that most Americans, who may have shared with the military the belief that it was "the media" that was responsible for the defeat of the United States in Vietnam, felt the press covering the war in the Persian Gulf should be muzzled because they felt that the media was anti-military.[16]

The *context*, or marketing environment of the United States in which these methods to suppress media coverage were employed was clearly agreeable to the aims and beliefs of the administration of President Bush.

Americans were prepared for its military to fight a short war in which a weak nation was protected from a bullying one, and U.S. strategic interests were protected.

The access that the reporters were allowed in the war zone was narrowly channeled into daily briefings, where media-trained military officers deftly handled questions from an increasingly frustrated press corps. The correspondents were not only manipulated to assure a positive image in the nation's media, but were also exploited successfully to disseminate false information, in order to persuade the Iraqis that a direct amphibious invasion of Kuwait by U.S. Marines was being readied.[17]

From the start, the U.S. government's strategy was two-pronged: one, to maintain tight control of media coverage in the Persian Gulf during the buildup and fighting phases; and two, to mobilize American public opinion in favor of support for U.S. involvement. To pursue these strategies, the government borrowed freely from state-of-the-art public relations techniques defined by PR pioneer Edward R. Bernays and perfected by American public relations agencies to "engineer the consent" of the American people.[18]

In some cases, PR agencies working directly for the Government of Kuwait in Exile or its front organizations, used techniques that included professional media training for those Kuwaiti citizens in the United States who were assigned the task of promoting the case for involvement of the United States in the Persian Gulf War. Former U.S. network television news professionals taught those people, who were trained to use the same on-camera techniques commonly used by TV news reporters and anchors on nightly news and talk shows, thereby maximizing their credibility when testifying at Congressional hearings or appearing on television news shows. It was estimated by U.S. Congressman Jimmy Hayes that the government of Kuwait funded as many as twenty public relations, law and lobby firms as part of its determined effort to win the American support in ousting Hussein's troops from its country.[19] While these organizations were required by law to register as foreign agents in Washington, few Americans were conscious of their affiliations.

A key to the success of the Persian Gulf operation was the willingness of the top management of the major American news outlets (i.e., ABC, CBS, NBC, and CNN) to accept military control over their correspondents covering the fighting (despite the field correspondents' unhappiness with the situation). The administration's successful public relations campaign was further ensured by the American news managements' acceptance of the use of military "minders" (military public information officers trained to accompany and monitor correspondents), who would make certain that those correspondents allowed into the war zone only were given access to what these "minders" considered beneficial to the overall government image management campaign during the Persian Gulf War. These "minders" guaranteed that the correspondents in their charge did not interview personnel or witness events contrary to the stories and pictures that the U.S. government wanted to communicate to the American people.

The top management of some news organizations did complain about the infringement of the press's First Amendment rights when these constraining policies were imposed, and the Center for Constitutional Rights (on behalf of several minor news organizations), the American Civil Liberties Union and the French news agency Agence France-Presse also challenged the Defense Department press restrictions in a series of lawsuits. However, despite the bitter experiences they had had in Grenada and Panama, the major American news media never seriously fought these restrictive policies aggressively, and ultimately agreed to abide by them.[20]

Why the News Media Protests against Government Control Were Ineffective

The reason why U.S. print and particularly broadcast media responded so passively to these restrictions right from the onset of the Persian Gulf War buildup probably was a result of the dramatic changes American mass media had been undergoing since the end of World War II. In those years before and following the end of the Second World War, the dominant American newspapers, news magazines, and broadcast news outlets were owned or controlled by strong individualists like William Randolph Hearst, who controlled a powerful chain of newspapers, Henry Luce at Time/Life, William Paley of CBS, and David Sarnoff of NBC. Hearst had openly promoted the U.S. war with Spain in 1898, and Luce had been a passionate supporter of the campaign to widen the Korean War by having U.S. forces attack the Chinese mainland. These media magnates possessed enormous egos, and their decisions were greatly influenced by their own personal beliefs, judgments, and prejudices. With the power they wielded, they were then largely able to maintain their organization's independence

But the *use and control of public media* changed in the decades that followed, and experienced radical changes in ownership, technology, cultural, and institutional biases. In contrast with earlier era, the heads of almost all the influential news media operating during the Persian Gulf War were now middle managers accountable to chief executive officers of publicly owned multinational media conglomerates. These CEOs were, and continue to be, essentially businessmen, not newsmen. Their primary concern was a positive perception of their financial performance by their company's stockholders and the security analysts covering the media industry. Unlike the Hearsts, Luces, Paleys, and Sarnoffs of earlier decades, the future compensation and employment of these CEOs were dependent on the stockholders' confidence that the companies they had invested in would continue to generate ever-increasing revenues and profits. Issues like maintaining the integrity of the news, or government censors' infringements of First Amendment rights, were not a priority, if they were considered at all. The middle managers heading the various news divisions had won their jobs by understanding their bosses' and the stockholders' bottom-line priorities. Therefore, they were less than stalwart when Pentagon officials began curtailing their correspondents' ability to report on the war freely.

Another major change that made it difficult for many of the American news organizations to stand up to government press censorship and restrictions in war coverage was the extraordinary fragmentation occurring in electronic media after the advent of cable and satellite television. Since the beginning of the 1980s, the American people were being offered an expanding array of alternative electronic news programming sources, beginning with cable TV network CNN in the early 1980s. As a result, ABC, CBS, and NBC television networks lost large portions of their audiences and their budgets, and, by the time of the Persian Gulf War, were being forced to compete with a growing array of other broadcast, cable, and satellite television networks for a shrinking share of America's television households. Thus, no news medium had the same extraordinary power and influence that major mass media possessed in the past to demand that their correspondents be given access to the war zone the way they had done in earlier American military conflicts.

A Reversal of U.S. Policy

One of the greatest challenges facing President George H. W. Bush after Iraq invaded Kuwait was to dramatically reverse official U.S. foreign policy concerning Iraqi President Saddam Hussein, who had ordered the invasion. Before Hussein invaded Kuwait, his army had launched attacks against Iran as well as against the Kurds who were living in Iraq, but the U.S. government regarded these acts with some tolerance. This was because the realpolitik strategy of the United States identified the fundamentalist government of Iran as a greater security concern than Hussein's more secular government. Although Hussein had annihilated tens of thousands of his own citizens with poison gas, genocidal deeds like this didn't threaten any crucial U.S. strategic interests, so they were ignored.

In April 1990, a U.S. Congressional delegation visited Saddam Hussein in Iraq to demonstrate support for his policies. One of its members, Senator Alan K. Simpson, reportedly told the dictator; "...Democracy is a very irksome and confusing thing. I believe your problem is with the Western media, not with the U.S. government, because you are isolated from the media and the press. The press is spoiled and conceited....They do not want to see anything succeeding or achieving its objectives....They feed on each other. Each one of them eats part of the other." Only one week before Saddam Hussein's Iraq invaded neighboring Kuwait, U.S. Ambassador to Iraq April Glaspie sympathetically proposed to the Iraqi dictator that "an appearance [by Hussein] in the [U.S.] media, even for five minutes, would help [the administration] explain Iraq to the American people."[21]

However, seizing Kuwait, with its huge oil reserves that were then reliably providing America's industry and automobiles with inexpensive fuel, transformed Hussein from just another tinhorn Middle East dictator into a direct and immediate threat to American security interests. President Bush acted quickly to persuade the American people that Hussein's land grab must be resisted immediately and vigorously.

In the early stages of the crisis, Saddam Hussein was forging his own agenda, pursuing a propaganda campaign designed to enlist the support of not only the Iraqi people, but also the Arab world beyond Iraq. At first, Saddam Hussein was clearly misguided and heavy handed in his attempts to win world opinion, such as when he appeared on television with European and U.S. hostages, whom he described as "guests" of his government. Global television audiences will always remember seeing him demonstrating his kindly nature by patting the head of a captive—and very frightened—British child.[22]

But Saddam Hussein learned quickly from his early mistakes and subsequently used television, which he totally controlled in Iraq, to better PR advantage. As the air war commenced, Hussein strictly limited the number of Western journalists permitted to report from Baghdad, much as the U.S. military was doing with the press at its headquarters in Saudi Arabia. This tactic assured Hussein's government of both close scrutiny over the journalists' output, and tight rein over the impressions television audiences were receiving. Hussein favored CNN and refused to allow other U.S. TV networks to report from the Iraqi capital. Peter Arnett, CNN's Pulitzer Prize winning correspondent, and his camera crew were steered to carefully selected bombsites that had been approved for display. Arnett tried to provide balanced reportage in his commentary, but the devastating images of destroyed Iraqi homes, allegedly bombed by Coalition aircraft and missiles, provided much more powerful impressions than the mild verbal disclaimers he was allowed to provide under Iraqi censorship. Even Arnett's ironic observation that the signs adorning the wreckage of a purported Iraqi baby milk factory were printed in English, rather than in Arabic, were not sufficiently emphatic to overcome Hussein's public relations objective—to win the world's sympathy for his cause.[23]

Clearly, one of the Iraqi dictator's objectives was to influence American and European public opinion so as to undermine support of the U.S.-led Coalition's aims. But the primary targets for his PR program were the Iraqi people and ordinary citizens in other Arab countries. Until the final, crushing U.S.-led Coalition ground attack nearly wiped out his army, it seemed that Hussein had basically succeeded in using television to sway the Arab masses into believing he was their champion in his battle against the infidel West. In the years following the Persian Gulf War of 1991 and until the beginning of the new U.S. invasion of Iraq in 2003, Hussein regained considerable stature in the eyes of "the Arab Street" as an effective foe of the United States and its allies.[24]

In contrast to Hussein's absolute control of media within Iraq and his skill in manipulating Iraqi public opinion, the Bush administration's efforts to win public and Congressional support for its war aims met far greater challenges. The American people were by no means resolved to support the administration's plans to drive the Iraqi Army out of Kuwait at this point. In fact, 48 percent of those Americans interviewed in a December 1990 *New York Times*/*CBS News Poll* wanted President George H. W. Bush to wait before starting a war with Iraq if its troops did not withdraw from Kuwait by the U.S. mandated deadline of January 15, 1991.[25] This was the *pathos*, or state of mind, of almost half of the U.S. public at the time before the actual war was waged.

"Convincing Americans to fight a war to liberate a tiny Arab Sheikhdom ruled by a family oligarchy would require the demonization [of Hussein] in ways never contemplated by human rights groups," writes John R. MacArthur, author of *Second Front: Censorship and Propaganda in the Gulf War*. "It called for a frontal assault on public opinion such as had not been seen since the Spanish-American War. The war had to be sold. Fortunately for the president, there was talented help at hand."[26]

It didn't take long for a group calling itself "Citizens for a Free Kuwait" (a front organization created in the United States by the Kuwait government in exile to provide the appearance of wide public support) to hire political consultants close to President Bush and the Republican Party. "Citizens for a Free Kuwait," which was registered with the government as a nonprofit charity, was led by a small group of Kuwaiti citizens living in the United States. Its clear and single purpose was to persuade the American people and their representatives in Congress to pass legislation authorizing U.S. military forces to attack the Iraqi Army and drive them out of Kuwait. Shortly after its formation, "Citizens for a Free Kuwait" retained one of America's most powerful and prestigious public relations agencies, Hill & Knowlton, (a division of the British-owned WPP Group) to help achieve this objective.[27] Hill & Knowlton had a long and successful history of representing the interests of foreign governments to the American people. Indonesia, Turkey, and the People's Republic of China were among those countries retaining these PR experts to improve their image with the U.S. public[28]

To carry out its propaganda campaign, "Citizens for a Free Kuwait" attempted to disguise itself as a true American grass roots organization, broad-based in both its membership and its funding sources. In reality, almost all of the $12 million in contributions subsequently reported to the U.S. Justice Department came directly from the coffers of the Government of Kuwait.[29] A handful of other individual contributors in the United States and Canada made additional small financial donations.

The concept of establishing a "grass roots" front organization was one of Hill & Knowlton's tried and true techniques that the company had been employing on behalf of its clients for decades in order to disguise their true purpose and funding sources. A senior vice president and managing director of Hill & Knowlton acknowledged that his agency was employing a variety of communications tools on behalf of the "Citizens Committee for A Free Kuwait," including opinion sampling, video and print production, media placement and tracking, and grass roots support.[30] H & K also staged "Kuwait Information Days" on twenty U.S. college campuses, a national day of prayer for Kuwait, and distributed large quantities of "Free Kuwait" bumper stickers.[31] By the time Hill & Knowlton's as well as several other U.S. PR agencies' assignments were completed early in 1991, H & K alone had received more than $10 million as compensation from the Committee.[32]

In their campaign to mobilize Congressional and American public opinion in support of driving the Iraqis out of Kuwait, "Citizens Committee for a Free Kuwait" and Hill & Knowlton faced a climate of considerable controversy over committing American troops and other U.S. military resources to the conflict. For one thing, Kuwait itself was hardly a paragon of democracy. It had a long history of civil rights violations and exploitation of the non-Kuwaiti population that essentially did all the work in the tiny country while its few privileged native-born citizens lived a life of indulgence and leisure. Earlier, Kuwait had discarded all pretense of an open society, shutting down its legislative body and ruling the country by fiat. Selling the American people on the idea that our armed forces should be rushing to the defense of another endangered "democracy" was not going to be easy.

Ambivalence over the issue of dedicating American troops to this struggle was mirrored in the media and in protest rallies across the country. A sizeable and extremely vocal segment of American public opinion made it clear that it opposed U.S. entry into this conflict on moral grounds. They feared this could turn into another prolonged bloodbath for American soldiers, another Vietnam. In a series of public statements, Saddam Hussein encouraged the belief that such an American engagement would be costly to the United States, promising that American troops would face "the mother of all battles."

The Incubator Babies' Atrocity Story

About this time, a story about invading Iraqi troops pulling premature Kuwaiti babies out of incubators and leaving them to die on the cold floor of a Kuwaiti hospital began appearing in U.S. media. This often repeated tale was reminiscent of crude propaganda horror stories about German soldiers in World War I bayoneting Belgian infants (a story fabricated by the British government that later was discredited, but at the time contributed to the formation of negative attitudes toward Germany in the United States and elsewhere).

The tale of the Kuwaiti incubator babies first appeared in a British publication, *The London Daily Telegraph*, and was attributed to one of the exiled Kuwaiti government ministers. It was then carried in *The Los Angeles Times*. A growing number of other U.S. print and electronic news outlets subsequently ran the story. Eventually, President George H. W. Bush and members of the Congress embraced the report, repeatedly offering it as further evidence of the Iraqis' wickedness, fueling the growing American sentiment that the U.S. armed forces needed to step in to drive them out of Kuwait.

The Kuwaiti incubator atrocity story became the centerpiece of testimony at a special meeting of the Congressional Human Rights Caucus in Washington, chaired by U.S. Congressmen Tom Lantos and John Porter. While this hearing, which was widely covered by the news media, was regarded by most Americans as an official Congressional hearing of the U.S. government, it was not. In his book, *The Second Front: Censorship and Propaganda in the Gulf War*, John R. MacArthur said that both U.S. Congressmen were also cochairs of the Congressional Human Rights Foundation, "a legally separate entity that occupied free office space valued at $3,000 a year in Hill & Knowlton's Washington, DC office." The two Congressmen convened this unofficial meeting to consider evidence that might lead to the passage of a Congressional resolution supporting military intervention. Significantly, this setting did not require witnesses to testify under oath.

During the hearing, a young Kuwaiti girl named Nayirah testified that she had actually seen these atrocities perpetuated against newborn infants. Largely on the strength of her emotional testimony and subsequent reports of similar alleged inhumanities committed against the Kuwaiti population, Congress quickly passed a resolution committing the United States, in collaboration with its allies, to a course of armed intervention in the Persian Gulf. Some time after the end of the war against Iraq, it was revealed that Nayirah was the daughter of the Kuwaiti Ambassador to the United States. Furthermore, it was questionable whether she had actually even been in Kuwait when the Iraqi Army invaded, "doing volunteer work at the local hospital." A Hill & Knowlton agency executive later acknowledged that Nayirah was carefully scripted and rehearsed by an H & K team prior to her appearance at the hearing, another fact that was generally unknown at the time. When Nayirah's veracity was later challenged, her father, Kuwaiti Ambassador to the United States and Canada Saud Nasir al-Sabah retorted, "If I wanted to lie, or if we wanted to lie, if we wanted to exaggerate, I wouldn't use my daughter to do so. I could easily buy other people to do it."[33]

Several weeks after Nayirah testified in Washington, seven alleged witnesses to the Iraqi atrocities in Kuwait testified at the United Nations in New

York. They too were previously coached by Hill & Knowlton staffers. The United Nations Security Council then viewed a Hill & Knowlton-produced video about what was happening in Kuwait. Shortly afterwards, the UN authorized the use of force to eject Iraq from Kuwait. The American Congress followed suit in January 1991.[34]

American Media Provide Access

Once the decision to commit the American troops to military action in the Persian Gulf was made, the American news media began pulling out all the stops. Heavily censored correspondents at the front filed colorful stories depicting the buildup to the Coalition offensive that appeared in national news magazines like *Time* and *Newsweek* and on broadcast and cable television news shows. As the U.S. military and its Coalition allies achieved an overwhelming victory over the Iraqi Army, the flood of colorful and triumphant stories were embraced by an enthusiastic U.S. public as evidence that the stain of defeat in Vietnam had been totally erased. Virtually all voices questioning the wisdom of this engagement were stilled as America's superior military technology and prowess were showcased. Highly telegenic Army General H. Norman Schwarzkopf's regular briefings at his headquarters in Saudi Arabia had the effect of spellbinding both the media and the American people. General Schwarzkopf's now memorable briefing for the assembled world news media, when he suggested that his successful attack strategy was comparable to American football's classic "Hail Mary" play, established him as a media star.[35] When the final stages of the combat turned into a complete military rout for the Iraqi Army, consensus in the United States was almost complete.

The Public Supports the President

The American people were now in virtually total support of President George H.W. Bush's pursuit of the war, regarding it as a great victory for the United States and a dramatic demonstration of the country's military prowess. Even though President Bush ordered Coalition forces to end the slaughter after four days of combat (a judgment which caused consternation in many U.S. military leaders and members of the U.S. public, then and now), his decision to end hostilities and declare victory remains accepted and popular in the eyes of most Americans. A *New York Times* editorial observed, "the nation is already looking forward to a boisterous welcome home party.... [with] bands, balloons, flags galore and miles of yellow ribbon testifying that this war, as President Bush so often promised, will not end like Vietnam."[36]

The American people never questioned the blatant acts of media manipulation and tight censorship policies carried out by the administration, the

Pentagon, and the government of Kuwait during this period of conflict in terms of either their legitimacy or their zealous enforcement. A decade and a half after that war, there continues to be general public agreement that the demands of national security and the informational needs of the public were being responsibly fulfilled by the government.

Hollywood Films, Documentaries, Comics, Books, and Parades

As American troops returned triumphantly home from the battlefield in the Persian Gulf, the U.S. public's unhappy memories of the heavy casualties and defeat of the U.S. military in Vietnam was replaced with a new feeling of jubilance and pride in the prowess of U.S. fighting men and the advanced combat technology which helped them destroy the Iraqi Army with few American casualties.

"Operation Welcome Home" celebrations were staged across the United States, in small towns and large cities, to demonstrate the esteem that most Americans felt about the returning troops, with yellow ribbons now signifying the nation's appreciation of the military. President George H. W. Bush quickly exploited the public's spontaneous outpouring of positive feelings by arranging to visit military bases to greet the returning troops. The inevitable photo-ops greatly benefited both him and his administration. A writer for *The New York Times* observed that the war in the Persian Gulf "has produced extraordinary levels of support for President Bush and presented the Democrats with a daunting task in finding a candidate who can effectively oppose him in 1992, political professionals say."[37]

Military parades were held in many American cities, including Washington, DC in June 1991. On June 10, 1991, thousands of returning veterans of the Persian Gulf War paraded through the confetti-strewn, downtown canyons of lower New York City. It was the biggest ticker-tape parade in New York City's history, to that date, with U.S. Army Generals Colin H. Powell and H. Norman Schwartzkopf, and Defense Secretary Richard Cheney serving as Grand Marshals.[38]

During and after the war, Gary Trudeau's popular adult comic strip, *Doonesbury*, provided his usual humorous but skeptical views of both the Bush administration's buildup to the war and the conflict itself, to the readers of hundreds of American daily newspapers. A compilation of these comic strips, *The Portable Doonesbury*, was published in 1993 and was very successful. Marvel and DC Comics, two of the largest comic book publishers in the United States, also produced Gulf War action titles appealing to the young male American market. More realistic depictions of war in Iraq were created by Don Lomax and were published by Apple Comics.[39]

Hollywood studios produced several low-budget action films with the theme of the war in the Persian Gulf in the years following that engagement. These films were primarily distributed through videotape rental stores in the United States. They were *The Heroes of Desert Storm* (1991), starring Daniel Baldwin and Angela Bassett, *The Human Shield* (1992), starring Michael Dudikoff, and *Tactical Assault* (1999), starring Rutger Hauer. Two Hollywood-produced big budget feature films dealing with the war that received critical and box office success in the United States were *Courage Under Fire* (1996), starring Denzel Washington and Meg Ryan, and *Three Kings*, (1999) starring George Clooney, Mark Wahlberg, and Ice Cube. Film critic Roger Ebert, in the *Chicago Sun-Times*, described *Three Kings* as a "weird masterpiece," comparing it favorably with the best films of directors Martin Scorsese, Oliver Stone, Robert Altman, and Quentin Tarantino.[40] None of these motion pictures after the war caused the U.S. public to significantly modify its perception that the Persian Gulf War of 1991 was a masterful demonstration of America's armed might on the battlefield that resulted in few U.S. casualties.

Amazon.com lists 4,930 books that have been published about the Persian Gulf War of 1991.[41] Two of them were best-sellers. The first was *It Doesn't Take a Hero: The Autobiography of General H. Norman Schwarzkopf*, the senior field commander of Coalition forces during the engagement. The other is *Jarhead: A Marine's Chronicle of the Gulf War and Other Battles*, by Anthony Swofford, which offers a close-up view of the war through the eyes of a Marine sniper who saw limited combat in Iraq.

A large amount of filmed documentary footage was supplied by the American military to both U.S. and non-U.S. television networks for use on their nightly news broadcasts. In addition, U.S. network TV news teams, closely supervised by military public affairs officers, generated colorful combat footage. Throughout the battle, on-board video cameras mounted on Coalition aircraft captured the destruction wrought by "smart bombs" as they impacted on fortified Iraqi bunkers and aircraft hangers. Many "smart" missiles provided additional footage as the feedback video images of the targets just before they exploded. Much of this footage was fashioned into a series of dramatic documentaries that were frequently telecast on The History Channel, The Discovery Channel, The Learning Channel, and other U.S. cable and broadcast television channels. Some of the most popular documentary titles were "Operation Desert Storm," "Heroes of the Gulf War," "Special Ops," "Smart Bombs," and "M1 Abrams—the Supertank." They are now distributed widely in VHS videotape and DVD formats.

LESSONS LEARNED FOLLOWING THE PERSIAN GULF WAR—1991

"Selling In"—A Marketing Success

A fundamental principle of sales management is to never stop selling the customer, even after the customer has made the purchase decision. It's a technique called "selling in." Smart marketers understand that reinforcing the original buying decision is as important as making the initial sale. Except for purchases of little value, most people need to be reassured that they made the right decision after making the purchase decision. Going to war and sending our military into harm's way is one of the most significant purchase decisions that the country can make. The stream of positive images and cultural messages reinforcing the idea that America was triumphant in the 1991 war that the U.S. public has been continuously exposed to since that time has had an extremely positive reinforcing effect on assuring them that they made the correct decision twelve years ago. In that marketing communications respect, the Persian Gulf War of 1991 was an unqualified success.

With the exception of a small minority of the U.S. public, most Americans today continue to feel that President George H. W. Bush was right to wage war against Saddam Hussein and to drive the invading Iraqi forces out of Kuwait. By stopping the pursuit of the shattered Iraqi Army deeper into their country, he was able to bring Hussein's generals to the negotiating table and then quickly declare victory. As a result, the American military took few combat casualties and the majority of the military units swiftly returned home. In the eyes of most Americans, President Bush had performed the implicit promise he had made to force Saddam Hussein's Army out of Kuwait, thereby assuring a continuing flow of oil to the United States from the region. The fact that Saddam Hussein subsequently reneged on many of the agreements his defeated generals had accepted was largely ignored until the events following the attacks on the World Trade Center and the Pentagon were brought to the foreground of American consciousness as a basis for renewed war against Iraq.

Marketing Lessons from the Persian Gulf War

What can be learned from the lessons of the Persian Gulf War? There is no question that the public relations techniques employed by the George H. W. Bush administration worked very effectively, both before, during, and in the years after the Iraqi Army was defeated militarily in 1991. The American people were completely persuaded that Saddam Hussein, who had previously been tolerated as just another Middle Eastern dictator, and was tacitly supported by the United States in his battle against Iran, was now an arch demon. An overwhelming majority of the public believed that Saddam Hussein's attempt to take over Kuwait's oil fields and possibly threaten U.S. access to the oil fields in Saudi Arabia was a security threat to the nation.

To further justify American involvement in ousting Hussein's troops from Kuwait, the U.S. government claimed that the "totalitarian Iraqi dictatorship" had invaded, and was attempting to destroy the "freely elected democratic" nation of Kuwait. The fact that an unelected, small elite of officials ruled the Government of Kuwait did not deter the Bush administration from promoting this patently false image of the country's political status.[42] The reality was that neither the Iraqi nor Kuwaiti governments was governed by democratic principles; the "realpolitik" issue for the Bush administration was assuring continued American access to Kuwaiti and Saudi oil reserves that required the United States to now brand its former ally Saddam Hussein as a threat to democracy.

Although there were many other genuine examples of Hussein's inhumane behavior that could have been revealed (e.g., the regular use of torture on dissident Iraqis and the use of poison gas to exterminate his own Kurdish citizens), the "incubator baby" atrocity story was credibly presented as important evidence of Iraq's heinous and uncivilized behavior. This unproven atrocity story largely persuaded the U.S. Congress and the American people that the United States and its Coalition allies were obligated to drive out the Iraqi invaders, and rescue Kuwait. Complete control of news reports from the battlefield by the U.S. military assured that almost no contradictory voices were heard until long after the PR campaign's objectives were achieved. Saddam Hussein's policy of limiting and controlling Western media coverage before and during the conflict did little to minimize the effects of the U.S. propaganda campaign. A majority of the American people was swayed by the communications strategies and messages disseminated by the Kuwaiti Government in Exile and its American PR agencies that instigated the United States to drive the Iraqi Army out of Kuwait and attack Iraq. Even now, there is little evidence that the American people have changed their perceptions about the events that occurred in the Persian Gulf in 1991.

A fundamental reason why the American people continue to have a positive feeling about U.S. participation in the first Persian Gulf War was that the combat in Iraq produced minimal U.S. casualties. At the conclusion of "Operation Desert Storm," there were only 148 members of the U.S. Armed Forces killed in combat, as compared with more than 58,000 killed or missing in action during the war in Vietnam,[43] and more than 3,000 U.S. combat deaths in the conflict in Iraq. Further, the tight restrictions on television news coverage of these casualties successfully avoided the frightening imagery of American soldiers' coffins being loaded onto military transports that were displayed so regularly on television during the Vietnam War. As in other periods of war, there was little or no concern expressed by Americans about the enormous number of Iraqi casualties that resulted from this conflict. Also, the fact that this war was fought by professional volunteers, rather than by an army of reluctant, loudly complaining draftees (as was the case in both Korea and Vietnam), also contributed to the lack of public concern about U.S. involvement in this war.

The military's ability to totally control press reports of Persian Gulf War combat allowed this brief engagement to be presented as a triumph of

American technical and military superiority, reinforcing America's image as the undisputed dominant power in the world today. The fact that most of the munitions dropped on Iraqi troops and facilities during the war have subsequently been revealed to be gravity driven "dumb" bombs, rather than the precision laser-guided weaponry that was being continuously showcased in the media during the months leading up to the final assault, remains largely ignored by Americans. The public also has never questioned the brash endorsements of the infallibility of the Patriot Missile System by President George H. W. Bush and his spokesmen during the war, even though it has since been reported that the missiles rarely destroyed the Scud missiles they were aimed at, and when they did hit them, frequently caused them to shatter at high altitudes, producing even greater damage over "friendly" territory when the missile fragments hit the ground.

No news medium truly dominates the national consciousness anymore, with news programming being generated around the clock from every part of the world via satellite and on the Internet. This unprecedented proliferation of news sources, resulting in hordes of competing reporters all demanding equal access to the battlefield, has made it easier for the government to insist on limiting and controlling the press through pool coverage and close supervision of individual reporters who can be steered away from any event that might reflect badly on the way the government is conducting the war.

The scrutiny and control of the news media by the U.S. government during its armed conflicts have intensified considerably over the past three decades. It is true that U.S. military censors did monitor and edit the output of correspondents during World War II and the Korean conflict. However, there was little or no effort made by politicians or the military to control journalists' access to war zones, or to significantly interfere with their ability to report on anything they felt would interest their audiences, as long as it didn't directly threaten military security.

The marketing communications tactics employed by U.S. government agencies that were introduced during the military campaigns in Grenada, Panama City, and the Persian Gulf War clearly worked. However, these wars, which were relatively bloodless for the United States, were carried out swiftly against enemies that were militarily weak and lacking modern combat capabilities. Whether these techniques would be as effective in conflicts where the combat was prolonged, conscription was reintroduced, and American military casualties were great is doubtful.

It is likely in such circumstances, the credibility of the government might be more closely questioned and confidence in its ability to govern shaken. Despite the U.S. government's public relations successes of the Grenada, Panama, and Persian Gulf War (1991), there is a growing consciousness and skepticism about government "spinmeisters" and their tactics. This, coupled with the increasing fragmentation of international news media sources that are not so easily controlled by federal agencies (like those found on the

Internet), may produce a very different future scenario. The questionable tale of the incubator babies in Kuwait may yet come back to haunt future U.S. leaders, as did the fabricated stories of the bayoneted Belgian babies of World War I.

Overall, the Persian Gulf War was successfully sold to the American people by an administration that adhered to seven key principles: *One*, control the media environment by controlling media access to the war zone; *Two*, use sophisticated marketing and public relations strategies and techniques to justify the war by connecting it to the basic American myth of the Frontier and Regeneration through Violence; *Three*, line up an impressive army of coalition forces to signify global approval; *Four*, use and celebrate the latest technologies of war to overwhelm the enemy; *Five*, keep the active combat as brief and American casualties as low as possible; *Six*, don't ask the American people to make sacrifices to support the war (the volunteer military is a key element here); *Seven*, declare a complete and decisive victory and organize massive homecoming celebrations for the returning military forces. And be sure to tie a yellow ribbon around the entire package.

7

The Global War on Terror—Iraq

HOW TO SUCCESSFULLY SELL A WAR

Astute marketers know that no new product can successfully be sold to its target audience with only a brief campaign of advertising and related marketing communications activities. The campaign must not only be well conceived, but also intensive and sustained for a very long time. Even after the consumer makes the initial decision to purchase the product, the marketer must continue "selling it in" to assure that enthusiasm for the product purchase decision doesn't wane in the weeks and months following the original purchase. When the objective of the marketing campaign is to win, and then maintain public support for the U.S. administration's decision to invade and occupy another country, this axiom is even more applicable.

British military historian John Keegan notes that "The Iraq War of 2003 was exceptional in both beginning well for the Anglo-American force that waged it and ending victoriously.... The war was not only successful but peremptorily short, lasting only twenty-one days, from 20 March to 9 April [2003]."[1] If the war in Iraq had truly ended as did the Persian Gulf War in 1991, with the United States victorious after a brief battle resulting in few American casualties and Saddam Hussein's army shattered, Keegan's observation might have had lasting relevance.

However, the days and months following the occupation of Baghdad by American forces saw an insurgency generated by Saddam loyalists—and foreign fighters—mushroom throughout most parts of the country. This bloody aftermath of the invasion was clearly not what President George W. Bush's administration had expected, or what the U.S. public had been led to believe by the White House was going to happen. As the disparity between the Bush administration's initial promises of a short and affordable war evolved into a drawn out and bloody counterinsurgency campaign, the rising toll of U.S. combat casualties and huge financial costs began to sour many Americans on this Middle Eastern military adventure. Further, the compelling reasons that President Bush initially proposed to the American people as a rationale for a U.S. war with Iraq—Saddam Hussein's possession of weapons of mass destruction and his alliance with Al Qaeda—were never substantiated in the aftermath of the invasion despite intensive investigation.

Setting the Stage for the U.S. Invasion of Iraq

Watergate investigator Bob Woodward reports that the Bush administration's decision to invade Iraq was set in motion less than three months after the terrorist attacks in New York and Washington, DC, on September 11, 2001. At a November meeting of the National Security Council in the White House, President George W. Bush asked his Secretary of Defense Donald H. Rumsfeld what plans he had set for war with Iraq. When Rumsfeld acknowledged that no current war plan dealing with Iraq existed, the president told him to begin updating such a plan.[2] Rumsfield had initially brought up the idea of expanding America's reaction to the attacks to include an assault on Iraq as well as against Al Qaeda only one day after the attacks in New York and Washington. According to Bob Woodward, the Defense Secretary "was raising the possibility that they could take advantage of the opportunity offered by the terrorist attacks to go after Saddam immediately."[3]

George W. Bush would not have been the first American president who seized on a dramatic event to promote public support for a war he wanted to fight. President William McKinley (prodded by the popular press) used the sinking of the U.S. battleship *Maine* in Havana harbor, by causes unknown to this day, to incite a war against Spain. President Franklin D. Roosevelt waited until the Japanese fleet attacked Pearl Harbor before asking for Congress to declare war although he had considerable evidence that Japan was going to attack U.S. territory some time before the incident actually occurred. Lyndon B. Johnson delayed the launch of major U.S. air attacks on North Vietnam until that nation's torpedo boats allegedly staged several assaults on American destroyers cruising near its coast. In each of these cases, the president was preparing for a war and waiting for a dramatic event which he could use to mobilize public opinion to support the endeavor.

Some observers believe that the U.S. invasion of Iraq was being contemplated by Bush administration officials soon after George W. Bush won a narrow Electoral College victory. Among the war hawks were Vice President-elect Dick Cheney, National Security Advisor Condoleezza Rice, Defense Department Advisor Richard Perle, and Deputy Defense Secretary Paul Wolfowitz. However, when George Bush took office in January 2000, there is little doubt that these war plans were given a much higher priority. "They had come into office itching to replay the '91 war and try out their democracy domino theory in the Middle East—mirror imaging writ large," notes columnist Maureen Dowd.[4] Former U.S. Treasury Secretary Paul O'Neill also expressed this view, stating, "The United States began laying groundwork for an invasion of Iraq just days after President Bush took office in January 2001—more than two years before the start of the U.S.-led war that ousted Saddam Hussein."[5]

Richard Clarke, President Bush's former counterterrorism chief, said that shortly after the 9/11 attacks, the Bush administration's top officials were focusing more on plans to justify the attack on Iraq than on stopping Al Qaeda. According to Clarke, the president instructed him and others meeting in the White House Situation Room to "See if Saddam did this. See if he's linked in any way." When Clarke reminded him that Al Qaeda was responsible for the attacks, the President reportedly said, "I know, I know, but ... see if Saddam was involved. Just look. I want to know any shred. . . . " In a subsequent interview on the *CBS Television Network's* "Sixty Minutes," Clarke said that "an attack on Iraq under those circumstances was comparable to President Roosevelt, after Pearl Harbor, deciding to invade Mexico instead of going to war with Japan."[6]

Paul Wolfowitz, in a *Vanity Fair* interview, offered further evidence that the Bush administration was searching for a justification to invasion of Iraq: "We settled on the one issue that everyone could agree on, which was weapons of mass destruction."[7]

September 11, 2001, and Its Aftermath

Nine days after Islamic fundamentalist terrorists crashed three commercial airliners into the twin towers of New York's World Trade Center and the Pentagon in Washington, DC, President George W. Bush told a joint session of Congress that his administration was setting a new and forceful course for the nation. He said, " ... we will pursue nations that provide aid or safe haven to terrorism. Every nation, in every region, now has a decision to make. Either you are with us, or you are with the terrorists. . . . Whether we bring our enemies to justice or bring justice to our enemies, justice will be done."[8]

This blunt message set the tone for a presidency that had been struggling with economic issues and anemic public approval of administration policies since the president was narrowly elected in 2000. At that junction, he had lost the popular vote and narrowly won the electoral vote after a fiercely contested legal battle that was only resolved when the U.S. Supreme Court supported his claim for legitimacy as the victor in Florida and, then, in the national election. Prior to the events of 9/11, the polls indicated that George Bush's approval rating was less than 60 percent. One month after 9/11, the president's approval rating had spiked to nearly 90 percent.[9]

The events of 9/11 transformed his presidency. Almost immediately, Bush seized the initiative, rallying the nation to strike back against those who had attacked America. Only days after four U.S. airliners were hijacked to launch the attacks, both Houses of the U.S. Congress voted overwhelmingly to grant President Bush authority "to use all necessary and appropriate force" against those behind the terrorist attacks. "Just three days removed from these events, Americans do not yet have the distance of history," he said. "But our responsibility to history is already clear: to answer these attacks and rid the world of evil."[10]

The Afghanistan Sideshow

Before tackling the Iraq problem, there was the matter of finding Osama bin Laden and destroying him and his terrorist organization, Al Qaeda. Afghanistan had been a pawn in the Cold War, with the United States and other countries supporting the Mujahedin Resistance to the Soviet invasion. After the Soviet military evacuated the country in 1989, Afghan warlords fought for control, with the Islamic fundamentalist Taliban seizing power in 1996–1997. In providing sanctuary for bin Laden and Al Qaeda, the Taliban incurred the wrath of the United States.

After 9/11, the search for bin Laden intensified, with American and British planes attacking the Taliban in October 2001, helping anti-Taliban militias to capture Kabul, the capital, and other key cities. Although the Taliban were on the run, the situation remained unstable for some time, and in August 2003, NATO troops, including Americans, assumed control of the security of the country.

The American public loudly cheered this effort to rid the world of bin Laden, Al Qaeda, and the Taliban. But bin Laden escaped capture and the Taliban retreated to the border country with Pakistan from which they continued to attack NATO forces and to destabilize Afghanistan.

In America, the initial euphoria created by the search for bin Laden faded with the failure to capture him or to destroy Al Qaeda or the Taliban. Both the Bush administration and the news media seemed to lose interest in Afghanistan, relegating it to a minor story. But Afghanistan continued to fester and in January 2007, "Secretary of State Condoleezza Rice asked allies...to intensify their efforts to keep the Taliban from retaking parts of Afghanistan."[11] This came one "day after the Bush Administration said it would ask Congress for $10.6 billion to help the embattled Afghan government."[12]

Another headline story on the same front page of *The New York Times* reported a skeptical response from Rice's audience: "NATO Allies Wary of Sending More Troops to Afghanistan."[13] At that time, over 24,000 Americans and almost 20,000 other NATO military personnel were serving in Afghanistan. Clearly, Afghanistan had not become another "splendid little war" for America and did not rate a "Mission Accomplished" banner for President Bush.

In the days and weeks that followed the bombings, George W. Bush metamorphosed from an American president desperately pursuing his purpose to a national leader rallying the nation, seeking vengeance and justice against those who committed terrorist acts, as well as those nations providing them with safe havens and support. In the State of the Union address he delivered to the American public three and a half months after the 9/11 attacks, he said, "Our war against terror is only beginning," and singled out three nations—Iran, Iraq, and North Korea—that he said "constitute an axis of evil."[14]

This proposition, evoking clear moral issues contrasting the forces of good (the United States and its allies) versus the forces of evil (Iran, Iraq, and North Korea, as well as any other nation that offered shelter to terrorists) became President Bush's rallying cry to the U.S. electorate. It defined his presidency. In the months that followed, he returned to this theme again and again, attempting to persuade the American public that the time had come to defend the country against terrorist attacks by taking preemptive military measures against those countries he said possessed weapons of mass destruction and were willing collaborators of terrorist groups trying to harm the United States. With growing frequency, he expressed the conviction that if the UN or other nations were not prepared to act, the United States. would strike its enemies on a unilateral basis.

On October 7, 2002, President Bush further advanced his argument for war in a widely covered speech to the American people designed to prepare them for the war that was to come. Stating that Saddam Hussein could attack the United States or its allies "on any given day" with chemical or biological weapons, he warned the country that "confronting the threat posed by Iraq is crucial to winning the war on terror." He concluded that the United States had "an urgent duty to prevent the worst from occurring."[15]

An article in *The New Yorker* noted that the administration based its decision to invade and occupy Iraq on four assumptions: "first, that Saddam's regime was on the verge of acquiring nuclear explosives and had already amassed stockpiles of chemical and biological weapons; second, that the regime had meaningful links with Al Qaeda and (as was repeatedly suggested by Vice President Cheney and others) might have had something to do with 9/11; third, that within Iraq the regime's fall would be followed by prolonged celebration and rapid and peaceful democratization; and, fourth, that a similar democratic transformation would be precipitated elsewhere in the region, accompanied by a new eagerness among Arab governments and publics to make peace between Israel and a presumptive Palestinian state."[16]

Playing the Fear Card

Marketers of consumer products and services know that fear and anxiety are among the most powerful emotions in the human psyche that can be tapped to motivate a purchase decision. Early in the twentieth century, American marketers of deodorant soaps discovered how to successfully unleash and channel the public's fear of offending body odor. For many decades, cosmetic marketers have been skillfully convincing women of a certain age that their creams and lotions will arrest and reverse the ravages of time. By identifying Iraq as a direct and imminent threat to the security of Americans, President Bush played the fear card as effectively as any marketing campaign for L'Oreal Cosmetics, Dial Deodorant Soap, or the Slomin Shield home alarm system. His administration repeatedly conjured imminent threats to the country's security as a potent means of securing the continuing support of Congress and the U.S. public.

Bush Administration Is Accused of Timidity

In his speeches, President Bush repeatedly vowed to avenge the attacks on the Twin Towers and the Pentagon. However, he began finding himself under attack by some of the more hawkish news media for being too timid in his actual approach for seeking revenge against America's enemies. On Public Broadcasting Network's *News Hour with Jim Lehrer*, a military expert accused the president of practicing "the Bill Clinton approach to warfare . . . thinking small." Articles in the *New York Times* and *Washington Post* criticized him for taking only half measures in waging the war against terrorism, and warned that the first U.S. military strike, in Afghanistan, could mutate into another stalemate conflict like Vietnam. Expressing concern over this media criticism, President Bush acknowledged, "We're losing the public relations war."[17]

At a November 1, 2001, Pentagon press briefing, a reporter challenged Defense Secretary Rumsfeld, accusing him of selling the war to the American people rather than prosecuting it. The journalist asked, "How big a part of your job is the sales effort? . . . . And are the people that you're talking to buying?" Mr. Rumsfeld responded, saying it was an important job and that the administration had multiple audiences that it had to deal with. He cited the members of the armed services, the American people, and the press as the key audiences, saying that the administration had to "provide the calibration that we believe is the right calibration, the honest, true calibration."[18]

The Administration's War Marketing Campaign Goes into High Gear

President Bush and senior members of his administration began giving widely covered speeches and media interviews unequivocally branding Iraqi dictator Saddam Hussein and his regime as a serious security threat to America and the Free World. Further, they said that the United States was determined to remove him from power, with or without the support of the United Nations or any of America's traditional allies. Fundamental to this foreign policy position was the administration's conviction that American forces would be greeted as liberators by the Iraqi people once Saddam was deposed. Richard Perle, a leading war hawk and an influential advisor to Vice President Richard Cheney, told the news media that when American troops landed, the people of Iraq "will dance in the streets."[19]

The White House unambiguously acknowledged that "the administration was following a meticulously planned strategy to persuade the public, the Congress and the allies of the need to confront the threat from Saddam Hussein." *New York Times* writer Elisabeth Bumiller reported that administration officials began actively planning the campaign to market the war to Congress and the American people in July 2002. President Bush's aides, she said, examined the Congressional calendar to determine the most desirable time for hearings that would lead to a resolution supporting the war measure. "The White House decided, they said, that even with the appearance of disarray it was still more advantageous to wait until after Labor Day [2002] to kick off their plan," she wrote. Taking a page from the playbook guiding the launch strategy for most new consumer products campaigns in the U.S., White House Chief of Staff Andrew Card, who was responsible for coordinating the effort said, "From a marketing point of view, you don't introduce new products in August."[20] Media professionals know there is a significant increase in the size of U.S. television audiences in early September as Americans return from their summer holidays, benefiting both marketers of new consumer products as well as the administration's campaign to build a public consensus supporting its plan to attack Iraq. While Bush continued to seek public (and widely televised) national podiums to press his case for war, the White House began planning other marketing communication initiatives, just as marketers of consumer products create complex and well-coordinated strategies and programs to launch new soft drinks or cars.

One strategy explored by the Bush White House advisors and public relations consultants following the 9/11 attacks was "to keep Americans focused on the war effort" utilizing "a televised megaconcert with performers celebrating American values like freedom and democracy.... The event would be aimed at "educating a new generation of Americans on what war is all about." According to a story in *Time*, the White House PR team planned to recruit popular recording, television, and movie stars who had demonstrated their loyalty to President Bush as participants in this event. White House advisors believed that such an event would be more sympathetic to the sensibilities of more conservative voters, providing a counterpoint to a celebrity-filled show that had been carried on national television shortly after the bombings occurred. That program was "very nice, but a little too Hollywood and New York," i.e., liberal, in the words of one presidential advisor.[21] For reasons that were never explained, this televised "mega-event" never took place.

The Pseudo-Event

Ever since President Franklin D. Roosevelt began staging regular press conferences and broadcasting "fireside chats" on network radio in 1933, the pseudo-event has been employed as an effective marketing technique by those who followed him in the White House, according to historian Daniel J. Boorstin who defined pseudo-events as synthetically created events primarily generated to promote extensive coverage by the news media, or to directly reach a wide public audience. These events, he wrote, are largely characterized by the following characteristics: They are staged, not spontaneous; designed to be reported by the media; ambiguously related to the reality of events; and frequently "intended to be a self-fulfilling prophecy."[22]

As the kickoff for the president's campaign to gain public support for a U.S. invasion of Iraq, administration officials began planning a pseudo-event to exploit the first anniversary of the terrorist bombings, September 11, 2002. White House advisors suggested that the president make his nationally televised remarks on Ellis Island in the middle of New York Harbor with the Statue of Liberty illuminated behind him to maximize the dramatic visual effect. Dan Bartlett, President Bush's communications director, had previously sent a team to scout another island in New York Harbor as the potential site for the speech but his experts advised him that the Ellis Island location, now the site of a national historic monument, would provide better visuals for the network television cameras.[23]

On September 11, the president had a busy day, giving brief commemorative speeches first at the Pentagon in the nation's capital where the terrorists succeeded in crashing into their target; then at a field in Pennsylvania, where an airliner commandeered by some of the terrorists was forced to crash as the passengers fought to regain control of the aircraft; and finally at New York City where the two planes piloted by the terrorists destroyed the twin towers of the World Trade Center. At each stop on President Bush's busy itinerary there was enormous news media coverage, which culminated as he delivered his final address of the long day in the growing darkness of New York Harbor.

Speaking in somber and emotional tones, he told the huge U.S. and global live television audience that "he had no intention of ignoring or appeasing history's latest gang of fanatics." "We have made a sacred promise to ourselves and to the world," he said. "We will not relent until justice is done, and our nation is secure. What our enemies have begun, we will finish." This speech set the stage for the more pugnacious address he was to deliver at the United Nations the following day.[24] Moments after he finished his Ellis Island speech, White House aides began handing out copies of a lengthy report detailing the twelve-year history of Saddam Hussein's violations of United Nations Security Council resolutions to the news media. At the same time, Vice President Dick Cheney and other senior members of the Bush administration were giving continual interviews to the press, engaging in a "media blitz" to assure that the President's message was getting out.[25]

The next day, the president continued pursuing his campaign for justifying his case for war with Iraq in an address to the UN Security Council in New York. He urged its members to demand that Saddam Hussein destroy all his weapons of mass destruction and immediately comply with all of the previously passed UN resolutions requiring the Iraqi dictator to stop persecuting his nation's people, end support for terrorism, and finish paying reparations resulting from the Gulf War of 1991. After Hussein complied with these demands, President Bush said the United Nations would help "build a government that represents all Iraqis," clearly indicating that Saddam Hussein would not be part of this new government. A senior U.S. Defense Department official stated, "By going to the United Nations, we're trying to make people more comfortable with what we are trying to do, and that is to move toward a military engagement. We're doing things just to make people in the international community feel better."[26]

In the days and weeks following the president's talk at the UN, his administration intensified its drumbeat for war. The White House distributed stories to the news media describing Saddam's past atrocities and repeatedly asserted that Iraq was still developing weapons of mass destruction and harboring terrorists although "evidence of Saddam's terrorist connections and nuclear prospects is sketchy," an article in *Newsweek* observed. After the president delivered his speeches in New York, his approval rating soared from the low 60s to 70 percent. However, nearly two-thirds of those Americans polled still believed that the United States should attack Iraq only as part of a coalition of its European allies and the United Nations. To build greater public support for a unilateral American war with Iraq, the marketing campaign continued with the White House and government agencies disseminating a steady stream of facts and figures to the news media designed to generate stronger national backing. As one Bush aide said, "One thing this White House is good at is vividly telling a story."[27]

Three weeks after speaking at the United Nations, President Bush ratcheted up his efforts to win public support for military action against Iraq. In a television address seen by millions in the United States and around the world, he warned that "Saddam Hussein could attack the United States or its allies on any given day with chemical or biological weapons," arguing that "we have an urgent duty to prevent the worst from occurring." The president asserted that "Iraq's fleet of unmanned aerial vehicles was ultimately intended to deliver chemical and biological weapons to cities in the United States." Raising the specter of possible nuclear annihilation, he reprised John F. Kennedy's words at the time of the Cuban Missile Crisis: "Facing clear evidence of peril, we cannot wait for the final proof—the smoking gun—that could come in the form of a mushroom cloud." Following this speech, a *New York Times* reporter observed that the president's speech was part of a continuing administration initiative to sell his case against Saddam Hussein. The *New York Times* article said that at this point "His first audience, Congress, required the least persuasion.... His second audience, the American public, has been more problematic" because opinions polls revealed that while there was strong support for confronting Iraq, a majority of Americans still said that they didn't want the U.S. military to attack Iraq without allies, and felt that before any military action, the United Nations inspection process should be allowed to proceed.[28]

Selling the War to Congress and the United Nations

Only one month after President Bush presented his ultimatum to the UN Security Council demanding action against Iraq, both Houses of Congress overwhelmingly approved a resolution giving the president the authority to mobilize the armed forces for an attack on Saddam Hussein's regime. Following the vote, President Bush warned the Iraqi government that "it must disarm and comply with all existing UN resolutions, or it will be forced to comply. There are no other options for the Iraqi regime. There can be no negotiations. The days of Iraq acting as an outlaw state are coming to an end." While many members of Congress were reluctant to support the measure, the president persuaded the lawmakers to approve the resolution after he had presented his case to the United Nations with a clear indication that he was willing to keep trying to work within its framework to achieve broad coalition support. Democratic Congressman John Spratt reluctantly voted to pass it, but commented, "The president says he needs the authority to bolster his hand at the United Nations and get the arms inspections going." Democratic Senator Edward Kennedy added, "There's also a willingness to give the president the benefit of the doubt."[29] Unsaid, but a significant factor, was the concern of many Democrats in Congress facing close reelection contests in 2002 who feared the consequences of voting against the measure then being endorsed by a president riding high in popular opinion polls.

While the president was pressuring Congress to support his drive for war with Iraq, Secretary of State Colin Powell was working behind the scenes at the United Nations to overcome the resistance of France and other members of the Security Council to the passage of a more forceful resolution threatening possible military action against Iraq if it didn't immediately agree to permit the UN to resume its weapons inspections in the country. On November 8, 2002, four weeks after Congress authorized the administration to attack Iraq, the UN Security Council unanimously approved a resolution demanding that Saddam Hussein scrap his weapons programs or face "serious consequences," a clear signal of a likely American-led[30] attack. Five days later, Saddam Hussein begrudgingly agreed to allow UN weapons inspectors to return to Iraq after a four-year absence. A deadline for total compliance of the UN order was set for December 8, four weeks in the future.[31] That deadline was met with one day to spare when representatives of the Iraq government delivered nearly 12,000 pages of documentation to UN officials in Baghdad asserting that Iraq had no weapons of mass destruction nor was it developing them.[32] Two weeks later, the Bush administration concluded that Iraq was in "material breach" of United Nations resolutions and ordered the military to accelerate the deployment of U.S. troops to the Persian Gulf region.

Selling the War to the American Public

Winning Congressional approval was a crucial step in the administration's marketing campaign to gain public support to wage this war. With the endorsement of Congress now in hand, President Bush began focusing on his second major goal—winning the trust and backing of the American people to wage war in Iraq.

The administration's campaign was launched in late December 2002. In the days that followed, a host of senior administration officials gave speeches or made themselves available for interviews to make the administration's case for war on network television news shows and on major network affiliate stations in key U.S. TV markets. Secretary of State Colin Powell promoted the administration's case for war in a speech at the United Nations. Other advocates for the president's war policy included Deputy Secretary of State Richard Armitage, Defense Secretary Donald Rumsfeld, senior Pentagon advisor Paul Wolfowitz, and National Security Advisor Condoleezza Rice. As the administration's marketing operation progressed, Matthew Dowd, the White House pollster, said that "He was encouraged by other polls showing a rise in support for action to oust Saddam Hussein, with 60 percent favoring a war with Iraq."[33]

Ever since television became the dominant American medium, presidents have used their annual State of the Union address to the Congress as a potent way to win public support for their domestic and foreign policy programs. In addition to the vast TV audience watching the president speak "live" from the Capitol Building in Washington DC, the subsequent electronic and print media reportage of his remarks assures that anything he says will receive wide and detailed coverage. Near the end of January 2003, President Bush used his State of the Union address to step up the drumbeat for war with Iraq. While still offering to consult with the United Nations, he stated, ".... let there be no misunderstanding: if Saddam Hussein does not fully disarm, for the safety of our people and for the peace of the world, we will lead a coalition to disarm him."[34]

The president captured a national public audience again in early March 2003 at a rare televised prime time press conference at the White House to repeat his call to arms, warning that if the United Nations did not authorize a military strike against Iraq soon, "I will not leave the American people at the mercy of the Iraqi dictator and his weapons." When the president was asked to respond to a comment by Democratic Senator Edward Kennedy that Bush's "fixation on Saddam is making the world more dangerous for Americans" and that other critics have alleged that the president was taking the situation in Iraq personally because Saddam Hussein once tried to assassinate his father (former President George H. W. Bush), he denied having any other motive than to protect America.[35]

On March 17, 2003, President Bush warned Saddam Hussein that he had only forty-eight hours to leave Iraq or face military action, and criticized the United Nations for abdicating its responsibility to disarm the Iraqi regime. His remarks were covered by all of the country's television networks.[36] Commenting on intensive focus on getting maximum exposure of the administration message on television, David Gregory, the NBC TV correspondent in Washington said, "I knew things were getting serious when I saw a television makeup man at the Pentagon."[37]

A Gallup opinion poll taken four days earlier revealed that a majority of Americans (56%) approved of the way the president was handling the Iraq situation.[38]

As the U.S. Armed Forces prepared to launch their attack on Iraq, the administration's communications apparatus, in Washington, DC, in the Middle East, and around the world, went into high gear. Determined to maintain control of the news stories and images to a greater degree than any White House had done before in wartime, President Bush urged the spokesmen for all of the government's departments and agencies "to get out the news in a coordinated way that reflects the truth about our efforts." An article in the *Washington Post* said that the "administration plans to fill every information void in the 24-hour worldwide news cycle, leaving little to chance or interpretation." Expanding on the administration's plan to control America's understanding of what was happening in Iraq, Karen De Young described the following planned activities:

- At dawn of each day, White House spokesman Ari Fleischer will brief the major television networks and wire services so that morning news shows can have fresh updates.
- Thematic story lines for the day will be established among all the Administration's spokesmen and women to assure consistency in messages.
- Central Command headquarters in the Middle East will hold a regular afternoon news briefing timed to reach the noon news broadcast in the U.S. Early prime-time and late night broadcast in Europe will be fed each day from an afternoon briefing at the Pentagon in Washington, D.C.[39]

DELIVERING THE PROMISED WAR

On March 19, 2003, two days after delivering his final ultimatum to Saddam Hussein, President Bush appeared on network television again to inform the American people that "American and coalition forces are in the early stages of military operations to disarm Iraq, to free its people and to defend the world from grave danger. On my orders, coalition forces have begun striking selected targets of military importance to undermine Saddam Hussein's ability to wage war."[40] Less than two hours later, American and British Coalition ground forces began to swarm across the Iraqi border as strategic sites throughout Iraq came under aerial attack. The "shock and awe" phase of the military campaign promised by George W. Bush had begun.[41]

Traditionally, the public rallies round the president when American troops go into combat. A national Gallup Poll conducted one day after the invasion began found that 76 percent of Americans supported President Bush's decision to go to war.[42] Both Houses of Congress reflected this sentiment the day after the Coalition attacks started by overwhelmingly voting resolutions that "commends and supports the efforts and leadership of the President, as Commander in Chief, in the conflict against Iraq."[43]

Branding the War

The Bush administration's marketing specialists thought long and hard about the brand names they wanted to assign to various phases of the U.S. invasion of Iraq. As every marketer of consumer products knows, developing a positive and memorable brand name for your product plays a vital role in establishing a successful relationship with your target audience; in this case the target audience was primarily the American public.

Marketing and advertising veteran Jack Trout was recruited by the Bush administration in 2002 as part of the administration's "Brand America" program, an initiative to project a more positive image of America to the world. Marketing experts like Trout ultimately concluded that it was necessary to properly "brand" the impending preemptive war against Iraq to win the battle for public opinion in the United States and abroad. According to an article in the *Christian Science Monitor*, "The need to successfully brand the war . . . was particularly significant in this case, because of the long buildup before military action would be taken. No aggression or specific act of terrorism prompted action in Iraq, but rather a prolonged failure to play by the rules set forth by the United Nations." Regarding the war in Iraq, the article said that "some observers now cite a growing need for makers of foreign policy to embrace the image issue just as politicians have done for decades—and to hone their skill at selling war." "What we are really laying out here is that all the world has become a press conference," said Trout. "This is a battle for perception."[44]

So twelve years after President George H. W. Bush proclaimed "Operation Desert Storm" as the brand name for the first U.S. attack against Iraq, his son approved the brand name "Operation Iraqi Freedom" to characterize his war against Iraq as a liberating mission in the hope of persuading America and the world of his administration's altruistic intentions. And with the same kind of intuitive judgment that guided the Nazi High Command in World War II to term their combined air-land assault on surrounding nations a "Blitzkrieg," (or "Lightning War"), the president's advisors coined the phrase "Shock and Awe" to describe the air war that launched the second U.S. assault on Iraq.

"Linguists and marketing experts say the Bush administration is particularly adroit at using language to subtly influence debate," an article in the *Wall Street Journal* stated. "It's sort of as though the war makers have learned from the marketers," says David Burd, owner of Naming Co. "They are marketing the war to the public, packaging it and giving it a name. Even the list of countries supporting the U.S. effort has a name: The Coalition of the Willing."[45]

The Pentagon's Embedding Strategy

In February 2003, as the U.S. invasion of Iraq became increasingly a certainty, the Pentagon announced a new press policy: embedding accredited news correspondents with designated frontline military units in a move its officials called a historic shift in the decade-long conflict between the U.S. military and the press.

According to a report in *Editor & Publisher*, more than 500 reporters representing 300 U.S. and foreign news organizations as diverse as *Rolling*

Stone and *Al Jazeera* were advised that they would be given direct access to combat zones in Iraq and surrounding areas as embedded journalists. However, the Pentagon also demanded that those news correspondents taking part in the program abide by stringent security prohibitions on the "media products" they would be transmitting to their sponsoring news organizations. Violations of these ground rules would result in immediate expulsion from the theater of operations. Before the participating correspondents were provided with transportation to the Middle East accompanying the units they were embedded with, they were put through a brief and rudimentary training camp and issued military equipment to help them more readily adapt to the demands of the impending war zone.

Two weeks prior to the start of the invasion, George Allison, one of Hollywood's top art directors, was sent by the administration to U.S. Central Command Headquarters in Qatar to create a network TV quality stage set costing a quarter of a million dollars for U.S. generals to use as they presented daily updates to the press corps on the progress of the impending war. Mr. Allison had previously designed White House backdrops for President Bush's televised speeches. The *London Times* described the setup: "This is about bringing the level of technology up from the flipchart to the modern age. It is trying to send a clear message about the technology and our use of it."[46]

The Bush Administration Surrenders Some Control of the News

Until combat operations began in Iraq on March 20, 2003, the Bush administration was generally able to control the flow of information shaping the perceptions that the American public was forming about the impending war. They accomplished this by generating a continual stream of the president's nationally televised speeches, initiating a steady stream of media interviews using senior members of the administration who were adroit at staying "on message," and staging a series of "photo-ops" aimed at stimulating public support for the president's plan to wage war. At the same time, the administration was extraordinarily effective in stonewalling the press it considered unsupportive of the president's programs and limiting their capacity to get information that might weaken the White House's case for war: ".... it seems to me that the operative assumption at the Pentagon is, we will talk to you if it fits our specific narrow purpose and not if it doesn't," said David Wood, Newhouse News Service's national security correspondent. Since the American public depends on the news media to inform them about the daily activities and policies of the government, the Bush White House's ability to tightly control media access to such information was micromanaged to a greater degree than in any previous administration in recent U.S. history.[47]

However, once the attack against Iraq commenced, the Bush administration no longer had such tight control of the words and images that Americans would be accessing about the conflict. In this new era of advanced media technologies, journalists embedded with frontline units were transmitting words and imagery as the events were actually occurring on the battlefield, in the air over Iraq and on warships cruising in the Persian Gulf. Satellite technology, round-the-clock news coverage, and the diverse news sources offered by the Internet, much of it distributed by non-U.S. news organizations, had transformed the media environment and the ways in which the United States and global public learned what was happening. Military censors could now only react to violations of Pentagon ground rules after the public had already received the news. "The technology has improved to the point where one is relatively easily able to transmit voice and pictures from the field," said NBC vice president Bill Wheatley. "With a videophone, in theory you can broadcast from just about anywhere."[48]

In the initial stages of the war, beginning with the assault across the Iraq border until the envelopment of Baghdad, news coverage of the Coalition's campaign was almost universally positive. Some media critics observed that the general tone of the coverage, particularly on television, was skewed toward overly patriotic imagery of heroic American soldiers as they charged across the desert, and ignored the extent of the collateral damage to Iraqi civilians.

In the aftermath of the initial Coalition attack and occupation of Iraq, Bush administration officials said they were pleased with the success of the "embedding" program. And opinion polls taken in the weeks following the seizure of Baghdad indicated that a large majority of the U.S. public (74%) agreed that the media coverage of the war was excellent. Dismissing criticism that media outlets were too jingoistic in their coverage, CBS News President Andrew Heyward said, "American journalists are rooting for America to win. You're not going to find a lot of Americans rooting for Iraq. That doesn't mean they're not objective and fair in their reporting."[49]

Public Opinion and the Second Stage of the War

Inevitably, American forces began to suffer casualties as the war ensued. Despite the fact that the number of killed and wounded U.S. combatants was initially small, a public opinion poll taken three days after the start of the war found that the percentage of Americans who believed the war was "going well" plunged from 71 percent to 38 percent. A likely reason for this sudden loss in public confidence was the realization that despite the promised potency of the U.S. "shock and awe" air assault, the invasion was going to cost the lives of a growing number of American troops on the ground, as well as Saddam Hussein's soldiers. "Contrary to the expectations of political leaders and the media, the American public is willing to tolerate some casualties if they believe the operation is going to be successful, if we're going to win," said Christopher Gelpi, a professor of political science at Duke University. "The level of casualties the public is willing to accept also depends on how important they think the mission is."[50]

Rising to this challenge, President Bush stepped up to assume the role of commander in chief/cheerleader to sustain public confidence in the ultimate success and necessity of this preemptive war. In the days following the start of the war, he increasingly appeared in public to sell and spin the war[51]

Spontaneous and Premeditated Photo-Ops

Sometimes unplanned "photo-ops" benefit the marketers of a war better than any imagery of a preplanned pseudo-event could. The celebrated classic World War II photograph of five victorious Marines and one Navy corpsman raising the American flag atop Mount Suribachi on Iwo Jima was one iconic example. That picture became the classic image of American military power, lifting the spirits of war-weary America and its allies.

Such a spontaneous photo-op occurred in the early stages of the U.S. envelopment of Baghdad when Marines converging on the center of the city draped an American flag over the head of a gargantuan statue of Saddam Hussein, and then quickly replaced it with an Iraqi flag to enhance the Coalition's attempts to visually position its forces as liberators, not invaders. The Marines next used an armored vehicle to topple the statue from its pedestal, leaving only a pair of hollow boots standing. A crowd of jubilant Iraqis dragged the head of the deposed dictator through the streets of Baghdad as television and still photographers captured every moment. These iconic images, seen almost instantly on television screens in the United States and around the world, became the most powerful visual symbol of the Coalition's military triumph in Iraq and momentarily stilled the critics of President Bush's decision to invade that country.[52]

One month later on May 1, the president's marketing communications team staged a pseudo-event on the deck of the U.S. aircraft carrier *Abraham Lincoln* that was later described in a *New York Times* article "as one of the most audacious moments of presidential theater in American history ... using the powers of television and technology to promote a presidency like never before." Every aspect of this event was carefully choreographed by White House aides, many with extensive network TV experience. As the carrier cruised within thirty miles of its San Diego base, the president chose to fly to the carrier in a Navy aircraft which made a tail-hook landing on its flight deck. He emerged from the plane, wearing a "Top Gun"-style flight suit, to the cheers of the assembled crew.

Flight helmet tucked under his arm, the president then delivered a brief speech celebrating the end of major combat in Iraq. A large banner proclaiming "Mission Accomplished" was displayed on the ship's superstructure above him. This meticulously staged pseudo-event was shown on every television news show in the country and was featured on the front page of every American newspaper. Prominent Democrats and some in the media criticized the president for what they termed a "political stunt," but a nationwide opinion poll revealed that 59 percent of those Americans polled said that his behavior was appropriate and not an effort to make political gain.[53]

Mr. Bush later denied that his staff had arranged for the "Mission Accomplished" banner to be placed strategically behind him for the cameras to capture, claiming that it "was suggested by those on the ship. They asked us to do the production of the banner, and we did," he said. Somewhat ingenuously, he added, "They're the ones who put it up."[54]

Another photo-op and pseudo-event that was successfully organized by his communications staff in 2003 was the President's surprise Thanksgiving Day visit with the troops in Iraq. A *New York Times* article observed that this act successfully managed to defuse the hostile comments of critics who took umbrage at the image of him "swaggering across an aircraft carrier in front of a banner reading 'Mission Accomplished.'" The new image being carried into homes across America on Thanksgiving Day was "the picture of Mr. Bush, his eyes glistening with tears, addressing cheering troops on Thanksgiving Day."[55] In keeping with the pseudo-event nature of this visit, the turkey that the president carried on a platter was made of plastic. This time, not even the sizzle was being sold.

Saving Private Lynch

One photo-op that initially was exploited by the U.S. military to boost support for the war, but was later discredited as inaccurate hype, involved the filming of the rescue of Army Private First Class Jessica Lynch who was wounded and taken prisoner by the Iraqis in the early days of the invasion. Pfc. Lynch was rescued from a hospital in Southern Iraqi on April 1 by a U.S. Special Forces unit. This rescue was shot with dramatic night-vision imagery and video copies were quickly distributed by the Defense Department to media in the United States and around the world. Initially, military spokesmen at the Coalition's Central Command headquarters in Qatar told correspondents that Pfc. Lynch had engaged in a "to-the-death" gun battle before she was shot and captured. They also stated that she was mistreated at the Iraqi hospital where she was brought for treatment. A Central Command spokesman advised the journalists that "this was the first successful rescue mission of an American POW since World War II."

According to a story that later appeared in the *Chicago Tribune* and in other media, her serious injuries were not from gunshot wounds, but instead occurred when the truck in which she was riding crashed after it was ambushed by Iraqis. And contrary to earlier statements that she had been abused after her capture, she reportedly was professionally treated by the Iraqi doctors and nurses at the hospital who on several occasions shielded her from the Iraqi military and were attempting to repatriate her to Coalition forces when the Special Forces team arrived. Soon after these revelations, both the Bush administration and the media lost all interest in the Jessica Lynch rescue story.[56]

The Dover Test

Since the Vietnam War, American presidents have been wary of the "Dover Test," the images of caskets containing U.S. war dead arriving at Dover Air Force Base Mortuary in Delaware. During the Vietnam War, images of returning military caskets were screened nightly on television news shows and in the print media, triggering powerful emotional responses by the public about the human costs of war. Former astronaut and then U.S. Senator John Glenn coined the phrase, "Dover Test," when talking about publicized images of dead U.S. combatants arriving at Dover in 1994 from the conflict in Haiti. He then said "the more coffins that arrive from overseas, the Americans' appetite for war—any war—is dulled."[57]

Fearful of such demoralizing imagery in future wars, the military banned the media from covering the arrival of such remains in 1991. At the start of the war in Iraq, the military reiterated this ban to include all military installations, explaining that it was enforced "to be sensitive to the families of those killed." Nevertheless, in two separate cases early in the war, photographs of flag-draped caskets arriving from the Middle East were inadvertently released to the media. Since then, no images of returning military dead have been seen in the press.[58]

Those seriously wounded in Iraq are brought back in military transports that land at Andrews Air Force Base [near Washington, DC] after midnight, said U.S. Senator Patrick Leahy, "making sure the press does not see the planes coming in."[59] Further reflecting the administration's concern about public perceptions, the press was restricted in its ability to cover the funerals of Americans killed in Iraq at Arlington National Cemetery. "They don't want the public to see what the great difficulties are," Boston University historian Robert Dallek said. "They're fearful that the public is turning against the war because it's frustrated by the losses of blood and treasure, in this case Iraq and earlier in Vietnam."[60]

THE PRESIDENT'S APPROVAL RATINGS

Selling in the Peace Begins to Slip

Perhaps because of the successful selling of the war and the quick and seemingly decisive Coalition victories over the Iraqi military forces, the president continued to enjoy the support of the public in the initial aftermath of the major combat phase of the war in Iraq. At this point, significant insurgent action against the Coalition forces had not yet coalesced. In April 2003, public opinion polls showed that Americans were more optimistic about the direction the Bush administration was taking than before the war, with the president receiving a 71 percent job approval rating. Almost three-fourths of Americans polled now expressed support for George Bush's decision to take military action against Iraq, a substantially greater percentage than those who had supported this course before the war began.[61]

In the months that followed, however, the repeated assurances by senior administration officials that the American military would be warmly greeted as liberators began to ring hollow as an insurgency emerged in Iraq, causing a growing number of U.S. and allied casualties. Only 61 U.S. troops had been killed when the president made his triumphant announcement on the deck of the aircraft carrier *Abraham Lincoln* at the beginning of May. By early July 2003 more than 200 U.S. troops were dead and the body count continued to rise daily. The president blamed members of Saddam Hussein's Baath Party and other terrorist groups for sabotaging Coalition forces' attempts to rehabilitate the country. Despite intense efforts by the military to find evidence of weapons of mass destruction in Iraq, George Bush's primary justification for going to war, none were found. In addition, Saddam Hussein was still at large somewhere in Iraq and leading the insurrection. Public support for the war in the United States began slipping. A Gallup Poll released at the beginning of July reported that the number of Americans who now thought the war was not worth fighting had almost doubled.[62]

Through the summer of 2003, President Bush continued encouraging the American public to support his administration's commitment in Iraq as U.S. casualties mounted and the projected costs of rebuilding the shattered nation skyrocketed to one billion dollars a week. As the second anniversary of the September 11 attacks approached, Democrats eager to exploit the president's increased vulnerability with the electorate, began openly criticizing his Iraq strategies in the hope of weakening his chances for reelection in 2004. Key members of his administration like Defense Secretary Donald Rumsfeld and National Security Advisor Condoleezza Rice counterattacked, appearing on countless network TV talk shows and defending his policies in well-publicized speeches around the country.[63]

National public opinion polls showed that 35 percent of the nation now said they believed that the postwar operation was not going well, in contrast with 21 percent holding that view three months earlier. In response, the president shifted the theme of his marketing message to justify the continuing U.S. presence in Iraq. In the first prime-time nationally televised speech he delivered since announcing the launch of the "Shock and Awe" bombing campaign, and just a few days before the second anniversary of the September 11 bombings, the president now defined Iraq as a "central front" in the war on terrorism, although his administration still had not discovered any evidence of an Iraq–Al Qaeda connection. While calling on the UN and individual countries to help by providing military and financial aid to rebuild the shattered nation, he also asked Congress for an additional $87 billion to cover the costs of the stabilization operations in Afghanistan and Iraq.[64]

In this address, the president warned Americans that "there will be no going back to the era before September 11, 2001, to false comfort in a dangerous world.... The surest way to avoid attacks on Americans is to engage the enemy where he lives and plans [so that] we do not meet him again on our own streets, in our cities." In rebuttal, Howard Dean, a candidate for the Democratic presidential nomination, termed the speech "outrageous," saying that the president was "beginning to remind me of what was happening with Lyndon Johnson and Dick Nixon during the Vietnam War.... The government begins to feed misinformation to the American people in order to justify an enormous commitment of American troops, which turned out to be a tremendous mistake."[65]

With major combat operations in Iraq several months in the past, the American public's concerns were shifting to more domestic issues, primarily with the economy. While the public remained concerned about the possibility of future terrorist acts in the United States, opinion polls indicated that Americans' confidence in the administration's management of the economy was weak, representing a threat to the president's reelection hopes. However, since 9/11, the public still regarded George W. Bush as a strong and decisive leader, no small advantage at a time when America remained insecure and fearful of future terrorist attacks.[66]

The President Tries to Bypass the "Media Filter"

Like many U.S. presidents before him, George W. Bush chaffed at what he called the "media filter," which he defined as national news media and the Washington press corps that were limiting his ability to communicate the truth to the American people. His concern was based on his belief that the American people were beginning to think that the U.S. campaign in Iraq was faltering. The president attempted to bypass this perceived obstacle by addressing the nation personally on prime time network television, limiting the number of his White House press conferences and making himself available only for one-on-one interviews with local and regional U.S. news media outlets that he believed would be less adversarial in their approach.

"It was an effort to reach Americans that get their news from their local television stations," a White Spokesman said. In an interview with an interviewer with one local station group, President Bush said, "There's a sense that people in America aren't getting the truth. I'm mindful of the filter through which some news travels. And sometimes you just have to go over the heads of the filter and speak directly to the people, and that's what we will continue to do." A CBS Network spokesperson labeled it the "public relations equivalent of a declaration of war."[67]

President Bush was quite open in his criticism about the press, clearly indicating that he believed its reportage and commentary reflected a more leftist point of the view than that held by a majority of the U.S. public. He acknowledged spending little time watching television news or reading newspapers. When asked by a reporter how he then knows what the public thinks, he answered, "You're making a huge assumption—that you represent what the public thinks." An article in the *The New Yorker* noted that the Bush White House has an unusual skill "in keeping much of the press at a distance while controlling the news agenda. And for perhaps the first time the White House has come to see reporters as special pleaders—pleaders for more access and better headlines—as if the press were simply another interest group, and, moreover, an interest group that's not nearly as powerful as it once was."[68]

Unlike marketers of consumer products and services, presidents and their administration are limited by federal law from buying advertising time or space to forward their political policies, or paying organizations like public relations agencies to advance their political agendas. So like many previous U.S. presidents who experienced frustration with news media they judged was insufficiently enthusiastic in supporting their policies, George W. Bush announced that he was going to express his views to the American people "using regional news outlets more hospitable and less judgmental" because he said "There's a sense that people in America aren't getting the truth." White House "image makers" said that they were "pleased" with the results of the president's media bypass operation which they felt had allowed Mr. Bush to more fully inform the American people about the progress being made in Iraq since Saddam Hussein was deposed.[69]

The President's Credibility Begins to Be Questioned

Eight months after Coalition forces occupied Iraq, critics of the Bush administration, including members of Congress, former Pentagon officials, and a number of retired but still influential U.S. generals, began aggressively challenging the wisdom of the president's Iraq policy. Three hundred and eighty one U.S. soldiers had been killed by November 2003, and analogies with America's Vietnam War experience began to be drawn, particularly relating to allegations about the administration's lack of candor about what was really happening in Iraq.

A *USA Today* article noted "the Bush administration is making mistakes that are eerily similar to the ones Lyndon Johnson, Richard Nixon and military leaders made a generation ago." Throughout the fall months, Bush administration spokesmen repeatedly declared that media reports were not accurately reporting the positive progress being made in Iraq. Republican Senator John McCain, a prisoner of war in North Vietnam for five and a half years, said, "The American press and the American public saw our leaders talk about a 'light at the end of the tunnel' that did not exist during the Vietnam War. We can win the war in Iraq, but not if we lose popular support in the United States."[70]

Saddam's Capture Gives Bush a Bounce in Polls

While U.S. casualties continued to mount and public opinion polls reflected a growing concern about the course of the war, the capture of Saddam Hussein by U.S. troops in mid-December 2003 gave President Bush a dramatic boost in his approval ratings. Sixty-nine percent of Americans polled at the end of the year said that they believed the administration's repeated claims that the deposed dictator was linked to the September 11 bombings despite the fact that no evidence had been found to support this assertion.[71] However, the polls also indicated that Americans still feared U.S. forces would be forced to remain in Iraq for years and were not persuaded that the president had a plan to get U.S. troops out of Iraq.[72]

The run up to the presidential elections in the fall of 2004 was in full swing as the first anniversary of the war approached. The president's Democratic challenger, Senator John Kerry, was doing his best to undermine the country's faith in George W. Bush's handling of the war, as well as the U.S. economy. President Bush vigorously counterattacked, continuing to argue that the war being fought in Iraq was also a war against Al Qaeda and global terrorism, and that the United States would ultimately prevail. His single-minded message appeared to strike a resonant chord with the public, while Senator Kerry's proposals for a resolution of the conflict were considered vague and ill-defined. While the president's approval ratings declined somewhat from the earlier part of the year, a majority of Americans still believed that going to war was the right thing to do. And by a large margin, the polls showed that more Americans trusted the president than challenger Kerry to effectively handle the situation in Iraq.[73]

Abu Ghraib Photos Reach the Media

A shock wave of anger and disgust echoed across the United States and around the world when gruesome photos of hooded and naked Iraqi prisoners being humiliated and abused by smiling American soldiers in Baghdad's Abu Ghraib prison were shown on the CBS Television Network at the end of April 2004. Reacting quickly to this graphic proof of mistreatment, President Bush angrily condemned the abusive behavior saying, "I share a deep disgust that those prisoners were treated the way they were treated. Their treatment does not reflect the nature of the American people. That's not the way we do things in America. . . . " U.S. military authorities in Iraq, already aware of the existence of the photos, had brought charges against those soldiers involved in the incidents before the pictures reached the media, but the personal damage done to the image of President Bush and his administration in America, as well as in other countries, was significant as critics of his policies asserted that the wide exposure of the pictures "threatened to undermine a central justification for the Iraq war: freeing the Iraqi people from an abusive regime."[74]

White House advisors immediately went into a crisis management mode, denying that the president had any knowledge of the abuses before the pictures were aired on television, and attempting to insulate him from the damaging political consequences of the incident. However, the media soon learned that senior Pentagon officials had been trying to get CBS TV executives to delay exposing the story on its highly rated news show *Sixty Minutes* for several weeks before it actually aired.

The White House denied that it had been informed about these measures. Military officials also admitted preparing in advance "an extensive campaign to blunt the impact . . . including three dozen questions and answers anticipated from reporters," a *New York Times* story said. "Once the photographs were shown, the strategy was to have senior officials in Baghdad emphasize that an American soldier had brought the abuses to the attention of his superiors, that military commanders had quickly begun criminal and administrative inquiries, that criminal charges had been brought against six soldiers and that a new commander had been assigned to revamp detention facilities and practices in Iraq."[75]

Attitudes about the Abu Ghraib revelations were quickly reflected in public opinion polls taken shortly after the abuses were publicly revealed. "For the first time, a majority of Americans say they're dissatisfied with President Bush's performance, and 58 percent disapprove of his handling of the situation in Iraq," a *USA TODAY/CNN/Gallup Poll* reported. "The poll finds war opposition growing since news of the prisoner abuse broke 12 days ago. More than half of Americans—54% vs. 47% just a week ago—now say going to war was 'not worth it.'"[76]

Bush Rebounds from the Abu Ghraib Scandal and Mounting U.S. Casualty Count

As the summer of 2004 passed, the Bush administration seemed to weather the storm created by the negative impact on public opinion generated by the Abu Ghraib abuse story. Even as the number of U.S. war dead in Iraq rose above the 1,000 mark in September, public opinion polls indicated that President Bush had regained Americans' confidence by a margin of 53 percent to 37 percent over presidential challenger John Kerry when asked who they believed would do a better job of dealing with the war. Administration critics suggested that a primary reason why the public was still confident in the president was that the White House had been successful in distracting Americans with news of the handover of limited sovereignty to the Iraqis in June and the limited official mention of casualties. In a *Washington Post* story, retired Army general Barry R. McCaffrey said he believed "that the White House and Pentagon are even letting concern for political implications shape military strategy. We are fighting skillfully, but we are ceding large portions of the country, so we can get through the presidential elections."[77]

Countdown to the U.S. Presidential Elections

Following the major political parties' conventions, President George W. Bush and Democratic challenger John Kerry went head-to-head in national campaigns that were described by many observers as the most heated and adversarial in decades. In his speeches, the president continually raised the question, "Who can you trust?" and described his Democratic opponent as too weak on national defense, too irresolute on terrorism, and accused him of being a "flip-flopper." A story in the *Houston Chronicle* said, "The voters were given a stark choice: Stay the course laid out by the president, or fire him by electing Sen. John Kerry. If Bush is certified the winner, it will be because he convinced voters that change in the Oval Office would be too risky during a time of war and terrorist threats."[78]

Bush Wins Reelection

As it turned out, George W. Bush won reelection in November as much on the strength of his perceived position on moral and traditional values, as on his stewardship of the war in Iraq and the war against terrorism, according to a national survey of voters as they left their polling places. A key element in his victory was his ability to position his Democratic opponent as a multilateralist who lacked the necessary resolve to successfully end the war in Iraq and defeat global terrorism. Mr. Bush won the presidential election by a margin of 51 percent to 48 percent for Kerry, appealing overwhelmingly to voters on his handling of the terrorism issue, which they believed was inseparable from the war in Iraq.[79]

America's first Republican president, the martyred Abraham Lincoln, famously noted the need to preserve one's *ethos* with the people: "If you once forfeit the confidence of your fellow citizens, you can never regain their respect and esteem. It is true that you may fool all the people some of the time; you can even fool some of the people all the time; but you can't fool all of the people all the time." In the 2004 elections, President Bush and his campaign advisors proved that you only have to fool enough of the people at the right time to get reelected despite conducting a postwar struggle that was proving to be more lasting, costly, and uncertain than the war itself.

The "Fear Card" Prevailed

From the beginning of the administration's buildup to the U.S. invasion of Iraq following the attacks on 9/11, the Bush administration was successful in arousing Americans' feelings of fear. It accomplished this by executing a sophisticated and complex marketing program designed to convince the members of the U.S. Congress and the public that removing Saddam Hussein from power would importantly contribute to America's safety from future attacks. Three weeks after the presidential election, a national poll found an upswing in Americans' confidence that the United States was winning the war. The poll also showed that President Bush's approval rating had risen since the election.[80] Another national survey taken near the end of the year found that "Americans say they've given Mr. Bush a mandate to fight the antiterrorism war, overseas and on U.S. soil by a strong margin of 74% to 20%. By a narrower 52% to 41%, they say he has a mandate to keep American troops in Iraq as long as it takes to create a stable democracy there."[81]

Support for War in Iraq Begins to Fade

While support for President Bush remained relatively steady, Americans' support for the war in Iraq began to fade in the early months of 2005. A consensus seemed to be building that the Bush administration should be given more time to try to stabilize the country before it started withdrawing troops, but a national poll found "that the percentage of Americans who believed the situation in Iraq was 'worth going to war over' had sunk to a new low of 39%." Poll analysts interpreted these results to mean that "while Americans have grown more pessimistic about the chances for success in Iraq, most are willing to give President Bush some time to try to turn the operation into a success." Sixty-five percent of those surveyed said "they believed the war in Iraq had harmed the United States' image around the world."[82]

The Iraqis Vote

A little less that two years after the United States and its Coalition allies invaded Iraq and overthrew the regime of Saddam Hussein, the people of Iraq went to the polls in January 2005 to vote in the first free election that country had seen in fifty years. The polling places in Baghdad and other cities were closely guarded by Coalition and newly trained Iraqi military, and they proceeded with relatively little violence.

"The people of Iraq have spoken to the world, and the world is hearing the voice of freedom from the center of the Middle East," President Bush said in a nationally televised statement after the polls had closed in Iraq. In the same statement, Mr. Bush noted that more than 1,400 American troops had died since the beginning of the war. An article in the *New York Times* reported that "Mr. Bush and his aides were clearly concerned the [televised images showing jubilant Iraqis voting] would add to the pressures at home to set a clear timetable for withdrawing the 150,000 American forces now based there. So even while hailing the accomplishment, they spent much of the day tamping down expectations, issuing reminders that the American-led efforts to remake Iraq was still at a precarious stage."[83]

Bush Benefits from Iraqi Election

A national poll taken shortly after the January 30, 2005, Iraqi elections showed that Americans had given President Bush his highest job approval rating in more than a year and indicated the public's "cautious optimism" about Iraq's future. A majority of Americans now concluded that going to war with Saddam Hussein's regime was not a mistake. Further, the survey revealed that the U.S. public now believed that things are going well there and that it's likely democracy will be established in Iraq." A senior administration strategist observed, "Nothing breeds success like success."[84]

The question remains whether the pacification of insurgents will result in the relative success achieved by the American military forces and civilian administrators in winning the hearts and minds of Filipinos following the Spanish-American War, or in the military successes and political failures that plagued America's twenty-five-year effort to stem communist expansion in Vietnam. Thus far, the Bush administration has succeeded in "selling in" the Iraq War as something Americans need in order to avenge 9/11 (although no credible connection has been found between Al Qaeda and Saddam Hussein), destroy weapons of mass destruction (although none were found in Iraq), and bring democracy and peace to the Middle East (uncertain at this time). Events in Iraq and American elections will tell whether the "Gunfighter Nation" can regenerate the world through violence.

In his January 20, 2005, Inaugural Address, President George W. Bush used the words "freedom" twenty-seven times and "liberty" fifteen times, but made no references to "Axis of Evil" or to Iraq, Iran, North Korea, Osama bin Laden, Al Qaeda, or even Homeland Security. Instead, he proclaimed America's New Manifest Destiny: "So it is the policy of the United States to seek and support the growth of democratic movements and institutions in every nation and culture, with the ultimate goal of ending tyranny in our world." Later, he expanded on his evangelical call to arms: "America, in this young century, proclaims liberty throughout the world, and to all the inhabitants thereof."[85]

A *New York Times/CBS Poll* published the same day reported that the president had an approval rate of 49 percent, significantly below the ratings of Bill Clinton and Ronald Reagan, the last two presidents for eight years, at the start of their second terms in office. Three quarters of those polled said they believed the president had no clear plan for getting out of Iraq, a significant jump from the previous quarter. Asked to predict future events, 25 percent said the United States would be safer from terrorism in 2009 than now, 17 percent less safe, and 52 percent the same. Asked whether significant U.S. military force will still be in Iraq when the president leaves the White House in 2009, 75 percent said yes, 20 percent no, and 5 percent had no opinion.[86] The poll failed to ask people whether they thought that the United States *should* still be in Iraq in 2009.

National Strategy for Victory in Iraq

In November 2005, the Bush administration's National Security Council issued a thirty-five-page *National Strategy for Victory* in Iraq that identified eight pillars for winning the war. Essentially, this document acknowledges the continuing difficulties in bringing peace and stability to Iraq, but argues that the United States cannot "cut and run," that "Victory in Iraq is a vital U.S. interest," and that "Failure is not an option."[87] The document also claims that an American withdrawal from Iraq will seriously weaken American credibility and that " . . . the terrorists will pursue us and our allies, expanding the fight to the rest of the region and to our own shores."[88] This recycling of the "Domino Theory" espoused by the Eisenhower, Kennedy, and Johnson administrations is clearly intended to appeal to American fears as well as patriotism.

Despite the lack of historical evidence to support the "Domino Theory" in either Vietnam or Iraq, the terrorist attacks of 9/11 continue to resonate with many Americans. Indeed, the victory in Iraq strategy quotes President George W. Bush's words spoken June 28, 2005: "The only way our enemies can succeed is if we forget the lessons of September 11, if we abandon the Iraqi people to men like Zarqawi, and if we yield the future of the Middle East to men like bin Laden. For the sake of our Nation's security, this will not happen on my watch."[89]

What stands out in this strategic assessment is its focus on Iraq and Iraqi public opinion, with little or no attention paid to the American people. Past attempts to connect Osama bin Laden and the Al Qaeda attacks on 9/11 to Iraq have foundered on the hard rocks of reality; simply put, there is not one shred of credible evidence that Saddam Hussein even knew of the Al Qaeda plots, much less aided and abetted them. Still, some 30–34 percent of Americans polled consistently say they believed that Iraq was connected to 9/11, despite numerous news reports that such connections simply do not exist. Even denial of such connections by then Secretary of Defense Donald

Rumsfeld, Secretary of State Condoleezza Rice, Vice President Dick Cheney, and even President George W. Bush himself has failed to move these true believers from their views.

Falling Public Support

According to an *ABC/Washington Post Poll* of May 11–15, 2006, public support for President Bush's handling of the Iraq War fell from a high of 75 percent in April 2003 ("Mission Accomplished") to a low of 32 percent in May 2006. Asked whether the war in Iraq was worth fighting, 70 percent said yes in 2003 but only 37 percent agreed in 2006. On the question of whether the Iraq War helped America's long-term security, in 2003, 62 percent said yes; in 2006, that figure fell to 48 percent. To the question of whether people thought that the Bush administration had told the truth or intentionally misled the American people in selling the war in 2002, a similar shift in opinion occurred. In July 2004, 55 percent said that Bush and his aides believed that they told the truth while 42 percent said that the administration had deliberately misled the people. In May 2006, 46 percent still believed in Bush's ethos while 52 percent believed that they had been manipulated.

An *ABC News/Washington Post Poll* report of May 16, 2006, provides comparisons of a number of wars and their approved ratings. In March 1951, 51 percent of Americans called the Korean War "a mistake." In July 1971, 61 percent thought the same of the Vietnam War. In January 1991, 30 percent found the Persian Gulf War to be "a mistake." In November 2001, only 9 percent labeled the invasion of Afghanistan "a mistake." In May 2006, 59 percent thought that the war in Iraq is "a mistake."

A *CNN Poll* of May 2006 echoed these findings, reporting that " . . . 56 percent of those polled say the war is not worth U.S. lives and other costs." Of significance to this study are these findings; " . . . only 41 percent of those polled believed the United States is winning [the war in Iraq], although 50 percent said the country will win." Even when wars go badly, Americans still cling to their beliefs in the ultimate ability of Americans to triumph over perceived evils.

As the *ABC News/Washington Post Poll* of May 11–15, 2006, reported, only 38 percent of respondents thought that America "should remain on the current course," while 54 percent said "we should change directions and scale back our objectives." When asked to compare the expected conclusion of the Iraq War with three earlier wars, a mere 11 percent compared it to "World War II which unified America [and was] . . . an important turning point for the United States' role in the world." Thirty-four percent compared Iraq to the Vietnam War "which divided America and lowered United States' international prestige."

Overall President Bush's career job approval rate was now only 33 percent, with 65 percent disapproving. As ABC News analyst Gary Langer wrote on May 16, 2006, "The President's situation is fairly dire. His approval rating now matches his father's low in August, 1992, the summer before he lost the re-election. The current president's disapproval rating is the highest in ABC polls since 1981, and a single point from the highest in Gallup Poll history (that record is Richard Nixon's)."

The 2006 Elections

The 2006 midterm elections provided some evidence of whether voters were still buying Bush as president and commander in chief, with the Democrats narrowly winning the Senate by one vote and the House of Representatives by a margin of 233 to 201, gaining 31 seats. According to a November 8, 2006, *New York Times Poll*, almost 60 percent of the voters expressed disapproval of the war in Iraq. Voters cited their main concerns as the economy, corruption in politics, terrorism, the war in Iraq, values, and immigration. Significantly, the Democratic Party benefited from the support of independent voters. In this election, national issues seemed to dominate local politics.

As 2006 came to a close, the war in Iraq continued to defy easy solutions, with the American military death toll nearing 3,000 and Iraq increasingly moving toward civil war, pitting Sunnis, Shiites, and Kurds against each other with a national government unable to govern or even restore any semblance of order or security. The failure to contain the chaos cost Secretary of Defense Donald Rumsfeld his job, and he was replaced by Robert Gates to try to restore confidence in the Bush administration's ability to win the war. A December 11, 2006, *CBS News Poll* found that only 21 percent of Americans approved of President Bush's handling of Iraq while a staggering 75 percent disapproved. Asked about the "situation in Iraq," only 8 percent thought it was "staying the same," and 52 percent thought it was "getting worse." To the question of whether the United States will eventually succeed in Iraq, the results were similarly pessimistic: 9 percent thought success "very likely," 34 percent thought success "somewhat likely: and 53 percent thought success in Iraq was "not very/not likely at all." These are significant downward slides in customer satisfaction. The ratio of going well to going badly was 46–52 percent in December 2005, 30–67 percent in October 2006, and 25–71 percent in December 2006. Additionally, the poll reports that Americans were losing confidence in the American military's ability to win the war with only 15 percent thinking that the United States is winning the war; 55 percent think that the United States should have stayed out of the war with 39 percent still believing it was the right thing to do. Overall, President Bush's job approval rating sank to a new historic low, with only

31 percent approving and 63 percent disapproving. A similar percentage also questions the decision to fight a war in Iraq, with only 34 percent supporting the decision and 62 percent calling it a mistake.

Despite the Bush administration's fear and loathing of any Vietnam–Iraq comparisons, the public opinion polls indicate a similar pattern in the two conflicts. In Vietnam, the percentage of supporters versus doubters shifted from a 60–24 percent ratio in August 1965 to a 29–60 percent in January 1973.

The Iraq Study Report

The extend of the failure to sell this war to the American people and to win the actual war on the ground was revealed in the December 6, 2006, release of the *Iraq Study Group Report*, the results of a study undertaken by five prominent Democrats and five prominent Republicans with input from the Bush administration, former government officials, serving and retired military leaders, and various experts on the Middle East. With sponsorship from the United States Institute of Peace, the James A. Baker III Institute for Public Policy at Rice University, the Center for the Study of the Presidency, and the Center for Strategic and International Studies, the group worked from March 2006 to provide what it called in the subtitle of the report: *The Way Forward—A New Approach* with seventy-nine specific recommendations for changing the goals, strategies, and tactics for the war. The report's executive summary begins with these ominous words: "The situation in Iraq is grave and deteriorating. There is no path that can guarantee success, but the prospects can be improved."[90] Among the eerie reminders of Vietnam, the report urges that American forces be withdrawn as Iraq's forces become able to defend the country, a strategy that failed in Vietnam.

Within days of the release of this report, President Bush signaled his reluctance to abandon his "stay the course" strategy (a phrase the White House attempted to suppress in 2006) by objecting to two specific recommendations: withdrawing American troops from Iraq and negotiating with Iran and Syria on Mideast peace with stability. While admitting, "I thought we would succeed quicker than we did. And I am disappointed by the pace of success." As in the Vietnam War, the American president seemed to ignore the reality of events and continued to try to spin the story to sell a dud as a wonder product that the public would buy if it were packaged properly.

In selling the Iraq War, the White House tried a number of different brands and slogans—"Operation Iraqi Freedom," "Shock and Awe," "The Coalition of the Willing," "The Axis of Evil," and "Mission Accomplished." All failed to keep Americans convinced that the war would deliver peace and democracy to the Middle East and security and justice to the United States. Increasingly, as 2006 drew to a close, this war that had now lasted longer than American's involvement in World War II was beginning to resemble the now-legendary Ford Motor Company's fiasco with its launch of the Edsel automobile in 1958. A product designed by motivational research experts and marketed by skilled *spinmeisters*, the Edsel failed to win costumers and is now routinely cited in marketing and advertising courses and textbooks as one of the greatest marketing failures in the history of selling a product.

In selling this war, the Bush administration seemed to violate a number of principles central to successful marketing and to democracy itself. In the words of the cochairs of the Iraq Study Group, "...its success depends upon the unity of the American people in a time of political polarization...U.S./foreign policy is doomed to failure—as is any course of action in Iraq—if it is not supported by a broad sustained consensus."[91] In marketing terms, this is a clear warning to the Bush administration in "selling in" the Iraq War to the American people. The response of the administration to these recommendations and the continuing struggle in Iraq will play out in public opinion polls and the 2008 National Elections for control of the White House, the Senate, and the House of Representatives.

The New Sales Pitch

On January 10, 2007, President Bush gave a major speech on prime time television to announce his new strategy for victory in Iraq. Ignoring almost all of the recommendations of the Iraq Study Group, the president proposed an increase of 21,500 combat troops to pacify Baghdad and stabilize the Iraqi government of Prime Minister Nuri al-Maliki against the insurgents. According to a *CBS News Poll* of September 11, 2007, only about one-third of Americans watched the speech; of those only 37 percent approved of the "troop surge" plan while 50 percent disapproved. An *ABC News Poll* that same day reported that 61 percent of Americans opposed the proposal with 36 percent supporting it. Significantly, 57 percent believed that the United States was losing the war. To President Bush's key selling proposition that victory in Iraq is essential for victory in the Global War on Terror, opinion was evenly divided, with 45 percent accepting and 47 percent rejecting the *logos* of this message.

Clearly, what Aristotle labeled the *pathos of the audience* continues to play a significant role in how persuasion operates. The American mythic beliefs in American Exceptionalism, the Gunfight Nation founded in the Frontier Tradition, and the Regeneration through Violence provide responsive chords in this siren song to sell the Iraq War to the American people.

A front-page story in the September 24, 2006, *New York Times* reported that a Classified National Intelligence Estimate finds that the War in Iraq has actually encouraged worldwide Islamic radicalism, moving Muslims to join "the Global Jihadist Movement." The failures to justify the war by proving a link between Saddam Hussein and 9/11 or Al Qaeda by finding weapons of mass destruction (WMD), and by bringing peace and democracy to Iraq and the Middle East have now been joined by the failure to make America and the world safe by containing Islamic terrorism. In reality, the American efforts in Iraq may actually have facilitated its global expansion. In seeking to sell a war against terror to the American people, the Bush administration seems to have sold Islamic Jihadism to the entire Muslim World.[92]

What is oddly lacking in Bush's War on Terror are any clear plans or operations to contain those other two strands of his "Axis of Evil"—Iran and North Korea, both of which continue to claim competence in nuclear weaponry. Can the Bush administration sell the two new wars to make the world safe for democracy? Or, has President Bush, like President Woodrow Wilson after World War I, promised more than he can deliver?

On his European trip of February 21–24, 2005, the President said, "This notion that the United States is getting ready to attack Iran is simply ridiculous." He added "....diplomacy is just beginning...Iran is not Iraq."[93] Meanwhile, Osama bin Laden remains at large and Iran and North Korea continue to stonewall on nuclear arms and the Middle East continues to fester. President Bush's brave new world of peace and democracy may be just beyond the horizon or merely a figment of a super-salesman's pitch. Time will tell whether the Bush administration is selling the steak itself or only sizzle.

The entire question of protecting America from terrorist attacks has been answered with vague claims by the president and his advisors that the U.S. military efforts in Iraq are keeping the terrorists away from the homeland. In the homeland, the welcomed resignation of Tim Ridge as Secretary of Homeland Security was followed by the fiasco of former New York City Police Commissioner Bernard Kerick's nomination and quick withdrawal over charges of having hired an illegal alien; finally Michael Chertoff was appointed to the post, an event about which most Americans remain ignorant. In response to a strong recommendation by the National Commission on Terrorist Attacks Upon the United States and after stinging criticisms over White House delays by Commission members, a Director of National Intelligence was created to coordinate the intelligence activities—the Central Intelligence Agency (CIA), Federal Bureau of Investigation (FBI), and the Departments of Defense, Energy, Homeland Security, Justice, State and Treasury.[94]

With little evidence that America is safer now than on 9/11/01 or that Americans are now informed about and cognizant of the color schemes used to designate the various levels of security alerts used by the government, the War on Terror at home seems to be more a public relations gambit than a shield to protect America from those who would harm the country. As a *New York Times* front-page story on a Department of Homeland Security Internal Audit reported, serious criticisms have arisen over how funds were allocated for defense of U.S. ports, noting, "For example, Wyoming received four times as much anti-terrorism money per capita as New York did last year."[95] Along with news and politics, it now seems that all security is local, too.

Popular Culture and the War

One sign of the war's falling popularity was the almost total absence of its coverage by popular culture. The initial invasion and early victory were well covered in real time by the embedded news media and in follow-up documentaries that were shown on cable TV channels like Arts and Entertainment, The History Channel, and the Military Channel. The only major film about the war was Michael Moore's 2005 documentary *Fahrenheit 911* which scathingly attacked both Bush administrations for misleading America into two wars to serve the interests of Saudi Arabia, OPEC, and the Bush family, but Hollywood was silent.

On broadcast television, the war was not a central theme on any continuing domestic program. Despite the focus of Fox's highly rated TV series "24" on nuclear threats to America, Iraq was not even mentioned. Similarly, CBS's "The Unit" portrayed the adventures of an elite military unit that travels the globe to protect the United States without setting foot in Iraq. Another CBS program, "NCIS," detailed the cases handled by the Navy's criminal investigation section but never had a case dealing with the Iraq War.

One significant new avenue for communication utilized in the Iraq War was the Internet, with its capabilities for reaching a global audience with Web sites and blogs, available to official sources and freelancers alike. Indeed, the first images of the humiliation and abuse inflicted upon prisoners in Abu Ghraib prison were posted by American soldiers using their digital cameras and video recorders to post their "souvenirs" for the world to see. Individual military personnel have been keeping digital logs of their service experiences and sending them via the Internet.

The execution of Saddam Hussein on December 30, 2006, was captured in gruesome details by a witness with a cell phone capable of recording sight and sound and later transmitted over numerous Web sites. The negative fallout from their botched and macabre hanging was a public relations blunder for both the American and Iraqi governments and a propaganda coup for the Iraqi insurgents and their allies throughout the Middle East and the world.

In the brave new world of cyberspace, the Information War is now being fought with digital weapons that no longer favor only the official and the powerful sources. In resisting the globalization of ideas, products, and messages, the counterforces now employ the most sophisticated techniques and technologies of the cybernetic revolution in communication. Future wars will clearly be waged not only on actual battlefields but in the virtual world of instant digital communication. In addition to the force-of-arms, command, control, and communication of information will be needed for victory on the battlefield and for the hearts and minds of the American people and their allies.

Popular music, which played significant roles in the Spanish-American War, World War I, and World War II but was largely absent in Korea, Vietnam, and the Persian Gulf War, seemed to suffer from some identity problems with the Global War on Terror and Iraq. Immediately following 9/11, many songwriters and performers rallied around the flag and sang the praises of America, but after the singing group, The Dixie Chicks, criticized President Bush's war in 2003, the support for the war became less vocal. As Jon Pareles notes in a *New York Times* article

> The culture response to war in Iraq and the war on terrorism—one protracted, the other possibly endless—doesn't have an exact historical parallel. Unlike World War II, the current situation has brought little national unity; unlike the Vietnam era, ours has no appreciable domestic support for America's opponents. Iraq may be turning into a quagmire and civil war like Vietnam, but the current war has not inspired talk of generationwide rebellion (perhaps because there's no draft to pit young against old) or any colorful, psychedelically defiant counterculture. The war songs of the 21st century have been sober and earnest, pragmatic rather than fanciful.[96]

Although some country music performances continue to support Bush and the war, Pareles also cites the antiwar messages of some country musicians, including the Dixie Chicks, and some rappers, including Eminem, who challenged the administration's selling of the war, while continuing to support the American military forces still fighting in Iraq.[97] What we have here was a failure by the Bush administration to enlist and use American popular culture to help "sell through" the war in Iraq as being essential to defending America in the continuing Global War on Terror.

FUTURE GLOBAL CHALLENGES

The War on Terror promised Americans both retribution for the attacks of 9/11 and protection from further attacks on America and Americans. With the rising casualty rates in Iraq and the confusion and uncertainty at home, how well will the administration succeed in "selling" the war on terror that has now became a war to make the world safe for democracy? "Nation building" was scorned by candidate Bush in a 2000 presidential debate but embraced fully in his 2005 Inaugural Address: "The survival of liberty in our land increasingly depends on the success of liberty in other lands. The best hope for peace in our world is the expansion of freedom in all the world." Despite the failures to keep Afghanistan from being re-Talibanized, to bring peace and stability to Iraq, to ease tensions between the Arabs and Israelis, or to end the nuclear proliferation attempted by Iran and North Korea, the Bush administration continued in early 2007 to claim success on all fronts while warning of a "Long War" to combat "global terror." Once more, it is America's Manifest Destiny to enlighten the world with ideas and ideals and be the Gunfighter Nation that stops terror and tyranny with force-of-arms. Once more, some people need killing and some countries need changing. The Greeks had a word for America's mission: *hubris*.

8

What We Learned

This final chapter of the book summarizes what we learned about the ways American presidents have approached the challenge of mobilizing public opinion and winning America's endorsement for the wars it has fought since 1898. In this chapter, we will convey what lessons were learned from these successes or failures as they particularly relate to the current approach of George W. Bush and that of future presidents as they seek public support for the wars that are certain to be fought in the years ahead.

In the eight wars that Americans have fought during the past 109 years, every U.S. president has lied, withheld the truth, and/or distorted the facts to win Congressional and public support for the military adventures they wanted to wage. We have tried to understand the reasons why some presidents succeeded and others failed to persuade the American people to support these wars.

We looked at both the short-term effects of these wars on American public opinion and the public's attitude toward the president in office at the time, and we also considered the longer-term effects as the American people retrospectively judged how they were persuaded to support these wars, the manner in which they were waged, and the aftermath of these wars.

WHY AMERICANS GO TO WAR

Most Americans believe they are citizens of a peace-seeking nation. Yet for more than the ten decades we surveyed, the country has supported its presidents' determination to follow the path of war whenever it was demanded. Why and how Americans have managed to reconcile this pacifistic sense of self at the same time they invariably chose the warpath is the subject of this book.

The late nineteenth-century America, the era that we examined first, was radically different from early twenty-first-century America, the period in which we concluded our study. Deeply embedded beliefs of that earlier time—the sanctity of the Monroe Doctrine, belief in America's Manifest Destiny, and the importance of bringing Christian civilization to the uninitiated—are now artifacts of the country's past and are scarcely remembered, if recalled at all, by the vast majority of Americans. However, certain vestiges of those sentiments are still embedded in the American psyche and continue to influence vital decisions affecting the country's foreign policy and its commitment to the waging of war. Simply put, Americans are willing to go to war when they believe that their national honor and security are threatened.

DO AMERICANS LIKE WAR?

Few film images remain as indelibly implanted in the American psyche as the iconic scene in *Patton*, when U.S. Army General George S. Patton, Jr., portrayed by actor George C. Scott, addresses a crowded hall of soldiers preparing to go into combat under his command during World War II. General Patton's actual words, addressing members of the U.S. Army's 6th Armored Division in England a week before the invasion of Normandy was launched, follow:

> Men, all this stuff you've heard about America not wanting to fight, wanting to stay out of the war, is a lot of horse dung. Americans traditionally love to fight. All real Americans love the sting of battle. When you were kids, you all admired the champion marble shooter, the fastest runner, the big league ball players, the toughest boxers.... Americans love a winner and will not tolerate a loser. Americans play to win all the time. I wouldn't give a hoot in Hell for a man who lost and laughed. That's why Americans have never lost and will never lose a war. Because the very thought of losing is hateful to Americans...."[1]

Could it be true that Americans really like going to war? There is considerable historical evidence that it is. The ethos of the "Gunfighter Nation" has consistently influenced U.S. domestic and foreign policy decisions since the mid-nineteenth century. Of course, there are conditions and criteria which must be met before the American public is primed to fight a war. But it may be that most Americans possess an aggressive nature predisposing them to consistently embrace the war option without much reflection to a greater degree than the citizens of other countries.[2]

Americans have always admired "the man of action," best exemplified by Wyatt Earp and Theodore Roosevelt in real life, and by John Wayne and Clint Eastwood in Hollywood films. Theodore Roosevelt and the Hollywood actors in their movies played roles in which their characters were invariably impatient with long-winded palaver, choosing to substitute violent action for reflection, and demanding immediate results. And, while ignoring traditional rules of behavior, these revered "good guys" always seem to win. It's not surprising then that most Americans have become invested with the self-image of themselves as "the good guys," who feel justified in taking quick action through war to right the perceived wrongs of the world.

Further reinforcing this image of Americans as "the good guys" is the belief that America has been particularly blessed by God. The majority of its citizens believe they live in a God-fearing country, and when summoned to fight a war, it has been invariably accompanied by the president's assurance that "God is on our side." President George W. Bush echoed this sentiment continually in the speeches he made leading up to the invasion of Iraq. Armed with the belief that they are always on the side of right, and are particularly favored by God, Americans feel that any war they agree to fight is necessary and just, assuming that they have been properly indoctrinated in advance by an effective administration sales campaign. It's interesting to note that the followers of Osama bin Laden who hijacked airliners to attack the World Trade Center Towers and the Pentagon, and the insurgent suicide bombers now attacking civilians and military personnel in Iraq also believed that they are doing God's work.

There is considerable evidence that Americans believe they *do invariably win* on the battlefield. In the two wars we discuss in this book where this point of view is challenged, the Korean War and the War in Vietnam, most Americans believe the only reason that the American military didn't completely prevail over its communist foes was the incompetence or lack of resolution of its national leadership and civilian naysayers, and the liberal media's lack of patriotic support for the U.S. Armed Forces. In every other war, the conflict resulted in a clear-cut American military victory.

Throughout most of the country's history, Americans have been taught to believe that the United States is a nation of winners—the best in the world. Of course, global conflicts have frequently arisen in the past because other nations' peoples were convinced that they possessed the same uniquely superior quality. For example, at the start of World War II, both Germany and Japan confidently declared war on America because their respective leaderships felt that their armed forces were superior and would easily conquer any enemy that dared to oppose them, including the United States.

In the aftermath of some major American conflicts, the public's positive feelings at the start of the war turned negative as the cost in American lives rose and other personal sacrifices were demanded. In such cases, they came to believe that they were misled by their president, or the war that they had initially supported was later perceived as not worth fighting. The dramatic difference in the feelings of the American people in the years following World War I and World War II best exemplify this phenomenon.

THE EFFECT OF A VOLUNTEER OR CONSCRIPTED MILITARY

The Spanish-American War was fought by a professional U.S. military supplemented by enthusiastic volunteers who rallied to the flag in a wave of superpatriotism. Fortunately for the United States, the ineptness of the Spanish military in defending its colonial possessions spared the country a serious test of its military's combat effectiveness. Most U.S. casualties among those fighting in Cuba were the result of disease, primarily Yellow Fever.

As the United States moved from a position of neutrality to becoming a combatant in World War I, it became quickly clear that a major conscription of men would be necessary to bring the armed forces of the United States to a point of combat readiness. There was never any serious resistance to the Draft in World War I, in which the U.S. military was engaged for only its final year. While the United States sustained heavy casualties in several fiercely fought ground battles in Europe, the human cost for America did not come close to the enormous toll in human lives paid by its allies and its enemies.

However, in the aftermath of World War I, disillusionment among U.S. war veterans about the worth of that conflict began to set in. President Woodrow Wilson found he was unable to deliver on the utopian promises of a lasting peace he had made to the country. Many Americans became embittered at the mean-spirited squabbling over the spoils of the war by the European Allies and the refusal of our wartime allies to repay their debts.

Further, the revelations of the U.S. government's propaganda program to generate public enthusiasm for entry into the war left a bitter aftertaste about the sacrifices that had been made. The residue of this sense of disillusion was translated into a growing isolationist sentiment, at least toward involvement in European affairs, which was held by a significant majority of the American public in the decades following the end of World War I. This aversion pervaded the country until the Japanese Navy attacked the U.S. without warning on December 7, 1941, and the other major Axis Powers, Germany and Italy, declared war on the United States four days later.

A military conscription act had been passed by Congress in the summer of 1940. There were limited public protests against a draft at that time, but all resistance dissolved following the disastrous acts of war against the United States committed by Japan in December 1941. Throughout World War II and in the decades that have followed, there have never been any serious challenges to the legitimacy and necessity of the military draft that brought nearly 10 million American men under arms.

Military Selective Service laws were extended at the conclusion of World War II, and then transformed into the Universal Military Training and Service act which still required qualified men between the ages of eighteen and twenty-six to be available for active duty in the U.S. Armed Forces. When the Korean War erupted in June 1950 that conflict demanded many more troops than were available at the time because of the rapid demobilization of the military at the end of World War II. This short-term problem was partially solved by reactivating many servicemen who had previously served in World War II and were still bound by reserve military obligations. Many of these men returned to active duty to fight in Korea, angry and frustrated.

As previously discussed, the Korean War was ineffectively marketed to the American people as being critical to the country's national security. Not surprisingly, there was considerable passive resistance among draft age men who sought to avoid the military draft by claiming exemptions based on educational and other deferments or disqualification. In the years that followed, the negative feelings about their military experience by both these conscripted men, as well as the veterans of World War II who had been recalled to active duty for service in Korea, contributed to a general public sense of dissatisfaction about the entire U.S. involvement in that extended "Police Action."

Conscription became a major issue because of the diminishing popularity of the Vietnam War, particularly after President Lyndon Johnson began committing rising numbers of U.S. troops to fight and often die in that Southeast Asian country. Because of the many loopholes and technicalities allowing for exemption from the military draft in the late 1960s and early 1970s, the ranks of soldiers being sent to fight in Vietnam were largely filled by minorities, the poor and the working class. As U.S. casualty rates climbed, American involvement in the war became increasingly unpopular with a sizeable segment of the U.S. public; the draft was a major point of controversy.

After President Richard Nixon extricated the United States from that conflict, he abolished the draft in 1973 and replaced it with an all-volunteer military. That system for maintaining the strength of the U.S. Armed Forces remains at present.

It would seem that mass conscription of Americans in time of war is not in itself a cause for dissension and controversy. However, we believe that unless a president has made a clear and irrefutable case for war to the American people, as Franklin Delano Roosevelt did in 1941, a military composed of conscripted troops is likely to have a negative effect on the way the public views involvement in present and future conflicts. This view is strengthened by the almost certain necessity that if future U.S. administrations determine that it is necessary to reactivate the military draft, women may well face conscription as well as men because of social changes that have taken place regarding their equal status in American society. In the current war in Iraq, many women who are professional soldiers found themselves engaged in combat, although not technically assigned a combat responsibility. As of January 2007, sixty-nine female military personnel have died in Iraq since the war began in 2003, and in the future this could be an additional factor affecting civilian support for a president's decision to go to war.[3]

In general, however, we believe it is correct to assume that as long as America relies on volunteers to fill its military ranks, U.S. presidents will experience less dissension by the public about going to war than if large numbers of military conscripts are drafted for service.

HOW ADVANCES IN MARKETING COMMUNICATIONS TECHNIQUES AND THE PROLIFERATION OF MEDIA VEHICLES HAVE AFFECTED THE WAY WARS ARE SOLD

American presidents now have many more sophisticated marketing communications techniques and diverse media vehicles to promote their campaigns to wage war than ever before.

Spanish-American War

President McKinley's live voice and message could only be heard by those within earshot of him. While the availability of the telegraph allowed his words to be transmitted widely, the public's access to his utterances were accessible only by reading reports of them in local newspapers and other printed media. The role of the popular newspapers and other print media in interpreting his words largely depended on the political views of their owners and publishers, and those words were not necessarily reported fully or accurately. This communications problem between President McKinley and the electorate unquestionably accelerated America's entry into a war with Spain.

World War I

Advances in media technology were matched by the development of sophisticated marketing communications techniques in the years leading up to America's joining the side of the Allies in World War I. This period marked the birth and effective introduction of an array of advertising, public relations, and other marketing communications techniques which played an important role in bringing American public opinion to the point where it was ready to support President Wilson's decision to join the war. Motion pictures, although still silent, powerfully affected the patriotic emotions of the U.S. public and swayed its sympathy toward the Allied cause, while the films demonized their opponents. It was the first war America fought in which the propaganda function was formalized as an official government function under the Committee on Public Information.

World War II

President Franklin D. Roosevelt had an extraordinarily keen grasp of communication and how to best exploit the media to his advantage in the years leading up to America's declaration of war against the Axis Powers in World War II. His astute use of broadcast radio to establish a personal rapport with the U.S. public through his regular "Fireside Chats" played a crucial role in building his credibility as a respected leader in a time of crisis. The power of Hollywood films, now "talkies," was also harnessed to present sympathetic stories about the Allied war effort, and at the same time defile the image of their Axis enemies. Once the United States joined the war, all public media were coordinated by the government through the Office of War Information to assure the most effective and efficient use of all communications to support the war effort.

Korea and Vietnam

Inexplicably, during both the Korean and Vietnam Wars, the government did little to utilize effective marketing communications techniques in an organized way, or harness the power of television to influence U.S. public opinion in support of the government's war aims. In fact, during the Vietnam War, television in particular became a counterproductive medium to the government as television audiences viewed stories each night which visually and verbally contradicted much of what the government was telling the people. In the years that followed the withdrawal of U.S. troops from Vietnam that prolonged conflict came to be called "The Living Room War" because of the powerful impact television had on shaping American public opinion about the war.

The only Hollywood motion picture that supported the U.S. government's war policy during those years was John Wayne's *The Green Berets*, a film that was critically panned but commercially successful. None of the U.S. presidents who were in office during the course of that war ever attempted to formally establish a coordinating propaganda agency to enlist the public's support as the government had done so successfully during World War I and World War II. Succeeding U.S. administrations clumsily attempted to suppress or intimidate the news media into generating positive stories about the how the war was progressing, but only succeeded in losing credibility and triggering rancorous news media responses.

Grenada

It was while President Ronald Reagan was in office that the government began to embrace more sophisticated methods of getting its message across to the U.S. public during periods of combat, and at the same time using methods to effectively suppress the news media from disseminating information that might contradict the administration's version of events. President Reagan was an experienced Hollywood actor who used his professional savvy and his considerable charm to disarm the often hostile news media and earn the title of the "Great Communicator."

Shortly after 241 U.S. Marines were killed by a suicide bomber in Lebanon in 1983, he ordered the invasion of the island of Grenada in the Caribbean Ocean to thwart a Marxist attempt to take over the government. Despite the fact that President Reagan deliberately deceived the news media about the invasion plans and then permitted the U.S. military to discourage press attempts to land on the beaches of Grenada at the point of a gun, he managed retrospectively to win public approval of his actions, celebrated later in the Clint Eastwood blockbuster hit, *Heartbreak Ridge*.

Panama City

While not possessing the communication gifts of his predecessor in the White House, President George H. W. Bush used the same deceptive techniques when he launched a U.S. military attack on Panama City in 1989 in order to drive Panama's President Manuel Noriega from power. By this time, the Pentagon had agreed to a national press pool arrangement so that all the news media could be informed of developments on the ground in Panama City in a timely and accurate way. Once in Panama, however, the administration restricted this small contingent of authorized press from actually visiting the scene of the fighting for several days and forcefully discouraged other journalists who attempted to fly into Panama City. With extremely limited eye-witness news coverage in a position to contradict the official version of what was transpiring, the American people ultimately approved President Bush's actions and still consider his decision to invade Panama City as having been in the best interests of U.S. national security.

The Persian Gulf War

The administration of President George H. W. Bush continued to improve on the government's ability to manage or "spin" the news media in wartime in 1991 when the U.S. military and its Coalition allies drove the invading Iraqi army from neighboring Kuwait. From the very beginning of the operation, the military micromanaged the movement and access of the hundreds of journalists who descended on the scene so that the press corps was largely reduced to extremely restrictive press briefings and tightly supervised "photo-ops." Most film footage of the war that was seen by television audiences in the United States and around the world was supplied by sources controlled by the Pentagon. There was no opportunity to pursue independent news angles or stories because correspondents were inevitably shepherded around the battlefield by U.S. military "minders."

At the conclusion of the swiftly won war, resulting in few Coalition casualties and massive numbers of Iraqi dead and wounded, the American public immediately celebrated the military victory and continue to embrace its memory as one of the country's most impressive demonstrations of U.S. military prowess. The ability of the administration to consistently present a heroic and sanitized view of that conflict reinforced the administration's belief that suppressing independent news media coverage so that the public was primarily dependent on the government for battlefield reportage was the most effective formula for assuring public support of future U.S. military forays.

The Global War on Terror—Afghanistan and Iraq

The American/NATO attacks on the Taliban in Afghanistan were swift and sure retaliation for 9/11, requiring no special plans for public support from Americans. The extended nature of the conflict may test public enthusiasm but the Bush administration made few attempts to rally such support from the American people.

When President George W. Bush and his advisors decided to pursue a war with Iraq, they were faced with significant hurdles that had not burdened Presidents Reagan or George H. W. Bush before them. For one thing, the president did not have a clear-cut justification to invade Iraq. True, the catastrophic terrorist attacks in New York and Washington had traumatized the nation, and Americans were determined to revenge themselves on their attackers, but establishing convincingly that there was linkage between Al Qaeda and Saddam Hussein's regime proved impossible. In the end, no weapons of mass destruction were found in Iraq, raising new questions about the need for this war.

Nevertheless, the president continued to expand the presence of U.S. military forces in countries adjoining Iraq while his administration attempted to win the support of the United Nations and its traditional allies to join in this conflict. In the end, the president only succeeded in winning the total support of Great Britain and the titular support of a handful of other nations to his side.

Journalists embedded with Coalition forces reported favorably on the early military successes but later coverage questioned the entire war effort. In sum, the American media and public bought the war at first but continuing insurgency, the inability of the Iraq government to govern effectively, the failure to capture Osama bin Laden and to connect Iraq to 9/11 or the weapons of mass destruction resulted in disappointment and falling support. It is a classic example of good marketing killing a weak product.

TOWARD THE FUTURE

Unlike the presidents that we studied in earlier portions of this book, George W. Bush and the presidents who succeed him will be facing a bewildering assortment of media choices from which they must choose to channel their messages and ideas. While President John F. Kennedy could charm or President Richard Nixon could intimidate a small handful of network television presidents into presenting friendlier treatment of administration policies, the present array of print and electronic media vehicles has become so fragmented and numerous that it is virtually impossible to control coverage anymore.

The advent of fiercely independent news internet Web sites like *Drudgereport.com* and Internet blogs like *InstaPundit*, providing political commentary and criticism, are transforming the media environment as the distinction between traditional news media and these new media forms becomes blurred.

We believe that U.S. presidents in the future will have little concern about mainstream news media criticisms as their administrations pursue public backing for their war plans. Growing numbers of Americans are already migrating to the Internet, as well as to other electronic communications channels still evolving, for the information and commentary they need to form political judgments. In such a fragmented media environment, there will be no single news source that will be powerful enough to sway public opinion. This will be a double-edged sword for both the administration and its critics.

The central challenge for the American system of government is whether such marketing communications manipulations are compatible with democracy. Can Americans become more selective buyers of war or will they continue to allow superpatriotism to overwhelm careful critical analysis of the sales pitches used to sell wars? The question is whether Americans can act like the informed, enlightened, and thoughtful citizens necessary for any democracy to flourish or will they continue to be willing buyers of whatever war an administration is selling. We hope that the former is true but fear that the latter is more likely. As long as Americans continue to like war, any president selling a war has a customer base that is already half-sold; a few well-chosen slogans and images will complete the deal. Our hard advice is this: Buy a war if you want but be aware of exactly what you are buying.

SELLING WAR TO AMERICA

We found that Aristotle's 2500-year-old rules for successful persuasion (with some updating) are as relevant now to the selling of the eight wars we examined as they were in the times of Athenian antiquity. In each of these periods of armed conflict, U.S. presidents who engaged in the difficult task of persuading the country to go to war needed to understand the following:

First, the *context* (time, place, events, and circumstances within which the persuasion is to occur) must be examined. If the marketing environment is fertile for exploitation because of history and prior media efforts, the American public will support the administration, especially if the public believes that an unprovoked and cowardly attack on the country or its military forces has occurred ("Remember the *Maine*"; "Remember the *Lusitania*"; "Let's Remember Pearl Harbor"; "Remember 9/11").

Second, a U.S. president has *ethos* (trustworthiness and credibility as a source of information) simply by having been popularly elected. The president's credibility will be strengthened or diminished by a number of factors, primarily the success or failure of the U.S. military's efforts against the enemy and the administration's ability to control the negative effects of bad news. In the Philippines Insurrection, President Theodore Roosevelt's administration was able to explain away the atrocity charges against U.S. Marines as not representing official policy. More than one hundred years later, President George W. Bush did the same in the face of allegations about the abuse of Iraqi prisoners by U.S. soldiers in Abu Ghraib prison.

Third, the *logos* of the messages, or the selling proposition, will appeal to both logic and emotion if it is connected to some core American values like "freedom," "democracy," "peace," and America as the "Guiding Light of the World."

Fourth, a U.S. administration, either through happenstance or planning, will almost certainly attempt to control ("spin") the *public media* in order to influence how news organizations cover the war. While the American popular press was initially more war-minded than the first McKinley administration in the months leading up to the war against Spain, President Theodore Roosevelt, who succeeded McKinley after his assassination, later needed to work hard at damage control during the Waller trial. In general, however, despite frequent criticisms by the news media, most American public media traditionally support America's wars at the onset, although they frequently become critical as the wars progress.

Fifth, a president must understand the *pathos* of the people (the morale, biases, hopes, fears, and desires of the target audiences). In modern marketing parlance, understanding the "psychographics," or psychological composition of the public, is vital if a U.S. administration plans to shape "consumer behavior" to its own ends. In the Spanish-American War, the people's biases, morals, hopes, fears, dreams, and desires were shaped more by the press than by the presidency; that is not always the case and contemporary U.S. presidents can now ill-afford to allow the news media to shape their decisions.

Finally, since the *effects* of all persuasion include both positive and negative outcomes, administrations are successful in selling a war when they trumpet their successes (the victories at Manila Bay and Santiago Bay, D-Day, and Iwo Jima) while downplaying their failures (U.S. withdrawal from Vietnam). Increasingly, it is essential for U.S. presidents to continually monitor the effects of the marketing campaigns through increasingly sophisticated public opinion polls so that the White House can adjust their direction and execution.

BUYING WAR IN AMERICA

If Americans are to become more aware buyers of war, they need to grow more cognizant of the marketing techniques employed by the administration in its attempt to sell a war to the American people. To counter the techniques used by the government, we suggest the following critical-thinking strategies:

First, carefully examine the *context* to see if this war is really needed by the people and the nation or merely serves the interest of the president and others promoting U.S. entry into an armed conflict with one or more nations. In short, Americans need to debate the following: Why does the country need this war? What national security interests are being served by this war? What will this war cost the nation and the American people in terms of lives and other resources?

Second, scrutinize the *ethos* (truthfulness and credibility) of the president and the administration by asking some probing questions: Do you trust the president because he/she is president? Are you being asked to trust the president without examining the evidence that supports the call to war? Are you being asked to trust the president simply because the Constitution names him the Commander in Chief of the Armed Forces?

Third, critically evaluate the logical and emotional appeals of the key selling propositions by being wary of logic without evidence and emotional appeals to the shared myths of American Exceptionalism, Gunfighter Nation, and Manifest Destiny. Be especially suspicious of any messages that promise an easy and painless war. Above all, distrust all calls to patriotism without price. To Samuel Johnson, "Patriotism is the last refuge of a scoundrel"; to the warmongers, patriotism is the first technique to be employed to sell a war. If the war is necessary and just, ask why the president has not requested an Act of War from Congress.

Fourth, obtain as much information as you can from the widest variety of news sources, recognizing that American media tend to support any administration at the onset of any war. Seek out alternative sources, even foreign or hostile ones, and alternative media, especially the Internet.

Fifth, probe your own *pathos* concerning the war, noting your own hopes and fears. Question your own biases and ask if the administration is pandering to your hopes or exploiting your fears. Ask yourself what sacrifices you and your family are willing to make to support this war. Do not buy a war if you are not willing to bear the burden of the conflict.

Finally, be on the alert for the increasingly sophisticated marketing manipulation of public opinion by the administration. American administrations, especially in times of war, attempt to manipulate you on a daily basis. Therefore, you need to inoculate yourself each day against the propaganda disseminated by the White House, the Department of Defense, and the Department of Homeland Security. America's third president Thomas Jefferson is credited with this warning: "Eternal vigilance is the price of liberty." In this age of unending political marketing, all Americans need to develop what Ernest Hemingway said was essential to a critical mind: a built-in, shockproof shit detector.

TOWARD THE FUTURE

The Cold War between the United States and its allies and the Soviet Union and its allies lasted, according to official Department of Defense calculations, from September 2, 1945, to December 26, 1991, a total of forty-six years, three months, and twenty-four days. During that time, the United States fought two hot wars, financed and/or supported a number of conflicts, and waged a war of ideas with all available media of communication. While the American public were uneven in their support of the specific efforts during that time and American administrators were uneven in selling the conflicts and the Cold War itself, the end of the Soviet Union and its Warsaw Pact allies signaled victory for the West in that ideological struggle.

The present and future Global War on Terror can be said to have begun on September 11, 2001, with the terrorist attacks on the Pentagon and the World Trade Towers. How long this new "Long War," to use Pentagon-speak, will last is open to intelligence and military estimates, political prognostications, and specious speculations. The future will reveal how America will support this new long struggle and whether the country will buy the wars that future administrations try to sell.

The American way of war was forged in the Industrial Age and has followed Claus von Clauwitz's principles but it may be that wars now and in the foreseeable future may more closely resemble the guerilla wars that plagued the American military in the Indian Wars, the Filipino Insurrection, the Banana Wars in Central America before and after World War I, and the quagmire of Vietnam.[4] Although America was able to persevere and win the Cold War, the question of winning what the Pentagon calls the "Global War on Terror" and the "Long War" is still open.

The American way of selling war was formulated within the context of modern commercial advertising and marketing techniques developed in conjunction with popular mass media of communication (newspapers and magazines, and later film, and television). The wars of tomorrow will be waged and sold not only with the strategies, tactics, and techniques of the past but with the new realities of communication in the Information Age. Increasingly, the command and control of both military operations and marketing campaigns will be complicated by the increasing availability of new media technologies that provide access to audiences and that also provide these audiences with empowerment in terms of control of information flow. The media wars for the hearts and minds of the American and global audiences will be waged by governments and insurgents alike, by friends and foes, by dissidents and terrorists. This new "Long War" will be fought in both reality and virtual reality.

No central source will be able to control the messages by controlling the sources of the messages and the media that will carry these messages. As media continue to be decentralized, it may become more difficult for American presidents and their administrations to sell wars to Americans in the future. In the present Global War on Terror, as the memory of 9/11 faded and the War in Iraq failed to " clear, hold, build" while President Bush was unable to resell the war with new and modified slogans, public support for this war fell to its lowest levels ever. Public support for the Long War will continue to fade unless the terrorists commit new attacks on America. Another 9/11 would once again summon the Gunfighter Nation to arms.

Notes

INTRODUCTION

1. http://www.guardian.co.uk/notesandqueries/query/0,5753,-21510,00.html

2. Richard Leiby, "The Hilton's Strange Embed Fellows," *Washington Post* (March 7, 2003).

3. Frederick Jackson Turner, *Rereading Frederick Turner: "The Significance of the Frontier in American History" and Other Essays*, with Commentary by John Mack Faragher (New York: Henry Holt and Company, 1994), 32.

4. Richard Slotkin, *Gunfighter Nation: The Myth of the Frontier in Twentieth Century America* (New York: Antheneum, 1992), 10; See also his *Regeneration through Violence: The Mythology of the American Frontier, 1600–1860.* (Middletown, CT: Wesleyan University Press, 1973) and *The Fatal Environment: The Myth of the Frontier in the Age of Industrialization 1800–1890* (New York: Antheneum, 1985).

5. Lt. Col. Gary D. Solis USMC (ret.), "Terrorists, Due Process, and Military Commissions," *Marine Corps Gazette* (February 2002), 46–48.

6. See George Creel, *How We Advertised America: The First Telling of the Amazing Story of the Committee on Public Information.* (New York: Harper and Row, 1920) and S. L.Vaugh. *Holding Fast the Inner Lines: Democracy, Nationalism, and the Committee on Public Information* (Chapel Hill: University of North Carolina Press, 1980).

7. See Raymond Fielding, *The American Newsreel 1911–1967* (Norman: University of Oklahoma Press, 1972), Chapter 7; John Keegan, *The First World War* (New York: Alfred A. Knopf, 1999), 414–427; and Russell F. Weigley, *The American Way of War: A History of United States Military Strategy and Policy* (New York: Macmillan Publishing Co., Inc., 1973), Chapter 16.

8. See John W. Dower, *Embracing Defeat: Japan in the Wake of World War II* (New York: W. W. Norton and Company, 1999); John Keegan, *The Second World War* (New York: Viking Penguin, 1989), Chapter 33 (The Legacy of the Second World War); and Gerhard L. Weinberg, *A World At Arms: A Global History of World War II* (Cambridge: Cambridge University Press, 1994), Conclusion: The Cost and Impact of War.

9. See Michael J. Arlen, *The Living Room War* (New York: Farrah, Straus and Giroux, 1969); James William Gibson, *The Perfect War: Technowar in Vietnam* (Boston, MA: The Atlantic Monthly Press, 1986); and General Bruce Palmer, Jr., *The 25-Year War: America's Military Role in Vietnam* (Lexington: University of Kentucky Press, 1984).

10. See Craig LaMay, Martha FitzSimon, and Jeanne Sahadi, eds., *The Media at War: The Press and the Persian Gulf War* (New York: Gannett Foundation Media Center, 1971).

11. See George Kennedy, *The Art of Persuasion in Ancient Greece* (Princeton, NJ: Princeton University Press, 1963), Chapter 3.

12. Jacques Ellul, *Propaganda: The Formation of Men's Attitudes*, translated by Konrad Kellen and Jean Lerner (New York: Alfred A. Knopf, 1971), 256.

13. See Carl von Clausewitz, *On War*, edited and translated by Michael Howard and Peter Paret (Princeton, NJ: Princeton University Press, 1976), 75.

14. Ibid.

15. Ibid., 78–80.

16. Ibid., 80.

17. Ibid., 119.

18. Ibid., 186.

19. Elizabeth Becker and James Dao, "Hearts and Minds: Bush Will Keep the Wartime Operation Promoting America," *New York Times* (Wednesday, February 20, 2002), A 11; James Dao. "Hearts and Minds: New Agency Will Not Lie, Top Pentagon Officials Say," *New York Times* (Thursday, February 21, 2002), A 14.

1: The Splendid Little War—The Spanish-American War

1. Frederick Jackson Turner, *Rereading Frederick Jackson Turner*, with commentary by John Mack Faragher (New York: Henry Holt and Company, 1994).

2. Allan R. Millett and Peter Maslowski, *For the Common Defense: A Military History of the United States of America* (New York: The Free Press, 1984), 102–114.

3. Ibid., 117–137.

4. Ibid., Chapter 6; See also James M. McPherson, *Battle Cry of Freedom: The Civil War Era* (New York: Oxford University Press, 1988), especially Chapter 28.

5. Max Boot, *The Savage Wars of Peace: Small Wars and the Rise of American Power* (New York: Basic Books, 2002), 63–64.

6. Millett and Maslowski, *For the Common Defense*, 258–262.

7. Joseph E. Wilson, *The Cuban Crisis as Reflected in the New York Press* (NewYork: Columbia University Press, 1934), 460.

8. See James Coleman, *On the Great Highway* (Boston, MA: Lothrop Publishing, 1900), 178; Michael Emery and Edwin Emery, *The Press and America*, 6th

ed. (Englewood Cliffs, NJ: Prentice Hall, 1988), 236; L. Synder and R. Morris, eds., *A Treasury of Good Reporting* (New York: Simon and Schuster, 1962), 236; Phillip Knightley, *The First Casualty: The War Correspondent as Hero and Myth-Maker from the Crimea to Kosovo*, rev. ed. (Baltimore, MD: The Johns Hopkins Press, 2000), 58.

9. Millett and Maslowski, *For the Common Defense*, 267.

10. Raymond Fielding, *The American Newsreel 1911–1967* (Norman: University of Oklahoma Press, 1972), 30.

11. Millett and Maslowski, *For the Common Defense*, 270–271.

12. Ibid., 275.

13. Boot, *The Savage Wars of Peace*, 125.

14. Irwin Leigh Matus, "*Urbanography: Where the Dream Was Made*," The Composing Stack, Inc., http://Urbanography.com/urban/0006/index.htm.

15. Boot, *The Savage Wars of Peace*, 120–123.

16. Brigadier Edwin H. Simmons (U.S.M.C., ret.), *The United States Marines 1775–1975* (New York: The Viking Press, 1976), 75–76.

17. Millett and Maslowski, *For the Common Defense*, 273–282.

18. Fielding, *The American Newsreel*, 31–34.

19. Boot, *The Savage Wars of Peace*, 125.

20. Quoted in Ibid., 105.

21. Arthur M. Schlessinger, Jr., *Running for President: The Candidates and Their Images, Volume Two, 1900–1992* (New York: Simon and Schuster, 1994), 1–21.

22. Quoted in Millet and Maslowski, *For the Common Defense*, 291.

23. Ibid.

24. Ibid., 293.

25. Ibid., 292–297; see also Boot, *The Savage Wars of Peace*, 120–123; Allan R. Millett, *Semper Fidelis: The History of the United States Marine Corps* (New York: Macmillan Publishing Co., Inc., 1980), 152–155.

26. Emery and Emery, *The Press and America*, 242–243.

27. Boot, *The Savage Wars of Peace*, 127.

2: The Great War—World War I

1. This summary of the early years of the war used a number of sources, chiefly D. J. Goodspeed, *The German Wars 1914–1945* (Boston, MA: Houghton Mifflin, 1977); Walter Goerlitz, *History of the German General Staff, 1657–1945* (New York: Frederick A. Praeger, Inc., Publishers, 1953), 156–178; John Keegan, *The First World War* (New York: Alfred A. Knopf, 1999); and B. H. Liddell Hart, *The Real War 1914–1918* (New York: The Atlantic Monthly Press Books, 1930).

2. See Phillip Knightley, *The First Casualty: The War Correspondent as Hero and Myth-Maker from the Crimea to Kosovo*, rev. ed. (Baltimore, MD: Johns Hopkins Press, 2000), 163–165.

3. See Barbara Tuchman, *The Zimmermann Telegram* (New York: Ballantine Books, 1985).

4. See George B. Clark, *Devil Dogs: Fighting Marines of World War I* (Novato, CA: Presido Press, 1999); David Kennedy, *Over Here: The First World War and American Society* (New York: Oxford University Press, 1980); and Laurence

Stallings, *The Doughboys: The Story of the AEF, 1917–1918* (New York: Harper and Row Publishers, 1963).

5. Quoted in George Creel, *How We Advertised America: The First Telling of the Amazing Story of the Committee on Public Information that Carried the Gospel of Americanism to Every Corner of the Globe* (New York: Harper and Row, 1920).

6. Ibid., 5.

7. Ibid., 6.

8. Ibid., 85–92.

9. Ibid., 104–108.

10. Ibid., 276.

11. Ibid., 275.

12. Ibid., 281.

13. For an examination of this issue in contemporary times, see Benjamin R. Barber, *Jihad vs. McWorld: How Globalism and Tribalism are Reshaping the World* (New York: Ballantine Books, 1995).

14. For an excellent study of these war films see Michael T. Isenberg, *War on Film: The American Cinema and World War I, 1914–1941* (London: Associated University Presses, 1981).

15. Creel, *How We Advertised America*, 159.

16. George Theofiles, *American Posters of World War I: Price and Collector's Guide* (New York: Dafran House Publishers Inc., 1973).

17. John McCabe, *George M. Cohan, The Man Who Owned Broadway* (Garden City, NY: Doubleday and Co., 1973), Chapter 9.

18. Keegan, *The First World War*, 335–343.

19. Goodspeed, *The German Wars*, 245–253.

20. Stallings, *The Doughboys*, 295–302.

21. Creel, *How We Advertised America*, 184–207.

22. See Horace Peterson and Gilbert Fite, *Unfavorable to Mobilization: Opponents of War 1917–1918* (Madison: University of Wisconsin Press, 1957).

23. Keegan, *The First World War*, 414–420; and Richard Watt, *The Kings Depart, TheTragedy of Germany: Versailles and the German Revolution* (New York: Simon and Schuster, 1968), Chapter 7.

24. George Creel, *Rebel at Large: Reflections of Fifty Crowded Years* (New York: G. P. Putnam's Sons, 1942), 206.

25. Creel, *How We Advertised America*, 430; See also Robert Jackall and Janice M. Hirota, "America's First Propaganda Ministry: The Committee on Public Information during the Great War," in Robert Jackall, ed., *Propaganda* (New York: New York University Press, 1995); James R. Mock and Cedric Lawton, *Words That War The War: The Story of the Committee on Public Information* (Princeton, NJ: Princeton University Press, 1939); and S. L. Vaughan, *Holding Fast the Inner Lines: Democracy, Nationalism, and the Committee on Public Information* (Chapel Hill: University of North Carolina Press, 1980).

26. Watt, *The Kings Depart*, 501–530.

27. Creel, *How We Advertised America*, 401.

28. Edward L. Bernays, *Public Relations* (Norman: University of Oklahoma Press, 1952), 71.

29. George Seldes, *One Man's Newspaper Game: Freedom of the Press* (Indianapolis, IN: Bobbs-Merrill, 1935), 37.

30. Jeremy Noakes and Geoffrey Pridham, eds., *Documents on Nazism, 1919–1945* (New York: Viking Press, 1975), 38.

3: The Good War—World War II

1. Quoted in James MacGregor Burns, *Roosevelt: The Lion and the Fox* (New York: Harcourt, Brace and Company, 1956), 449.

2. For this chapter, we have drawn upon many sources, chiefly Herbert P. Bix, *Hirohito and the Making of Modern Japan* (New York: Harper Collins Publishers, 2000); D. J. Goodspeed, *The German Wars, 1914–1945* (Boston, MA: Houghton-Mifflin, 1977); John Keegan, *The Second World War* (New York: Viking, 1989); William L. O'Neill, *A Democracy at War: America's Fight at Home and Abroad in World War II* (Cambridge, MA: Harvard University Press, 1993); Ronald Spector, *Eagle against the Sun: The American War with Japan* (New York: The Free Press, 1984); Gerhard L. Weinberg, *A World at Arms: A Global History of World War II* (New York: Cambridge University Press, 1994).

3. Burns, *Roosevelt: The Lion and the Fox*, 262–263.

4. Alan R. Millet and Peter Maslowski, *For the Common Defense: A Military History of the United States of America* (New York: The Free Press, 1984), 394.

5. *New York Times* (Wednesday, September 4, 1939), 1.

6. *New York Times* (June 23, 1940), 1.

7. Keegan, *The Second World War*, 88–102.

8. A. M. Sperber, *Murrow: His Life and Times* (New York: Freundlich Books, 1986), 161–163; See also Stanley Cloud and Lynne Olson; *The Murrow Boys: Pioneers on the Front Lines of Broadcast Journalism* (Boston, MA: Houghton Mifflin Company, 1996), Chapter 6.

9. Quoted in Sperber, *Murrow*, 168–169.

10. Millet and Maslowski, *For the Common Defense*, 396–397.

11. *New York Times* (June 22, 1941), 1.

12. Kenneth S. Lynn, *Hemingway* (New York: Simon and Schuster, 1987), Chapter 19; See also Hugh Thomas, *The Spanish Civil War* (New York: Harper and Brothers, 1961).

13. Garth Jowett, *Film: The Democratic Art* (Boston, MA: Little, Brown and Company, 1976), 299.

14. Ibid., 300–304.

15. James MacGregor Burns, *Roosevelt: Soldier of Freedom 1940–1945* (New York: Harcourt Brace Jovanovich, Inc., 1970), 34.

16. Ibid.

17. Ibid., 154–161.

18. Burns, *Roosevelt: The Lion and the Fox*, 275.

19. Gordon Prange, *At Dawn We Slept* (New York: McGraw-Hill Book Company, 1981).

20. *New York Times* (December 8, 1941).

21. *New York Times* (December 9, 1941).

22. Ian Kershaw, *Hitler: 1936–1945 Nemesis* (New York: W. W. Norton and Company, 2000), 442–448.

23. *New York Times* (December 12, 1941).

24. Millet and Maslowski, *For the Common Defense*, 407–410.

25. Duane Schultz, *The Doolittle Raid* (New York: St. Martin's Press, 1988).

26. Gordan Prange, *Miracle at Midway* (New York: McGraw-Hill Book Company, 1982).

27. *New York Times* (November 8, 1942), 1.

28. Clayton R. Koppes and Gregory D. Black, *Hollywood Goes to War: How Politics, Profits, and Propaganda Shaped World War II Movies* (New York: The Free Press, 1987), 66–67.

29. Ibid., 193.

30. Elizabeth M. Norman, *We Band of Angels: The Untold Story of American Nurses Trapped on Bataan by the Japanese* (New York: Random House, 1999), 123–129.

31. Dorothy Jones, "Hollywood War Films," *Hollywood Quarterly* 1 (1945).

32. Robert Fyne, *Hollywood Fights a War*, unpublished Ph.D. dissertation, New York University, 1976, 366–367.

33. Ibid., 336.

34. Koppes and Black, *Hollywood Goes to War*, 186, 216–217.

35. Burns, *Roosevelt: Soldier of Freedom 1940–1945*, 34–35.

36. Bill Mauldin, *Up Front* (New York: Henry Holt and Company, 1945).

37. James Bradley, *Flags of Our Fathers* (New York: Bantam Books, 2000), 275–277.

38. Ibid., Chapter 16; On May 24, Ira Hayes was removed from the tour and ordered by the Commandant of the Marine Corps to rejoin his outfit. John Bradley and Renee Gagnon continued the tour. In the 1949 John Wayne film, *The Sands of Iwo Jima*, all three would reenact the flag raising in the Mount Surabachi scene.

39. Kershaw; *Hitler: 1936–1945 Nemesis*, 798–833.

40. George Feifer, *Tennozan: The Battle of Okinawa and the Atomic Bomb* (New York: Ticknor and Fields, 1992).

41. Ibid., 568–573.

42. John W. Dower, *Embracing Defeat: Japan in the Wake of World War II* (New York: W. W. Norton and Company/The New Press, 1999), 33–39; Bix, *Hirohito and the Making of Modern Japan*, 525–530.

43. *New York Times* (July 29, 1945), 1.

44. Keegan, *The Second World War*, 590–591; Weinberg, *A World at Arms*, 894–895.

45. *New York Times* (October 2, 1946), 1.

46. Dower, *Embracing Defeat*, Chapter 15.

47. Bix and Dower make strong arguments for a more balanced and judicious look at the "Japanese miracle."

4: The Forgotten War–Korea

1. Clay Blair, *The Forgotten War: America in Korea 1950–53* (New York: Times Books, 1987), 7–8.

2. I. F.Stone, *The Hidden History of the Korean War* (New York: Monthly Review Press, 1952), 12.

3. David E. Sanger, "How North Korea Became North Korea," *New York Times* (July 27, 2003), WK 5.

4. Stone, *The Hidden History of the Korean War*, 77–78.

5. John E. Mueller, *War, Presidents, and Public Opinion* (New York: John Wiley & Sons, Inc., 1973), 51.

6. Franklin D Mitchell, *Harry S. Truman and the News Media: Contentious Relations, Belated Respect* (Columbia: University of Missouri Press, 1998), 64–65.

7. *Television Daily*, July 20, 1950.

8. Phillip Knightley, *The First Casualty: The War Correspondent as Hero and Myth-Maker from the Crimea to Kosovo* (Baltimore, MD: The Johns Hopkins University Press, 1975), 365–367.

9. Ibid., 371.

10. Mueller, *War, Presidents, and Public Opinion*, 44–47.

11. James I. Matray, "Truman's Plan for Victory: National Self-Determination and the Thirty-Eighth Parallel Decision in Korea," *The Journal of American History* 66 (September 1979),314–333.

12. Major Philip D. Caine, "The United States in Korea and Vietnam: A Study in Public Opinion," *Air University* Review (November–December 1968). (1951), 78–79.

13. Steven Casey, "White House Publicity Operations during the Korean War, June 1950–June 1951," *Presidential Studies Quarterly*, Washington, DC 35(4) (December 2005), 691.

14. NSC 81/1, "A Report to the President by the National Security Council on United States Courses of Action with Respect to Korea," http,://trumanlibrary.org/whistlestop/study collections/korea/large/sec4/nsc81-3.htm, 2–3.

15. Knightley, *The First Casualty*, 365–367.

16. Malcolm W. Cagle and Frank A. Manson, *The Sea War in Korea* (Annapolis, MD: U.S. Naval Institute, 1957), 120.

17. Foreign Relations of the United States, Vol. VII, 1950, 1076 (text); "History of the JCS III," 294–295.

18. Published Papers of the President of the United States: Harry S. Truman, 1950, 724–728.

19. David McCullough, *Truman* (New York: Simon & Schuster, 1992), 837.

20. Blair, *The Forgotten War*, 525.

21. McCullough, *Truman*, 847–848.

22. Alexander Bevin, *Korea: The First War We Lost* (New York: Hippocrene Books, Inc., 1986), 414–418.

23. Ibid., 433–437.

24. Blair, *The Forgotten War*, 960.

25. Robert Leckie, *Conflict: The History of the Korean War, 1950–53* (New York: Da Capo Press, 1962), 366–367.

26. Ibid., 387.

27. Dean Acheson, *The Korean War* (New York: W. W. Norton & Company, 1969), 113–114.

28. Adam B. Ulam, "Washington, Moscow, and the Korean War," in *Korea: Cold War and Limited War*," Allen Guttmann, ed. (Lexington, MA: D.C. Heath and Co., 1972), 284.

29. Trends in Television, Television Bureau of Advertising (TvB), June 1987, 3.

30. Tim Brooks and Earle Marsh, *The Complete Directory to Prime Time Network TV Shows: 1946–Present* (New York: Ballantine Books, 1985), 1030.

31. Nancy E. Bernhard, "Clearer than Truth: Public Affairs Television and the State Department's Domestic Information Campaigns," *Diplomatic History* (21)(1997), 561–563.

32. Adair Gilbert, *Vietnam on Film: From the Green Berets to Apocalypse Now* (New York: Proteus Books, 1981), 14.

33. Dan Ford, *Pappy: The Life of John Ford* (New York: Prentice-Hall, 1979), 234–236.

34. General Bruce Palmer, Jr., *The 25-Year War: America's Military Role in Vietnam* (Lexington: The University Press of Kentucky, 1984), 5.

35. Leckie, *Conflict*, 386.

5: The Domino Theory War–Vietnam

1. Jean Prescott, "Rise of the Baby Boomers/A & E Special 'Nation' Examines the Lives and Times of Generation," *Houston Chronicle* (June 12, 2004)

2. David Caute, *The Great Fear: The Anti-Communist Purge Under Truman and Eisenhower* (New York: Simon and Schuster, 1978), 49.

3. "The Younger Generation," *Time* (November 4, 1951).

4. Caute, *The Great Fear*, 541.

5. F. M. Kail, *What Washington Said: Administration Rhetoric and the Vietnam War: 1949–1969* (New York: Harper and Row, 1979), 66.

6. "'We Won't Surrender!' Is Last Word As Dien Bien Phu Falls Before Red Host; Ike Calls Parley; Unity Urged by Dulles," *The Washington Post* (May 8, 1954).

7. Ray F. Herndon, "Stories That Shaped the Century," *Los Angeles Times* (November 13, 1999).

8. Stanley Karnow, *Vietnam: A History* (New York: The Viking Press, 1983), 170.

9. Ibid., 213.

10. "U.S. Due to Train Vietnamese Army," *New York Times* (November 17, 1954).

11. Karnow, *Vietnam*, 247, 250.

12. Ibid., 259.

13. Robert Mann, *A Grand Delusion: America's Descent into Vietnam* (New York: Basic Books, 2001), 259.

14. David Halberstram, "Curbs in Vietnam Irk U.S. Officers: Americans Under Orders to Withhold News," *New York Times* (November 22, 1962).

15. Foreign Relations of the United States (FRUS), 1961–1963, 4:140–143.

16. James William Gibson, *The Perfect War: Technowar in Vietnam* (Boston, MA: The Atlantic Monthly Press, 1986), 87.

17. Karnow, *Vietnam*, 22.

18. David Halberstram, "GI's Told Not to Criticize Vietnam," *New York Times* (June 24, 1963).

19. Louis Harris, "U.S. Handling of Vietnam Issue Has Public Confused, Cautious," *Washington Post* (March 30, 1964).

20. The Gallup Poll, "Less than 40% of People Follow Vietnam Events," *Washington Post* (May 27 1964).

21. William M. Hammond, *Reporting Vietnam: Media and Military at War* (Lawrence: University Press of Kansas, 1998), 22.

22. Ibid., 24.

23. Ibid., 30.

24. Leo Bogart, *Cool Words, Cold War: A New Look at the USIA's Premises for Propaganda* (Washington, DC: American University Press, 1995), 55–56.

25. Thomas Powers, *The War at Home: Vietnam and the American People, 1964–1968* (New York: Grossman Publications, 1972), 14.

26. Gibson, *The Perfect War*, 89.

27. Karnow, *Vietnam*, 295.

28. Michael R. Beschloss, ed., *Taking Charge: The Johnson White House Tapes, 1963–1964* (New York: Harper and Row, 1966), 398.

29. Foreign Relations of the United States (FRUS), 1964–1968, 1:523.

30. Gibson, *The Perfect War*, 5.

31. Eugene Marlow and Eugene Secunda, *Shifting Time and Space: The Story of Videotape* (New York: Praeger Publishers, 1991), 30–34.

32. Ibid., 35.

33. Karnow, *Vietnam*, 412.

34. Lewis H. Lapham, "Seen but Not Heard," *Harper's Magazine* (July 1995).

35. Jack Raymond, "3,500 U.S. Marines Going to Vietnam to Bolster Base," *New York Times* (March 7, 1965).

36. From *The Fog of War*, a film documentary by Errol Morris featuring an interview with Robert J. McNamara, released by Sony Pictures Classics, 2003.

37. Frank Rich, "Oldest Living Whiz Kid Tells All," *New York Times* (January 25, 2004).

38. *Time*, "Reagan's TV Troubles," April 5, 1982.

39. McCandlish Phillips, "Now the Teach-In: U.S. Policy in Vietnam Criticized All Night," *New York Times* (March 27, 1965).

40. Mann, *A Grand Delusion*, 428.

41. "Senate Passes Penalty Bill for Burning of Draft Cards," *New York Times* (August 14, 1965).

42. Powers, *The War at Home*, 57, 59.

43. Congressional Record, April 26, 1965, 8440, 43.

44. Mann, *A Grand Delusion*, 497.

45. Phil G. Goulding, *Confirm or Deny* (New York: Harper and Row, 1970), 75.

46. William Raspberry, "Don't Forget King on War," *New York Post* (January 19, 2004).

47. Hammond, *Reporting Vietnam*, 104–105.

48. Michael J. Arlen, *Living Room War* (New York: The Viking Press, Inc., 1969), 114.

49. Personal interview with Gus Kerkoulas, New York City, February 7, 2004.

50. Hammond, *Reporting Vietnam*, 107.

51. Karnow, *Vietnam*, 546.

52. Austin Ranney, *Channels of Power: The Impact of Television on American Politics* (New York: Basic Books, 1983), 5.

53. "Westmoreland Requests 206,000 More Men; Stirring Debate in Administration," *New York Times* (March 10, 1968).

54. Joan Barthel, "John Wayne, Superhawk," *New York Times* (December 24, 1967).

55. Renata Adler, "Screen: 'Green Berets' as Viewed by John Wayne," *New York Times* (June 20, 1968).

56. Gilbert Adair, *Vietnam on Film: From the Green Berets to Apocalypse Now* (New York: Proteus Books, 1981), 169–190.

57. H. Bruce Franklin, *The Vietnam War: In American Stories, Songs, and Poems* (Boston, MA: Bedford Books of St. Martin's Press, 1996), 203.

58. George Gent, "Seeger Accuses C.B.S. Over Song," *The New York Times* (September 13, 1967).

59. James P. Sterba, "Marines Leaving South Vietnam Are Briefed on How to Act in a Peace Zone," *New York Times* (July 14, 1969).

60. Louis Calta, "Wounded Veteran Writes Song on Vietnam War," *New York Times* (February 1, 1966).

61. Franklin, *The Vietnam War in American Stories, Songs & Poems*, 206.

62. Michael Ellison, "This Is My Last Hurrah," *The Guardian* (October 18, 2000).

63. Franklin, *The Vietnam War in American Stories, Songs & Poems*, 205–206.

64. Robert Weissberg, *Public Opinion and Popular Government* (Englewood Cliffs, NJ: Prentice-Hall, 1976), 234–237.

65. Karnow, *Vietnam*, 582.

66. Godfrey Sperling, "Nixon's 'Secret Plan' That Never Was," *Christian Science Monitor* (December 9, 1997).

67. Daniel C. Hallin, *The Uncensored War* (Los Angeles, CA: University of California Press), 182.

68. Hammond, *Reporting Vietnam*, 128.

69. U.S. Department of State, American Opinion Summary, February 26–March 12, 1969; 13–27; George Gallup, "Favor Extreme Steps to End the War," *Chicago Sun-Times* (March 23, 1969).

70. Paul W. Valentine, "Candlelight Walk Caps Day in City," *Washington Post* (October 16, 1969).

71. "Text of President Nixon's Address to Nation on U.S. Policy in the War in Vietnam," *New York Times* (November 4, 1969).

72. Hammond, *Reporting Vietnam*, 148.

73. Richard Homan, "Pentagon Aides Assail Press," *Washington Post* (June 7, 1969).

74. Hammond, *Reporting Vietnam*, 216, 218.

75. "Returnees Jeered," *Washington Post* (July 11, 1969).

76. John Herbers, "Nixon Pushes Hard for Support of Vietnam Policy," *New York Times* (November 14, 1969).

77. Hammond, *Reporting Vietnam*, 600.

78. Robert M. Smith, "Two in Congress Ask Study of Massacre Report," *New York Times* (November 21, 1969).

79. "World-Wide," *Wall Street Journal*, (May 5, 1970), 611.

80. Mann, *A Grand Delusion*, 661.

81. Ibid., 661.

82. Karnow, *Vietnam*, 625

83. Mann, *A Grand Delusion*, 682.

84. "The Covert War," *New York Times* (June 15, 1971).

85. Mann, *A Grand Delusion*, 671.

86. James Reston, "'Mr. Nixon' Policy and Propaganda," *New York Times* (March 28, 1971).

87. Walter Pincus and George Lardner Jr., "Nixon Hoped Antitrust Threat Would Sway Network Coverage; Colson Advised Constant Pressure, Tapes Show," *Washington Post* (December 1, 1997).

88. Ibid.

89. Ibid.

90. Karnow, *Vietnam*, 653–654.

91. Philip Knightey, *The First Casualty: The War Correspondent as Hero and Myth-maker from the Crimea to Kosovo* (Baltimore, MD: The Johns Hopkins University Press, 2000), 462.

92. Karnow, *Vietnam*, 654.

93. "International," *New York Times* (January 28, 1973).

94. Mann, *A Grand Delusion*, 714.

95. Karnow, *Vietnam*, 667.

6: Operation Desert Storm—The Persian Gulf War

1. Henry E. Catto, Jr., "Dateline Grenada: The Media and the Military Go at It," *Washington Post* (October 30, 1983).

2. Richard Reeves, "Military Defeats Press Pool Again," *Montgomery Advertiser* (January 15, 1990).

3. Lou Cannon, "White House Resigns in Row Over Grenada Policy," *Washington Post* (November 1, 1983).

4. George H. Quester, "Grenada and the New Media," in Peter M. Dunn and Bruce W. Watson, eds., *American Intervention in Grenada* (Boulder, CO: Westview Press, 1985), 115.

5. Christina Jacqueline Johns and P. Ward Johnson, *State Crime, the Media, and the Invasion of Panama* (Westport, CT: Praeger Publisher, 1994), 67.

6. Leonard Maltin, *Leonard Maltin's Movie and Video Guide 1995* (New York: Penguin, 1994), 551.

7. "The Pentagon Pool, Bottled Up," *New York Times* (January 15, 1990).

8. Johns and Johnson, *State Crime, the Media, and the Invasion of Panama*, 78.

9. Tom Wicker, "Bush's Double Vision," *New York Times* (January 8, 1990).

10. John R. MacArthur, *Second Front: Censorship and Propaganda in the Gulf War* (New York: Hill and Wang, 1992), 7.

11. Everett E. Dennis, *The Media at War: The Press and the Persian Gulf Conflict* (New York: Gannett Foundation Media Center, 1991), 1–2.

12. Neil Hickey, "Lessons from the Gulf," *TV Guide* (April 6, 1991), 1.

13. Curtis Wilkie, "Simon's Chilling, Poetic Account of Captivity," *Boston Globe* (May 1, 1992).

14. "Censors Screen Pooled Reports," *New York Times* (February 28, 1991).

15. Neil Hickey, interview by Eugene Secunda, September 12, 2002.

16. David Gergan, "Why America Hates the Press," *U.S. News & World Report* (March 11, 1991), 57.

17. Edwin Diamond, "Who Won the Media War," *New York* (March 18, 1991), 27.

18. Edward L. Bernays, *Public Relations* (Norman: University of Oklahoma Press, 1952), 160.

19. "H&K Leads PR Charge in Behalf of Kuwaiti Cause," O'Dwyer's PR Services Report, Vol. 5, No. 1, January 1991, 8.

20. David Stebenne, "The Gulf Conflict in Historical Context," *The Media at War*, 20–21.

21. MacArthur, *Second Front*, 39–40.

22. John Pavlik, and Mark Thalhimer, "The Charge of the E-Mail Brigade," *The Media at War*, 36.

23. Walter Goodman, "Critic's Notebook: CNN in Baghdad: Danger of Propaganda vs. Virtue of Reporting," *New York Times* (January 29, 1991).

24. C. Henderson "The Filtered War," *New Statesman & Society* (April 5, 1991), 16.

25. *New York Times/CBS News* Poll, as reported in O'Dwyer's PR Services Report, January 1991, 3–4.

26. MacArthur, *Second Front*, 41–42.

27. Ibid., 46–49.

28. Robin Pogrebin, "Hill & Knowlton and Its Own P.R. Problems," *New York Observer* (February 10, 1992).

29. MacArthur, *Second Front*, 48–49.

30. *Jack O'Dwyer's Newsletter*, December 5, 1990.

31. Tom Regan, "When Contemplating War, Beware of Babies in Incubators," *Christian Science Monitor* (September 6, 2002).

32. Ibid.

33. John Stauber and Sheldon Rampton, *Toxic Sludge Is Good for You: Lies, Damn Lies and the Public Relations Industry* (Monroe, MA: Common Courage Press), 143.

34. Regan, "When Contemplating War, Beware of Babies in Incubators."

35. "Excerpts from Schwarzkopf News Conference on Gulf War," *New York Times* (February 28, 1991).

36. "Homecoming, Without Honors," *New York Times* (February 28, 1991).

37. Robin Toner, "Bush's War Success Confers an Aura of Invincibility in '92," *New York Times* (February 27, 1991).

38. Drudge Report, "Bush Circle Debates Whether to Hold Iraq Victory Parade for Military," April 20, 2003, http://www.drudgereport.com/parade.htm

39. http://www.brokenfrontier.com/columns/retroflect./archive/rfjune07.htm

40. Roger Ebert, "Three Kings," *Chicago Sun Times* (October 1, 1999).

41. http://www.amazon.com/exec/obidos/search-handle-form

42. Garth S. Jowett, and Victoria O'Donnell, *Propaganda and Persuasion*, 3rd ed. (Thousand Oaks, CA: Sage Publications, Inc., 1999), 314–315.

43. *New York Times 2003 Almanac*, Penguin Reference, 2002, 148.

7: The Global War on Terror—Iraq

1. John Keegan, *The Iraq War* (New York: Alfred A. Knopf, 2004), 1.

2. Bob Woodward, *Plan of Attack* (New York: Simon & Schuster, 2004), 1.

3. Bob Woodward, *Bush at War* (New York: Simon & Schuster, 2002), 49.

4. Maureen Dowd, "The Mirror Has Two Faces," *New York Times* (February 1, 2004).

5. "Ex-Aide: U.S. Planned Iraq War Pre-9/11," *New York Times* (January 11, 2004).

6. Bob Herbert, "The Wrong War," *New York Times* (March 26, 2004).

7. Sam Tannenhaus, "Bush's Brain Trust," *Vanity Fair* (May 2003).

8. http://www.defenselink.mil/cgi-bin/dlprint,cgi?http.defenselink.mil/transcripts/20

9. Tannenhaus, "Bush's Brain Trust"; Woodward, *Bush at War*, 206.

10. http://www.bushcountry.org/bush/bush_speeches/president_bush_speech_092001.htm

11. "Rice Seeks Allies' Help with Afghanistan," *New York Times* (January 26, 2007), A1.

12. Ibid.

13. Helene Cooper, "NATO Allies Wary of Sending More Troops to Afghanistan," *New York Times* (January 27, 2007), A1.

14. Woodward, *Bush at War*, 206.

15. David E. Sanger, "Threats and Responses: The President's Speech; Bush Sees 'Urgent Duty' to Pre-empt Attack by Iraq," *New York Times* (October 8, 2002).

16. The Editors, "The Choice," *The New Yorker* (November 1, 2004).

17. Woodward, *Bush at War*, 278–279.

18. DoD News Briefing—Secretary Rumsfeld and Gen. Myers, November 1, 2001, http://www.defenselink.mil/transcripts/2001/t11012001_t1101sd.html

19. Mary McGrory, "Selling War or Making Peace," *Washington Post* (March 24, 2002).

20. Elisabeth Bumiller, "Traces of Terror: The Strategy; Bush Aides Set Strategy to Sell Policy on Iraq," *New York Times* (September 7, 2002).

21. James Carney, "Selling a Long and Slow War," *Time* (October 8, 2001).

22. Daniel J. Boorstin, *The Image: A Guide to Pseudo-Events in America* (New York: Antheneum, 1987), 11–12.

23. Bumiller, "Traces of Terror."

24. David E. Sanger and Julia Preston, "Bush to Warn U.N.: Act on Iraq or U.S. Will; He Leads Nation in Mourning at Terror," *New York Times* (September 12, 2002).

25. Marc Sandalow, "9.11.01/One Year Later/ Warning from Bush on Day of Tears/President Pledges 'What Our Enemies Have Begun, We Will Finish,'" *San Francisco Chronicle* (September 12, 2002).

26. John Donnelly, "Bush Sets Course That Points Toward Attack," *Boston Globe* (September 13, 2002).

27. Tamara Lipper, Brant Martha, and Michael Hirsh, "'What Our Enemies Have Begun...We Will Finish': Selling the World on War," *Newsweek* (September 23, 2002).

28. Sanger, "Threats and Responses."

29. Susan Milligan, "Congress Gives Bush OK to Act Alone Against Iraq/Senate Follows House in Voting Strong Support," *Boston Globe* (October 11, 2002).

30. Colum Lynch, "U.S. Orders Iraq to Disarm; 'Serious Consequences' Threatened if Baghdad Does Not Comply," *Washington Post* (November 9, 2002).

31. Julia Preston, "Iraq Tell the U.N. Arms Inspections Will Be Permitted," *New York Times* (November 14, 2002).

32. Rajiv Chandrasekaran, "Baghdad Delivers Weapons Data to U.N.; 12,000-Page Declaration Reiterates Iraqi Denials," *Washington Post* (December 8, 2002).

33. Elisabeth Bumiller, "White House Memo: War Public Relations Machine Is Put on Full Throttle," *New York Times* (February 9, 2003).

34. Bennett Roth, "State of the Union/Bush: 'Decisive Days' Ahead/Address Spotlights Economy, Iraq threat," *Houston Chronicle* (January 29, 2003).

35. Anne E. Kornblutt and Michael Kranish, "Bush Says US Ready to Move on Iraq, President Ties Hussein to Threat of Terrorism," *Boston Globe* (March 7, 2003).

36. Anne E. Kornblut, "Bush Tells Hussein to Leave Within 48 Hours or Face War, Calls Mission on Iraq 'Course Toward Safety,'" *Boston Globe* (March 18, 2003).

37. David Gregory, in interview on the Don Imus radio program, WFAN, New York, March 19, 2003.

38. Michael Tackett, "Bush Taps America's New Fear," *Chicago Tribune* (March 18, 2003).

39. Karen DeYoung, "Bush Message Machine Is Set to Roll with Its Own War Plan," *Washington Post* (March 19, 2003).

40. "Bush's Speech on the Start of War," *New York Times* (March 20, 2003).

41. John Donnelly and Marcella Bombardieri, "Iraq War Begins: US Strikes at 'Sites of Opportunity'; Bush Vows Broad Campaign," *Boston Globe* (March 20, 2003).

42. Andy Netzel, "America at War/ Polls Say U.S. Public Backs President, Invasion of Iraq," *Houston Chronicle* (March 21, 2003).

43. Jim VandeHei, "Hill Resolutions Supporting Bush, Troops Are Approved; House Goes Beyond Senate in Praise of President," *Washington Post* (March 21, 2003).

44. Noel C. Paul, "Selling War: A Review of the Campaign," *Christian Science Monitor* (March 24, 2003).

45. Rebecca Blumenstein and Matthew Rose, "Name That Op: How U.S. Coins Phrases of War," *Wall Street Journal* (March 24, 2003).

46. David Charter, "Movie Men Add Special Effects to Media War," *London Times* (March 11, 2003).

47. Lori Robertson, "In Control," *American Journalism Review* (February/ March 2005).

48. Howard Kurtz, "Media Weigh Costs, Fruits of 'Embedding'; News Outlets Stretch Budgets for Chance to Witness Iraq War from Front Lines," *Washington Post* (March 11, 2003).

49. Mark Jurkowitz, "The Media's Conflict Experts Say Access to Troops Helped More than Hurt," *Boston Globe* (April 22, 2003).

50. Bill Duryea, "Can the U.S. Take Losses? Yes, if Victory Is in Sight," *St. Petersburg Times* (March 30, 2003).

51. Dan Balz and Mike Allen, "CEO Bush Takes over Management of Message," *Washington Post* (March 28, 2003).

52. Matthew Gilbert and Suzanne C. Ryan, "Snap Judgments: Did Iconic Images from Baghdad Reveal More about the Media than Iraq?" *Boston Globe* (April 10, 2003).

53. Elisabeth Bumiller, "Keepers of Bush Image Lift Stagecraft to New Heights," *New York Times* (May 15, 2003).

54. "Bush Steps Away from Victory Banner," *New York Times* (October 29, 2003).

55. Adam Nogourney, "Democrats Temper Praise for Bush Visit with Criticism," *New York Times* (November 28, 2003).

56. Hugh Delios and E. A. Torriero, "Sorting Fact from Fiction in POW's Gripping Story; Doubts about the Tale of Jessica Lynch's Rescue Aren't Limited to the Details; Questions Also Swirl about Who Is to Blame for the Hype," *Chicago Tribune* (May 26, 2003).

57. Pat Morrison, "Consequences of War: What You Won't See on TV," *Los Angeles Times* (November 11, 2003).

58. Jonathan Alter, "Yes, We Can Handle the Truth," *Newsweek* (May 3, 2004).

59. Morrison, "Consequences of War."

60. Gregg Zoroya, "Return of U.S. War Dead Kept Solemn, Secret; Process of Military Honor Guards Carrying Caskets of Slain Troops Kept from Public Eye," *USA Today* (December 31, 2003).

61. John Harwood, "The Wall Street Journal/NBC News Poll: War's Success Is Boon to Bush—Poll Shows President Gains on Issues on Home Front and Abroad," *Wall Street Journal* (April 14, 2003).

62. Bennett Roth, "America in Iraq/ Bush: U.S. to Stay in Iraq/ Poll Shows Slippage in Support for War," *Houston Chronicle* (July 2, 2003).

63. Linda Feldmann, "How 'Pushback' Plays for Bush on Iraq; Administration Vows 'No Retreat' This Week, as Casualty Count Raises Concern," *Christian Science Monitor* (August 28, 2003).

64. Bob Kemper, "Bush Wants UN in Iraq: Asks Congress for $87 billion, Defends Troop Levels; 'We Will Do . . . Spend What Is Necessary,'" *Chicago Tribune* (September 8, 2003).

65. Elisabeth Bumiller, "Bush Seeks $87 Billion and U.N. Aid for War Effort," *New York Times* (September 8, 2003).

66. Andrew Kohut, "A Chink in the Armor," *New York Times* (September 18, 2003).

67. Doug Halonen and Michele Greppi, "Bush Pulls Press Corps Bypass," *Television Week* (October 20, 2003).

68. Ken Auletta, "Fortress Bush; Annuals of Communications," *The New Yorker* (January 19, 2004).

69. Elisabeth Bumiller, "Trying to Bypass the Good-News Filter," *New York Times* (October 20, 2003).

70. Dave Moniz, "Some Veterans of Vietnam See Iraq Parallel in Lack of Candor; 'We Can Win the War,' McCain Says, 'but Not if We Lose Popular Support,'" *USA Today* (November 11, 2003).

71. Cindy Rodriquez, "Iraqi Tyrant Capture Fuels Myth of Safety," *Denver Post* (January 2, 2004).

72. "Capture of Saddam Leads to Boost for Bush in Polls," *Houston Chronicle* (December 17, 2003).

73. Dana Milbank, "Election 2004/Bush Rhetoric Keeps Public from Turning against War," *Houston Chronicle* (April 25, 2004).

74. Farah Stockman, "Bush Voices Disgust over Abuse Photos; Threat Is Seen to Iraq Mission," *Boston Globe* (May 1, 2004).>

75. Eric Schmitt and Richard W. Stevenson, "White House and Pentagon Scurry to Draft Responses," *New York Times* (May 5, 2004).

76. John Ritter, "Poll: War Opposition up Amid Iraqi Abuse Scandal; Americans Appalled by Images of Prisoners' Mistreatment," *USA TODAY* (May 11, 2004).

77. John F. Harris and Thomas E. Ricks, "Polls Suggest War Isn't Hurting Bush; Mounting Deaths in Iraq Have Not Resulted in Major Backlash in Public Opinion," *Washington Post* (September 10, 2004).

78. Gebe Martinez, "Election 2004/ U.S. Vote Essentially Was Decided in Iraq," *Houston Chronicle* (November 3, 2004).

79. Katharine Q. Seelye, "The 2004 Elections: The Electorate—The Voters," *New York Times* (November 4, 2004).

80. Dan Balz, "Bush Wins Second Term; Kerry Concedes Defeat; Both Speak of Need for Unity," *Washington Post* (November 4, 2004).

81. David W. Moore, "Despite Fallujah, Americans Skeptical about Ultimate Success in Iraq," (November 23, 2004), www.gallup.com/poll/content/login

82. Doyle McManus, "The Nation; The Times Poll: Support for War in Iraq Hits New Low; Most No Longer Back the Administration's Basis for Invading, but a Majority Say U.S. troops Should Stay Longer to Assist with Stabilization," *Los Angeles Times* (January 19, 2005).

83. David E. Sanger, "Bush Hails Vote," *New York Times* (January 31, 2005).

84. Jill Lawrence, "Bush Approval Rating Rebounds after Iraq Vote," *USA TODAY* (February 8, 2005).

85. Inaugural Address by George W. Bush, *New York Times* (January 20, 2005).

86. New York Times/CBS Poll, January 14–18, 2005, *New York Times* (January 20, 2005).

87. National Security Council, *National Strategy for Victory in Iraq* (Washington, DC, 2005), 1.

88. Ibid., 6.

89. Ibid., 13.

90. The Iraq Study Group Report, *The Way Forward—A New Approach* (New York: Vintage Books, 2006), xiii.

91. Ibid., x.

92. Mark Manzetti, "Spy Agencies Saw Iraq War Worsens Terrorism Threat; U.S. Intelligence Assessment Is Said to Find a Rise in Global Islamic Radicalism," *New York Times* (September 24, 2006), 1.

93. "Conversing His Way Across Europe," *New York Times* (February 27, 2005).

94. Daniel Eisenberg, "Bush's New Intelligence Czar," *Time* (February 28, 2005), 32–25.

95. Eric Lipton, "Audit Faults U.S. for Its Spending on Port Defense," *New York Times* (February 20, 2005).

96. Jon Pareles, "Pop Music and the War," *New York Times* (January 2, 2007).

97. Ibid.

8: What We Learned

1. http://www.turtletrader.com/patton.html

2. See Robert Kagan, *Dangerous Nation* (New York: Alfred A. Knopf, 2006).

3. http://www.npr.org/templates/story/story.php?storyId.

4. See Max Boot, *War Made New: Technology, Warfare, and the Course of History, 1500 to Today* (New York: Gotham Books, 2006).

Bibliography

Acheson, Dean. *The Korean War*. New York: W.W. Norton & Company, 1969.

Adler, Renata. "Screen: 'Green Berets,' as viewed by John Wayne." *New York Times* (June 20, 1968).

Alter, Jonathan. "Yes, We Can Handle the Truth." *Newsweek* (May 3, 2004).

Arlen, Michael J. *The Living Room War*. New York: Farrah, Straus and Giroux, 1969.

Auletta, Ken. "Fortress Bush; Annals of Communication." *New Yorker* (January 19, 2004).

Balz, Dan. "Bush Wins Second Term; Kerry Concedes Defeat: Both Speak of Need for Unity." *Washington Post* (November 4, 2004).

Balz, Dan, and Mike Allen. "CEO Bush Takes over Management of Message." *Washington Post* (March 28, 2003).

Barber, Benjamin R. *Jihad vs. McWorld: How Globalization and Tradition are Reshaping the World*. New York: Ballantine Books, 1995.

Barthel, Joan. "John Wayne, Superhawk." *New York Times* (December 24, 1967).

Becker, Elizabeth, and James Dao. "Hearts and Minds: Bush Will Keep the Wartime Operation Promoting America." *New York Times* (February 20, 2002).

Bernays, Edward L. *Public Relations*. Norman: University of Oklahoma Press, 1952.

Bernhard, Nancy E. "Clearer than Truth: Public Affairs Television and the State Department's Domestic Information Campaigns." *Diplomatic History*, 21(4) (Fall 1997), 561–563.

Beschloss, Michael R., ed. *Taking Charge: The Johnson White House Tapes, 1963–1964*. New York: Harper and Row, 1966.

Bevin, Alexander. *Korea: The First War We Lost*. New York: Hippocrene Books, Inc., 1986.

Bix, Herbert P. *Hirohito and the Making of Modern Japan.* New York: Harper Collins Publishers, 2000.

Blair, Clay. *The Forgotten War: America in Korea 1950–53.* New York: Times Books, 1987.

Blumenstein, Rebecca, and Matthew Rose. "Name That Op: How U.S. Coins Phrases of War." *Wall Street Journal* (March 24, 2003).

Bogart, Leo. *Cool Words, Cold War: A New Look at the USIA's Premises for Propaganda.* Washington, DC: American University Press, 1995.

Boot, Max. *The Savage Wars of Peace: Small Wars and the Rise of American Power.* New York: Basic Books, 2002.

———. *War Made Easy: Technology, Warfare, and the Course of History, 1500 to Today.* New York: Gotham Books, 2006.

Bradley, James. *Flags of Our Fathers.* New York: Bantam Books, 2000.

Brooks, Tim, and Earle Marsh. *The Complete Directory to Prime Time Network TV Shows: 1946–Present.* New York: Ballantine Books, 1985.

Bumiller, Elisabeth. "Bush Aides Set Strategy to Sell Policy on Iraq." *New York Times* (September 7, 2002).

———. "Bush Seeks $87 Billion and U.N. Aid for War Effort." *New York Times* (September 8, 2003).

———. "Keepers of Bush Image Lift Stagecraft to New Heights." *New York Times* (May 15, 2003).

———. "Trying to Bypass the Good News Filter." *New York Times* (October 29, 2003).

———. "White House Memo: War Public Relations Machine is Put on Full Throttle." *New York Times* (February 9, 2003).

Burns, James MacGregor. *Roosevelt: The Lion and the Fox.* New York: Harcourt, Brace and Company, 1955.

———. *Roosevelt: Soldier of Freedom 1940–1945.* New York: Harcourt, Brace Jovanovich, Inc., 1970.

Bush, George W. "Inaugural Address." *New York Times* (January 20, 2005).

Cagle, Malcom W., and Frank A. Manson. *The Sea War in Korea.* Annapolis, MD: U.S. Naval Institute, 1975.

Caine, Major Philip D. "The United States in Korea and Vietnam: A Study in Public Opinion," (November–December 1968): 49–56.

Calta, Louis. "Wounded Veteran Writes Song on Vietnam War." *New York Times* (February 1, 1966).

Cannon, Lou. "White House Press Aide Resigns in Row over Grenada Policy." *Washington Post* (November 1, 1983).

Carney, James. "Selling a Long and Slow War." *Time* (October 8, 2001).

Casey, Steven. "White House Publicity Operations during the Korean War: June 1950–June 1951." *Presidential Studies Quarterly*, 35(4) (December 2005), 691–717.

Catto, Henry E. Jr. "Dateline Grenada: The Media and the Military Go at It." *Washington Post* (October 30, 1983).

Caute, David. *The Great Fear: The Anti-Communist Purge Under Truman and Eisenhower.* New York: Simon & Schuster, 1978.

Chandrasekaren, Rajiv. "Baghdad Delivers Weapons Data to U.N.; 12,000-Page Declaration Reiterates Iraqi Denials." *Washington Post* (December 8, 2002).

Charter, David. "Movie Men Add Special Effects to Media War." *London Times* (March 11, 2003).

Clark, George B. *Devil Dogs: Fighting Marines of World War I.* Novato, CA: Presidio Press, 1999.

Clausewitz, Carl von. *On War*, edited and translated by Michael Howard and Peter Paret. Princeton, NJ: Princeton University Press, 1976.

Cloud, Stanley, and Lynne Olson. *The Murrow Boys: Pioneers on the Front Lines of Broadcast Journalism.* Boston, MA: Houghton Mifflin Company, 1996.

Coleman, James. *On the Great Highway.* Boston, MA: Lothrop Publishing, 1900.

Congressional Record (April 26, 1965) 8440, 43.

Creel, George. *How We Advertised America: The First Telling of the Amazing Story of the Committee on Public Information.* New York: Harper and Row, 1920.

———. *Rebel at Large: Reflections of Fifty Crowded Years.* New York: G.P. Putnam's Sons, 1942.

Dao, James. "Hearts and Minds: New Agency Will Not Lie, Top Pentagon Officials Say." *New York Times* (February 21, 2002).

Delios, Hugh, and E.A. Torriero. "Sorting Fact from Fiction in POW's Gripping Story." *Chicago Tribune* (May 26, 2003).

Dennis, Everett E. *The Media at War: The Press and the Persian Gulf Conflict.* New York: Gannett Foundation Media Center, 1991.

DeYoung, Karen. "Bush Message Machine Is Set to Roll with Its Own War Plans." *Washington Post* (March 19, 2003).

Diamond, Edwin. "Who Won the Media War?" *New York* (March 18, 1991).

Donnelly, John. "Bush Sets Course That Points Toward Attack." *Boston Globe* (September 13, 2002).

Donnelly, John, and Marcella Bombardieri. "Iraq War Begins; U.S. Strikes at 'Sites of Opportunity'; Bush Vows Broad Campaign." *Boston Globe* (March 20, 2003).

Dowd, Maureen. "The Mirror Has Two Faces." *New York Times* (February 1, 2004).

Dower, John W. *Embracing Defeat: Japan in the Wake of World War II.* New York: W.W. Norton and Company/The New Press. 1999.

Drudge Report. "Bush Circle Debates Whether to Hold Iraq Victory Parade for Military." (April 20, 2003). http://www.drudgereport.com/parade.htm

Duryea, Bill. "Can the U.S. Take Losses? Yes, if Victory Is in Sight." *St. Petersburg Times* (March 30, 2003).

Ebert, Roger. "Three Kings." *Chicago Sun Times* (October 1, 1999).

The Editors. "The Choice." *New Yorker* (November 1, 2004).

Eisenberg, Daniel. "Bush's New Intelligence Czar." *Time* (February 29, 2005).

Ellison, Michael. "This is My Last Hurrah." *The Guardian* (October 10, 2000).

Ellul, Jacques. *Propaganda: The Formation of Men's Attitudes*, translated by Konrad Kellen and Jean Lerner. New York: Alfred A. Knopf, 1971.

Emery, Michael, and Edwin Emery. *The Press and America*, 9th ed. Englewood Cliffs, NJ: Prentice Hall, 1999.

Feifer, George H. *Tennozan: The Battle of Okinawa and the Atomic Bomb.* Boston, MA: Houghton Mifflin Company, 1992.

Feldmann, Linda. "How 'Pushback' Plays for Bush in Iraq; Administration Vows 'No Retreat' this Week, as Casualty Count Raises Concern." *Christian Science Monitor* (August 28, 2003).

Fielding, Raymond. *The American* Newsreel *1911–1967*. Norman: University of Oklahoma Press, 1992.

Ford, Dan. *Pappy: The Life of John Ford*. New York: Prentice Hall, 1979.

Foreign Relations of the United States (1950) 7:1076.

Foreign Relations of the United States (1961–63) 4:140–143.

Foreign Relations of the United States (1964–1968), 1:523.

Franklin, H. Bruce. *The Vietnam War in American Stories, Songs & Poems*. Boston, MA: Bedford Books of St. Martin's Press, 1996.

Fyne, Robert. J. *Hollywood Fights a War*, unpublished Ph.D. dissertation, New York: New York University, 1976.

Gallup, George. "Favor Extreme Steps to End the War." *Chicago Sun Times* (May 23, 1969).

Gallup Poll, "Less than 40% of People Follow Vietnam Events." *Washington Post* (May 27, 1964).

Gent, George. "Seeger Accuses CBS over Song." *New York Times* (September 13, 1967).

Gergen, David. "Why America Hates the Press." *U.S. News & World Reports* (March 11, 1991).

Gibson, James William. *The Perfect War: Technowar in Vietnam*. the New York: Atlantic Monthly Press. 1986.

Gilbert, Adair. *Vietnam on Film: From the Green Berets to Apocalypse Now*. New York: Proteus Books, 1981.

Gilbert, Matthew, and Suzanne C. Ryan. "Snap Judgments: Did Iconic Images from Baghdad Reveal More About the Media than Iraq?" *Boston Globe* (April 10, 2003).

Goerlitz, Walter. *History of the German General Staff, 1657–1945*. New York: Frederick A. Praeger, Inc., Publishers, 1953.

Goodman, Walter. "Critic's Notebook: CNN in Baghdad: Danger of Propaganda vs. Virtue of Reporting." *New York Times* (January 29, 1991).

Goodspeed, D.J. *The German Wars 1914–1945*. Boston, MA: Houghton Mifflin, 1977.

Goulding, Phil G. *Confirm or Deny*. New York: Harper and Row. 1970.

Halberstram, David. "Curbs in Vietnam Irks U.S. Officers; Americans Under Orders to Withhold News." *New York Times* (November 22, 1962).

———. "GI's Told Not to Criticize Vietnam." *New York Times* (June 24, 1963).

Hallin, Daniel C. *The "Uncensored War."* Los Angeles, CA: University of California Press, 1989.

Halonen, Doug, and Michele Greppi. "Bush Pulls Press Corps Bypass." *Television Week* (October 20, 2003).

Hammond, William M. *Reporting Vietnam: Media and the Military at War*. Lawrence, Kansas: University Press of Kansas, 1998.

Harris, John F., and Thomas E. Ricks. "Polls Suggest War Isn't Hurting Bush; Deaths in Iraq Have Not Resulted in Major Backlash in Public Opinion." *Washington Post* (September 10, 2004).

Harris, Louis. "U.S. Handling of Vietnam Issue Has Public Confused, Cautious." *Washington Post* (March 30, 1964).

Harwood, John. "The Wall Street Journal/NBC News Poll: War's Success Is Boon to Bush—Poll Shows President Gains on Issues on Home Front and Abroad." *Wall Street Journal* (April 14, 2003).

Henderson, C. "The Filtered War." *New Statesman & Society* (April 5, 1991).

Herbers, John. "Nixon Pushes Hard for Support of Vietnam Policy." *New York Times* (November 14, 1969).

Herbert, Bob. "The Wrong War." *New York Times* (March 26, 2004).

Herndon, Ray F. "Stories That Shaped the Century." *Los Angeles Times* (November 13, 1999).

Hickey, Neil. "Lesson from the Gulf." *TV Guide* (April 6, 1991).

Homan, Richard. "Pentagon Aides Assail Press." *Washington Post* (June 7, 1969).

The Iraq Study Group Report. *The Way Forward—A New Approach*. New York: Vintage Books, 2006.

Isenberg, Michael T. *War on Film: The American Cinema and World War I, 1914–1941*. New Brunswick, NJ, London and Toronto: Associated University Presses, 1981.

Jackall, Robert, and Janice M. Hirota. "America's First Propaganda Ministry: The Committee on Public Information during the Great War." In Robert Jackall, ed., *Propaganda*. New York: New York University Press, 1995.

Johns, Christina Jacqueline, and P. Ward Johnson. *State Crime, The Media, and The Invasion of Panama*. Westport, CT: Praeger Publishers, 1994.

Jones, Dorothy. "Hollywood War Films." *Hollywood Quarterly* 1(1) (1945), 1–19.

Jowett, Garth S. *Film: The Democratic Art*. Boston, MA: Little, Brown and Company, 1976.

Jowett, Garth S., and Victoria O'Donnell. *Propaganda and Persuasion*, 3rd ed. Thousand Oaks, CA: Sage Publications, Inc., 1999.

Jurkowitz, Mark. "The Media's Conflict Experts Say Access to Troops Helped More than Hurt." *Boston Globe* (April 22, 2003).

Kagan, Robert. *Dangerous Nation*. New York: Alfred A. Knopf, 2006.

Kail, F.M. *What Washington Said: Administration Rhetoric and the Vietnam War: 1949–1969*. New York: Harper and Row, 1979.

Karnow, Stanley. *Vietnam: A History*. New York: The Viking Press, 1983.

Keegan, John. *The First World War*. New York: Alfred A. Knopf, 1999.

———. *The Iraq War*. New York: Alfred A. Knopf, 2004.

———. *The Second World War*. New York: Viking Penguin, 1989.

Kemper, Bob. "Bush Wants UN in Iraq; Asks Congress for $87 Billion; Defends Troop Levels; 'We Will Do ... Spend What Is Necessary.'" *Chicago Tribune* (September 8, 2003).

Kennedy, David. *Over Here: The First World War and American Society*. New York: Oxford University Press, 1980.

Kennedy, George. *The Art of Persuasion in Ancient Greece*. Princeton, NJ: Princeton University Press, 1963.

Kershaw, Ian. *Hitler: 1936–1945 Nemesis*. New York and London: W.W. Norton and Company, 2000.

Knightly, Phillip. *The First Casualty: The War Correspondent as Hero and Myth-Maker from the Crimea to Kosovo*, rev. ed. Baltimore, MD and London: The Johns Hopkins Press, 2000.

Kohut, Andrew. "A Chink in the Armor." *New York Times* (September 18, 2003).

Koppes, Clayton R., and Gregory D. Black. *Hollywood Goes to War: How Politics, Profits, and Propaganda Shaped World War II Movies*. New York: The Free Press, 1987.

Kornblut, Anne E. "Bush Tells Hussein to Leave Within 48 Hours or Face War, Calls Mission in Iraq 'Course Towards Safety.'" *Boston Globe* (March 18, 2003).

Kornblut, Anne E., and Michael Kranish. "Bush Says US Ready to Move on Iraq, President Ties Hussein to Threat of Terrorism." *Boston Globe* (March 9, 2003).

Kurtz, Howard. "For Media After Iraq, a Case of Shell Shock; Battle Assessment Begins for Saturation Reporting." *Washington Post* (April 28, 2003).

———. "Media Weigh Costs, Fruits of 'Embedding': News Outlets Stretch Budgets for Chance to Witness Iraq War from Front Lines." *Washington Post* (March 11, 2003).

LaMay, Craig, Martha FitzSimon, and Jeanine Sahadi, eds. *The Media at War: The Press and the Persian Gulf War*. New York: Gannett Foundation Media Center, 1971.

Lapham, Lewis H. "Seen but Not Heard." *Harper's Magazine* (July 1995).

Lawrence, Jill. "Bush Approval Rating Rebounds After Iraq Vote." *USA Today* (February 8, 2005).

Leckie, Robert. *Conflict: The History of the Korean War, 1950–53*. New York: Da Capo Press, 1962.

Leiby, Richard. "The Hilton's Strange Embed Fellows." *Washington Post* (March 7, 2003).

Liddell Hart, B.H. *The Real War 1914–1918*. New York: The Atlantic Monthly Press Books, 1930.

Lipper, Tamara, Martha Brant, and Michael Hirsh. "'What Our Enemies Have Begun ... We Will Finish': Selling the World on War." *Newsweek* (September 23, 2002).

Lipton, Eric. "Audit Faults U.S. for Its Spending on Port Defense." *New York Times* (February 20, 2005).

Lynch, Colum. "U.S. Orders Iraq to Disarm; 'Serious Consequences' Threatened if Baghdad Does Not Comply." *Washington Post* (November 9, 2002).

Lynn, Kenneth S. *Hemingway*. New York: Simon and Schuster, 1987.

MacArthur, John R. *Second Front: Censorship and Propaganda in the Gulf War*. New York: Hill and Wang, 1992.

Maltin, Leonard. *Leonard Maltin's Movie and Video Guide*. New York: A Penguin Book, 1994.

Mann, Robert. *A Grand Delusion: America's Descent into Vietnam*. New York: Basic Books, 2001.

Marlow, Eugene, and Eugene Secunda. *Shifting Time and Space: The Story of Videotape*. New York: Praeger Publishers, 1991.

Martinez, Gebe. "Election 2004/ U.S. Vote Essentially Was Decided in Iraq." *Houston Chronicle* (November 3, 2004).

Matray, James I. "Truman's Plan for Victory: National Self-Determination and the Thirty-Eighth Parallel Decision in Korea." *The Journal of American History* 66 (September 1979).

Matus, Irwin Leigh. "Urbanography: Where the Dream Was Made." The Composing Stack, Inc. http://urbanography.com/urban/00061/index.htm.

Mauldin, Bill. *Up Front*. New York: Henry Holt and Company, 1945.

Mazetti, Mark. "Spy Agencies Say Iraq War Worsens Terrorism Threat; U.S. Intelligence Assessment Is Said to Find a Rise in Global Islamic Radicalism." *New York Times* (September 24, 2006).

McCabe, John. *George M. Cohan, The Man Who Owned Broadway.* Garden City, NY: Doubleday and Co., 1973.

McCullough, David. *Truman.* New York: Simon & Schuster, 1992.

McGrory, Mary. "Selling War or Making Peace." *Washington Post* (March 24, 2002).

McManus, Doyle. "The Nation; The Time Poll: Support for War in Iraq Hits New Low; Most No Longer Back the Administration's Basis for Invading, but a Majority Says U.S. Troops Should Stay Longer to Assist with Stabilization." *Los Angeles Times* (January 19, 2005).

McPherson, James M. *Battle Cry of Freedom: The Civil War Era.* New York and Oxford: Oxford University Press, 1988.

Millbank, Dana. "Election 2004/Bush Rhetoric Keeps Public from Turning against War." *Houston Chronicle* (April 25, 2004).

Miller, Greg, and Richard Simon. "America Attacked: Nation Mobilizes; Congress OKs Use of Force; On Day of Remembrance, a Nation Mourns; Government Lawmakers United to Give President Full Power to Fight Terrorism; They Approve $40 Billion in Aid; Bush Calls up 3,500 Reservists; Later He Tries to Give Strength to a Grieving New York City." *Los Angeles Times* (September 15, 2001).

Millett, Allan R. *Semper Fidelis: The History of the United States Marine Corps.* New York: Macmillan Publishing Co., Inc., 1980.

Millett, Allan R., and Peter Maslowski. *For the Common Defense: A Military History of the United States of America.* New York: The Free Press, 1984.

Milligan, Susan. "Congress Gives Bush OK to Act Alone against Iraq/Senate Follows House in Voting Strong Support." *Boston Globe* (October 11, 2002).

Mitchell, Franklin D. *Harry S. Truman and the News Media: Contentious Relations, Belated Respect.* Columbia: University of Missouri Press, 1998.

Mock, James R., and Cedric Lawton. *Words That Won the War: The Story of the Committee on Public Information.* Princeton, NJ: Princeton University Press, 1939.

Moniz, Dave. "Some Veterans of Vietnam See Iraq Parallel in Lack of Candor; 'We Can Win the War,' McCain Says, 'but Not if We Lose Popular Support.'" *USA Today* (November 11, 2003).

Moore, David W. "Despite Fallujah, Americans Skeptical about Ultimate Success in Iraq." (November 23, 2004). www.gallup.com/poll/content/login/

Morris, Errol. *The Fog of War.* Sony Pictures Classics (2003).

Morrison, Pat. "Consequences of War: What You Won't See on TV." *Los Angeles Times* (November 11, 2003).

Mueller, John E. *War, Presidents, and Public Opinion.* New York: John Wiley & Sons, Inc., 1973.

National Security Council. *National Strategy for Victory in Iraq.* Washington, DC, 2005.

National Security Council 81/1. "A Report to the President by the National Security Council on United States Courses of Action with Respect to Korea." http://trumanlibrary.org/whistlerstop/studycollections/korea/large/nsc81-3.htm

Netzel, Andy. "America at War/Polls Say U.S. Public Backs President, Invasion of Iraq." *Houston Chronicle* (March 21, 2003).

New York Times 2003 Almanac. Penguin Reference, 2002.

"New York Times/CBS News Poll." O'Dwyer's PR Services Report, Vol. 5, No. 1, January 1991.

"New York Times/CBS News Poll, January 14–18, 2005." *New York Times* (January 20, 2005).

Noakes, Jeremy, and Geoffrey Pridham, eds. *Documents on Nazism, 1919–1945.* New York: Viking Press, 1975.

Nogourney, Adam. "Democrats Temper Praise for Bush Visit with Criticism." *New York Times* (November 28, 2003).

Norman, Elizabeth M. *We Band of Angels: The Untold Story of American Nurses Trapped on Bataan by the Japanese.* New York: Random House, 1999.

O'Neill, William L. *A Democracy at War: America's Fight at Home and Abroad in World War II.* Cambridge, MA: Harvard University Press, 1993.

Palmer, General Bruce, Jr. *The 25-Year War: America's Military Role in Vietnam.* Lexington: University of Kentucky Press, 1984.

Pareles, Jon. "Pop Music and the War." *New York Times* (January 2, 2007).

Paul, Noel C. "Selling War: A Review of the Campaign." *Christian Science Chronicle* (March 24, 2003).

Pavlik, John, and Mark Thalhimer. "The Charge of the E-Mail Brigade." In Everette E. Dennis, *The Media at War: The Press and the Persian Gulf Conflict.* New York: Gannett Foundation Media Center, 1991.

Peterson, Horace, and Gilbert Fite. *Unfavorable to the Mobilization: Opponents of War 1917–1918.* Madison: University of Wisconsin Press, 1957.

Phillips, McCandlish. "Now the Teach-In: U.S. Policy in Vietnam Criticized All Night." *New York Times* (March 27, 1965).

Pincus, Walter, and George Lardner Jr. "Nixon Hoped Antitrust Threat Would Sway Network Coverage; Colson Advised Constant Pressure, Tapes Show." *Washington Post* (December 1, 1997).

Pogrebin, Robin. "Hill & Knowlton and Its P.R. Problems." *New York Observer* (February 10, 1992).

Powers, Thomas. *The War at Home: Vietnam and the American People, 1964–1968.* New York: Grossman Publications, 1972.

Prange, Gordon. *At Dawn We Slept.* New York: McGraw-Hill Book Company, 1981.

———. *Miracle at Midway.* New York: McGraw-Hill Book Company, 1982.

Prescott, Jean. "Rise of the Baby Boomers/A&E Special 'Nation' Examines the Lives and Times of a Generation." *Houston Chronicle* (June 12, 2004).

Preston, Julia. "Iraq Tells the U.N. Arms Inspections Will Be Permitted." *New York Times* (November 14, 2002).

Public Papers of the Presidents of the United States: Harry S. Truman, 1950, "The President's News Conference of November 30, 1950," 724–728. http://quod.lib.umich.edu/cache/7/e/d/7edc649d29cdc31715fbc6ccff

Quester, George H. "Grenada and the New Media." In Peter M Dunn and Bruce W. Watson, eds., *Intervention in Grenada.* Boulder, CO: Westview Press, 1985.

Ranney, Austin. *Channels of Power: The Impact of Television on American Politics.* New York: Basic Books, 1983.

Raspberry, William. "Don't Forget King on War." *New York Post* (January 19, 2004).

Raymond, Jack. "3,500 U.S. Marines Going to Vietnam to Bolster Base." *New York Times* (March 7, 1965).

Reeves, Richard. "Military Defeats Press Pool Again." *Montgomery Advertiser* (January 15, 1990).

Regan, Tom. "When Contemplating War, Beware of Babies in Incubators." *Christian Science Monitor* (September 6, 2002).

Reston, James. "Mr. Nixon's Policy and Propaganda." *New York Times* (March 28, 1971).

Rich, Frank. "Oldest Living Whiz Kid Tells All." *New York Times* (January 25, 2004).

Ritter, John. "Poll: War Opposition Up Amid Iraqi Abuse Scandal; Americans Appalled by Images of Prisoners' Mistreatment." *USA Today* (May 11, 2004).

Robertson, Lori. "In Control." *American Journalism Review* (February/March 2005).

Rodriquez, Cindy. "Iraq Tyrant Capture Fuels Myth of Safety." *Denver Post* (January 2, 2004).

Roth, Bennett. "America in Iraq/Bush: U.S. to Stay in Iraq/Poll Shows Slippage in Support for War." *Houston Chronicle* (July 2, 2003).

———. "State of the Union/Bush: 'Decisive Days' Ahead/Address Spotlights Economy, Iraq Threat." *Houston Chronicle* (January 29, 2003).

Sandalow, Marc. "9.11.01/One Year Later." *San Francisco Chronicle* (September 12, 2002).

Sanger, David E. "Bush Hails Vote." *New York Times* (January 31, 2005).

———. "How North Korea Became North Korea." *New York Times* (July 27, 2003).

———. "The State of the Union: The Overview; Bush Focusing on Terrorism, Say Secure U.S. Is Top Priority." *New York Times* (January 30, 2002).

———. "Threats and Responses: The President's Speech; Bush Sees 'Urgent Duty' to Pre-empt Attack by Iraq." *New York Times* (October 8, 2002).

Sanger, David E., and Julia Preston. "Bush Warns U.N.: Act on Iraq or U.S. Will; He Leads Nation in Mourning at Terror." *New York Times* (September 12, 2002).

Schlessinger, Arthur M. *Running for President: The Candidates and Their Images, Volume Two, 1900–1992.* New York: Simon and Schuster, 1994.

Schmitt, Eric, and Richard W. Stevenson. "White House and Pentagon Scurry to Draft Responses." *New York Times* (May 5, 2004).

Schultz, Duane. *The Doolittle Raid.* New York: St. Martin's Press, 1988.

Seelye, Katherine Q. "The 2004 Elections: The Electorate—The Voters." *New York Times* (November 4, 2004).

Seldes, George. *One Man's Newspaper Game: Freedom of the Press.* Indianapolis, IN: Bobbs-Merrill, 1935.

Simmons, Brigadier General (ret.) Edwin H. *The United States Marines 1775–1975.* New York: The Viking Press, 1976.

Slotkin, Richard. *Gunfighter Nation: The Myth of the Frontier in Twentieth Century America*. New York: Antheneum, 1992.

Smith, Robert M. "Two in Congress Ask Study of Massacre Report." *New York Times* (November 21, 1969).

Snyder, L., and R. Morris, eds. *A Treasury of Good Reporting*. New York: Simon and Schuster, 1962.

Solis, Gary. "Terrorists, Due Process, and Military Commissions." *Marine Corps Gazette* (February 2002).

Spector, Ronald. *Eagle against the Sun: The American War with Japan*. New York: The Free Press, 1984.

Sperber, A.M. *Murrow: His Life and Times*. New York: Freundlich Books, 1986.

Sperling, Godfrey. "Nixon's 'Secret Plan' That Never Was." *Christian Science Monitor* (December 9, 1997).

Stallings, Laurence. *The Doughboys: The Story of the AEF, 1917–1918*. New York: Harper and Row, Publishers, 1963.

Stauber, John, and Sheldon Rampton. *Toxic Sludge Is Good for You: Lies, Damn Lies, and the Public Relations Industry*. Monroe, MA: Common Courage Press, 1995.

Stebenne, David. "The Gulf Conflict in Historical Context." In Everett E. Dennis, *The Media at War: The Press and the Persian Gulf Conflict*. New York: Gannett Foundation Media Center, 1991.

Sterba, James P. "Marines Leaving South Vietnam Are Briefed on How to Act in a Peace Zone." *New York Times* (July 14, 1969).

Stockman, Farah. "Bush Voices Disgust Over Abuse Photos; Threat is Seen to Iraq Mission." *Boston Globe* (May 1, 2004).

Stone, I.F. *The Hidden History of the Korean War*. New York: Monthly Review Press, 1952.

Tackett, Michael. "Bush Taps America's New Fear." *Chicago Tribune* (March 18, 2003).

Tannenhaus, Sam. "Bush's Brain Trust." *Vanity Fair* (May 2003).

Theofiles, George. *American Posters of World War I: Price and Collector's Guide*. New York: Dafran House Publishers Inc., 1973.

Thomas, Hugh. *The Spanish Civil War*. New York: Harper and Brothers, 1961.

Toner, Robin. "Bush's War Success Confers an Aura of Invincibility in '92." *New York Times* (February 27, 1991).

Tuchman, Barbara. *The Zimmermann Telegram*. New York: Ballantine Books, 1985.

Turner, Frederick Jackson. *Rereading Frederick Jackson Turner: The Significance of the Frontier in American History and Other Essays*, with commentary by John Mack Faragher. New York: Henry Holt and Company, 1994.

Ulan, Adam B. "Washington, Moscow, and the Korean War," in *Korea: Cold War and Limited War*, edited by Allen Guttmann. Lexington, MA: D.C. Heath and Co., 1972.

Valentine, Paul W. "Candlelight Walk Caps Day in City." *Washington Post* (October 16, 1969).

VandeHei, Jim. "Hill Resolutions Supporting Bush, Troops Are Approved; House Goes Beyond Senate in Praise of President." *Washington Post* (March 21, 2003).

Vaugh, S.L. *Holding Fast the Inner Lines: Democracy, Nationalism, and the Committee on Public Information.* Chapel Hill: University of North Carolina Press, 1980.

Watt, Richard. *The Kings Depart, the Tragedy of Germany; Versailles and the German Revolution.* New York: Simon and Schuster, 1968.

Weigley, Russell F. *The American Way of War: A History of United States Military Strategy and Policy:* New York: Macmillan Publishing Co., Inc., 1973.

Weinberg, Gerhard L. *A World at Arms: A Global History of World War II.* Cambridge, UK: Cambridge University Press, 1994.

Weissberg, Robert. *Public Opinion and Popular Government.* Englewood Cliffs, NJ: Prentice-Hall, 1976.

Wicker, Tom. "Bush's Double Vision." *New York Times* (January 8, 1990).

Wilkie, Curtis. "Simon's Chilling, Poetic Account of Captivity." *Boston Globe* (May 1, 1992).

Wilson, Joseph E. *The Cuban Crisis as Reflected in the New York Press.* New York: Columbia University Press, 1934.

Woodward, Bob. *Bush at War.* New York: Simon & Schuster, 2002.

———. *Plan of Attack.* New York: Simon & Schuster, 2004.

Zoroya, Gregg. "Return of U.S. War Dead Kept Solemn, Secret." *USA Today* (December 31, 2003).

Index

About the Authors

EUGENE SECUNDA is a Fulbright Scholar, and a member of the faculty in the Department of Culture and Communication, Steinhardt School of Culture, Communication and Human Development at New York University. He is the coauthor of *Shifting Time and Space: The Story of Videotape* (Praeger, 1991).

TERENCE P. MORAN is Professor in the Department of Media, Culture, and Communication, Steinhardt School of Culture, Communication, and Human Development at New York University. He shares an Emmy Award for the documentary "McSorley's New York" (1986) and was the coeditor of *Language in America* (Pegasus, 1969).